W9-CMZ-910

NORWAY
PREKESTOLEN

Etter en fottur på ca 2 timer i norsk villmark, er vi på Preikestolen, et av Norges mest attraktive reisemål. Lysefjorden er over 4 mil lang. Fjellene som omkranser fjorden er over 1000 meter høye og stuper mange steder rett ned i fjorden. Det er nesten utrolig å tenke seg at fjordene er gravet ut av is og stein under siste istid. Må oppleves.

A two-hour walk in the Norwegian wilderness brings us to Pulpit Rock, one of Norwayís most attractive destinations. Lysefjorden below is over 40 km long, surrounded by mountains over 1000 m high and many places plunging straight into the fjord. It is hard to believe that the fjords were dug out by ice and rock during the last Ice Age. Not to be missed.

Nach einer etwa zweistündigen Wanderung durch die norwegische Wildnis gelangen wir zur «Kanzel», einem der beliebtesten Ausflugsziele in Norwegen. Der Lysefjord ist über 40 km lang. Die Berge, die den Fjord umgeben, sind über 1000 m hoch und stürzen an einigen Stellen senkrecht in den Fjord. Es ist fast unvorstellbar, daß die Fjorde während der letzten Eiszeit von Eis- und Steinmassen ausgegraben wurden. Das muß man erlebt haben !

NORDKAPP

NORGE
NORWAY
NORWEGEN

OSLO

Snorre   SD152   Natur og Kulturforlaget ©. Norway. ☎ +47 51 88 19 95. Trykk: Industritrykk. Repro: Reprobanen. Foto: Pål Hermansen ©

Perry

Fodor's

FOURTH
New
EDITION

Norway

Bug repellent
Travellers checks

Tips hotels
NKr 5 – NKr 10

weight 44 pounds
Bird Book
need Converter

Kroner
NKr
"crown"

exchange save $
before you go –

The complete guide, thoroughly up-to-date

Take cash to

Packed with details that will make your trip _rural areas_

The must-see sights, off and on the beaten path

What to see, what to skip

Mix-and-match vacation itineraries

City strolls, countryside adventures

Smart lodging and dining options

Essential local do's and taboos

Transportation tips, distances and directions

Key contacts, savvy travel tips

When to go, what to pack

Clear, accurate, easy-to-use maps

Books to read, videos to watch

Reprinted from _Fodor's Scandinavia_

Fodor's Travel Publications, Inc.
New York • Toronto • London • Sydney • Auckland
www.fodors.com/

Fodor's Norway

EDITOR: Rebecca Miller

Editorial Contributors: Robert Andrews, David Brown, Daniel Cooper, Melody Favish, Christina Knight, Marius Meland, Shelley Pannill, Jennifer Paull, Karina Porcelli, Heidi Sarna, Helayne Schiff, M. T. Schwartzman (Gold Guide editor), Fiona Smith, Dinah A. Spritzer, Chunglu Tsen

Editorial Production: Tom Holton

Maps: David Lindroth, *cartographer*; Steven K. Amsterdam, *map editor*

Design: Fabrizio La Rocca, *creative director*; Guido Caroti, *associate art director*; Jolie Novak, *photo editor*

Production/Manufacturing: Mike Costa

Cover Photograph: E. Nagele/FPG International

Copyright

Fourth Edition

ISBN 0–679–03513–3

Special Sales

CONTENTS

Maps

ON THE ROAD WITH FODOR'S

WE'RE ALWAYS THRILLED to get letters from readers, especially one like this:

It took us an hour to decide what book to buy and we now know we picked the best one. Your book was wonderful, easy to follow, very accurate, and good on pointing out eating places, informal as well as formal. When we saw other people using your book, we would look at each other and smile.

Our editors and writers are deeply committed to making every Fodor's guide "the best one"—not only accurate but always charming, brimming with sound recommendations and solid ideas, right on the mark in describing restaurants and hotels, and full of fascinating facts that make you view what you've traveled to see in a rich new light.

About Our Writers

Our success in achieving our goals—and in helping to make your trip the best of all possible vacations—is a credit to the hard work of our extraordinary writers and editors.

While working as a journalist in Oslo, native Texan **Shelley Pannill** interviewed scores of Norwegians, including Liv Ullmann, and covered topics ranging from whaling to travel to the Nobel Peace Prize. A graduate of the Columbia University Graduate School of Journalism, Shelley has written news and features for United Press International, *The European* (London), and *The Star-Ledger* (NJ).

A huge fan of Scandinavian culture, editor **Rebecca Miller** lived in Norway for several years. While there, she tried everything from *lutefisk* to glacier skiing. She now resides in New York City.

New This Year

We're proud to announce that the American Society of Travel Agents has endorsed Fodor's as its guidebook of choice. ASTA is the world's largest and most influential travel trade association, operating in more than 170 countries, with 27,000 members pledged to adhere to a strict code of ethics reflecting the Society's motto, "Integrity in Travel." ASTA shares Fodor's devotion to providing smart, honest travel information and advice to travelers, and we've long recommended that our readers consult ASTA member agents for the experience and professionalism they bring to the table.

On the Web, check out Fodor's site (www.fodors.com/) for information on major destinations around the world and travel-savvy interactive features. The Web site also lists the 85-plus radio stations nationwide that carry *Fodor's Travel Show,* a live call-in program that airs every weekend. Tune in to hear guests discuss their wonderful adventures—or call in to get answers for your most pressing travel questions.

How to Use This Book

Organization

Up front is the **Gold Guide,** an easy-to-use section divided alphabetically by topic. Under each listing you'll find tips and information that will help you accomplish what you need to in Norway. You'll also find addresses and telephone numbers of organizations and companies—including visitor information offices—that offer destination-related services and detailed information and publications.

The first chapter in the guide, **Destination: Norway,** helps get you in the mood for your trip. What's Where gets you oriented, Fodor's Choice showcases our top picks, Books and Videos suggests pretrip research, from recommended reading to movies on tape with Norway as a backdrop, and Festivals and Seasonal Events alerts you to special events you'll want to seek out.

Chapters in *Fodor's Norway,* each dealing with a major region or city, contain recommended walking or driving tours. Within each city, sights are covered alphabetically. Within each region, towns are covered in logical geographical order, and attractive stretches of road and minor points of interest between them are indicated by the designation *En Route.* Off the Beaten Path sights appear after the places from which they are most easily accessible. Within town sections, all restaurants and lodgings are grouped together. The A-to-Z section at the end of each region or city covers getting to your destination, getting around, and helpful contacts and resources.

At the end of the book you'll find Portraits, with a chronology of the history of Norway.

Icons and Symbols

★   Our special recommendations
✕   Restaurant
🏠   Lodging establishment
✕🏠   Lodging establishment whose restaurant warrants a special trip
⚠   Campgrounds
🦆   Good for kids (rubber duckie)
☞   Sends you to another section of the guide for more information
✉   Address
☎   Telephone number
🕐   Opening and closing times
🎟   Admission prices (those we give apply to adults; substantially reduced fees are almost always available for children, students, and senior citizens)

Numbers in white and black circles that appear on the maps, in the margins, and within the tours correspond to one another.

Dining and Lodging

The restaurants and lodgings we list are the cream of the crop in each price range. Price categories are as follows:

For restaurants:

CATEGORY	COST*
$$$$	over NKr450
$$$	NKr300–NKr450
$$	NKr150–NKr300
$	under NKr150

*per person for a three-course meal, including tax and 12½% service charge

For hotels:

CATEGORY	MAJOR CITIES*	OTHER AREAS*
$$$$	over NKr1,300	over NKr1,000
$$$	NKr1,000–NKr1,300	NKr850–NKr1,000
$$	NKr800–NKr1,000	NKr650–NKr850
$	under NKr800	under NKr650

*All prices are for a standard double room, including service and 23% VAT.

Hotel Facilities

We always list the facilities that are available—but we don't specify whether they cost extra: When pricing accommodations, always ask what's included. Assume that all rooms have private baths unless otherwise noted. Breakfast is almost always included in the price of Scandinavian hotels.

Restaurant Reservations and Dress Codes

Reservations are always a good idea; we note only when they're essential or when they are not accepted. Book in advance, and reconfirm when you get to town. Unless otherwise noted, the restaurants listed are open daily for lunch and dinner. We mention dress only when men are required to wear a jacket or a jacket and tie.

Credit Cards

The following abbreviations are used: **AE**, American Express; **D**, Discover; **DC**, Diners Club; **MC**, MasterCard; and **V**, Visa.

Don't Forget to Write

You can use this book in the confidence that all prices and opening times are based on information supplied to us at press time; Fodor's cannot accept responsibility for any errors. Time inevitably brings changes, so always confirm information when it matters—especially if you're making a detour to visit a specific place. In addition, when making reservations be sure to mention if you have a disability or are traveling with children, if you prefer a private bath or a certain type of bed, or if you have specific dietary needs or other concerns.

Were the restaurants we recommended as described? Did our hotel picks exceed your expectations? Did you find a museum we recommended a waste of time? If you have complaints, we'll look into them and revise our entries when the facts warrant it. If you've discovered a special place that we haven't included, we'll pass the information along to our correspondents and have them check it out. So send us your feedback, positive *and* negative: email us at editors@fodors.com (specifying the name of the book on the subject line) or write the Scandinavia editor at Fodor's, 201 East 50th Street, New York, New York 10022. Have a wonderful trip!

Karen Cure

Karen Cure
Editorial Director

Scandinavia

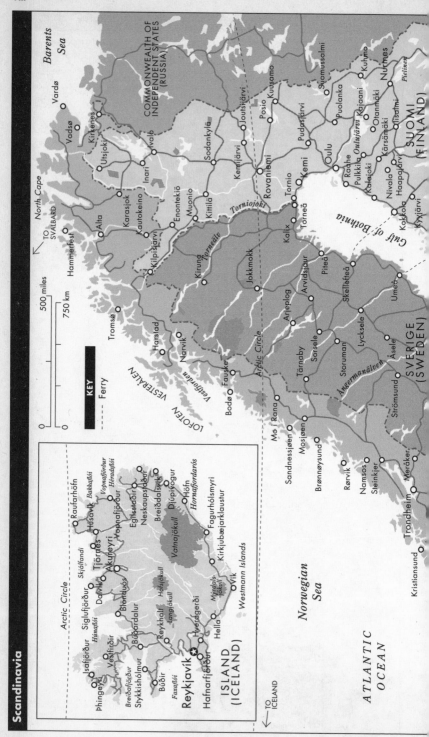

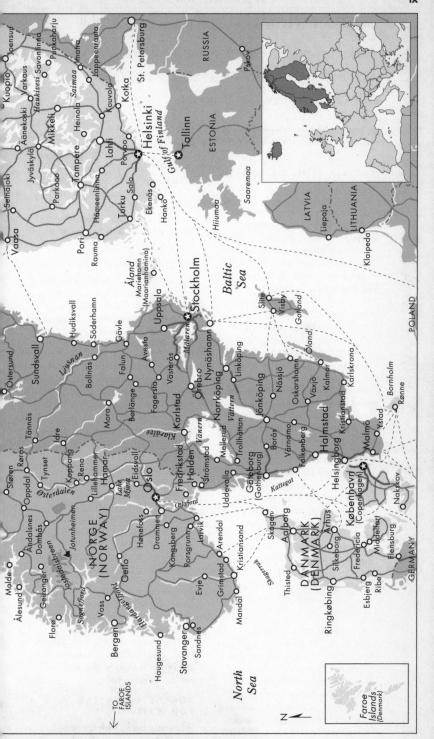

SMART TRAVEL TIPS A TO Z

Basic Information on Traveling in Norway, Savvy Tips to Make Your Trip a Breeze, and Companies and Organizations to Contact

A

AIR TRAVEL

MAJOR AIRLINE OR LOW-COST CARRIER?

Most people choose a flight based on price. Yet there are other issues to consider. Major airlines offer the greatest number of departures; smaller airlines—including regional, low-cost, and no-frill airlines—usually have a more limited number of flights daily. Major airlines have frequent-flyer partners, which allow you to credit mileage earned on one airline to your account with another. Low-cost airlines offer a definite price advantage and fewer restrictions, such as advance-purchase requirements. Safety-wise, low-cost carriers as a group have a good history, but **check the safety record before booking** any low-cost carrier; call the Federal Aviation Administration's Consumer Hotline (☞ Airline Complaints, *below*).

➤ MAJOR AIRLINES: **Scandinavian Airlines (SAS)** (☎ 800/221–2350) has daily nonstop flights to Oslo from Newark; daily connections to Oslo via Copenhagen from Chicago, Los Angeles, and Seattle; and twice-weekly connections (also via Copenhagen) from Toronto and Anchorage. **Finnair** (☎ 800/950–5000) offers flights to Norway via Helsinki. **Icelandair** (☎ 800/223–5500) flies from New York and Baltimore to Oslo via Reykjavík.

➤ FROM THE U.K.: **SAS** (☎ 0171/734–4020, FAX 0171/465–0125) flies from Heathrow to Oslo, Stavanger, and Bergen, and from Aberdeen to Stavanger. **Braathens SAFE** (☎ 0191/214–0991) operates flights from Newcastle to Stavanger, Bergen, and Oslo, and from London Gatwick to Oslo. **AirUK** (☎ 0345/666–777) has several flights weekly from Aberdeen to Stavanger and Bergen. **British Airways** (☎ 0345/222–111) offers nonstop flights from Heathrow to Bergen, Oslo, and Stavanger. **Aer Lingus** (☎ 0181/899–4747; in Ireland, ☎ 0001/377–777), **Cimber Air** (☎ 0645–737–747), **Business Air** (☎ 01382/66345), **Midtfly** (☎ 01224/723357), and **Icelandair** (☎ 0171/388–5599; 0181/745–7051 at Heathrow Airport) all have flights between Great Britain or Ireland and Norway.

GET THE LOWEST FARE

The least-expensive airfares to Norway are priced for round-trip travel. Major airlines usually require that you **book far in advance and stay at least seven days** and no more than 30 to get the lowest fares. Ask about "ultrasaver" fares, which are the cheapest; they must be booked 90 days in advance and are nonrefundable. A little more expensive are "supersaver" fares, which require only a 30-day advance purchase. Remember that penalties for refunds or scheduling changes are stiffer for international tickets, usually about $150. International flights are also sensitive to the season: **plan to fly in the off season** for the cheapest fares. If your destination or home city has more than one gateway, **compare prices to and from different airports.** Also price flights scheduled for off-peak hours, which may be significantly less expensive.

To save money on flights from the United Kingdom and back, **look into an APEX or Super-PEX ticket.** APEX tickets must be booked in advance and have certain restrictions. Super-PEX tickets can be purchased at the airport on the day of departure—subject to availability.

DON'T STOP UNLESS YOU MUST

When you book, **look for nonstop flights** and remember that "direct" flights stop at least once. International flights on a country's flag carrier are almost always nonstop; U.S. airlines often fly direct. Try to **avoid connecting flights,** which require a change of plane. Two airlines may jointly operate a connecting flight, so ask if your airline operates every segment—you may find that your preferred carrier flies you only part of the way.

USE AN AGENT

Travel agents, especially those who specialize in finding the lowest fares (☞ Discounts & Deals, *below*), can be especially helpful when booking a plane ticket. When you're quoted a price, **ask your agent if the price is likely to get any lower.** Good agents know the seasonal fluctuations of airfares and can usually anticipate a sale or fare war. However, waiting can be risky: The fare could go *up* as seats become scarce, and you may wait so long that your preferred flight sells out. A wait-and-see strategy works best if your plans are flexible, but if you must arrive and depart on certain dates, don't delay.

CHECK WITH CONSOLIDATORS

Consolidators buy tickets for scheduled flights at reduced rates from the airlines then sell them at prices that beat the best fare available directly from the airlines, usually without advance restrictions. Sometimes you can even get your money back if you need to return the ticket. Carefully read the fine print detailing penalties for changes and cancellations, and **confirm your consolidator reservation with the airline.**

➤ CONSOLIDATORS: **United States Air Consolidators Association** (✉ 925 L St., Suite 220, Sacramento, CA 95814, ☎ 916/441–4166, FAX 916/441–3520).

CONSIDER A CHARTER

Charters usually have the lowest fares but are not dependable. Departures are infrequent and seldom on time, flights can be delayed for up to 48 hours or can be canceled for any reason up to 10 days before you're scheduled to leave. Itineraries and prices can change after you've booked your flight, so you must **be very careful to choose a legitimate charter carrier.** Don't commit to a charter operator that doesn't follow proper booking procedures. Be especially careful when buying a charter ticket.

Read the fine print regarding refund policies. If you can't pay with a credit card, **make your check payable to a charter carrier's escrow account** (unless you're dealing with a travel agent, in which case his or her check should be made payable to the escrow account). The name of the bank should be in the charter contract.

Airlines routinely overbook planes, knowing that not everyone with a ticket will show up, but sometimes everyone does. When that happens, airlines ask for volunteers to give up their seats. In return these volunteers usually get a certificate for a free flight and are rebooked on the next flight out. If there are not enough volunteers the airline must choose who will be denied boarding. The first to get bumped are passengers who checked in late and those flying on discounted tickets, **so get to the gate and check in as early as possible,** especially during peak periods.

Always **bring a photo ID to the airport.** You may be asked to show it before you are allowed to check in.

ENJOY THE FLIGHT

For more legroom, **request an emergency-aisle seat;** don't however, sit in the row in front of the emergency aisle or in front of a bulkhead, where seats may not recline.

If you don't like airline food, **ask for special meals when booking.** These can be vegetarian, low-cholesterol, or kosher, for example.

Some carriers have prohibited smoking throughout their systems; others allow smoking only on certain routes or even certain departures from that route, so **contact your carrier regarding its smoking policy.**

COMPLAIN IF NECESSARY

If your baggage goes astray or your flight goes awry, complain right away. Most carriers require that you file a claim immediately.

➤ AIRLINE COMPLAINTS: U.S. Department of Transportation **Aviation Consumer Protection Division** (✉ C-75, Room 4107, Washington, DC 20590, ☎ 202/366–2220). **Federal Aviation Administration (FAA) Consumer Hotline** (☎ 800/322–7873).

THE GOLD GUIDE / SMART TRAVEL TIPS

WITHIN NORWAY

Norway is larger than it looks on a map, and many native travelers choose to fly, using trains and buses for shorter travel. If you are traveling from south to north, flying is a necessity: Stavanger in southern Norway is as close to Rome, Italy, as it is to the northern tip of Norway.

A number of special fares are available within Norway year-round, including air passes, family tickets, weekend excursions, and youth (up to the age of 26) and senior (older than 67) discounts. Youth fares are cheapest when purchased from the automatic ticket machines at the airport on the day of departure. All Norwegian routes have reduced rates from July through the middle of August, and tickets can be purchased on the spot.

For international travelers, one or two stopovers can often be purchased more cheaply along with an international ticket. With SAS, the least expensive tickets (Jackpot) are round-trip, must include a Saturday night, and can be bought only within Scandinavia from 7 to 14 days ahead. Ask about low rates for hotels and car rental in connection with Jackpot tickets. Weekend Jackpot tickets can be bought right up to flight time. SAS also gives couples traveling together a discount off some tickets and significant discounts on SAS hotels and car rentals. Low-priced round-trip weekend excursions from one Scandinavian capital to another (minimum three-day stay) can be bought one day in advance from SAS.

Braathens SAFE sells a **Visit Norway** pass, which includes the Scandinavian BonusPass. It is available at **Passage Tours of Scandinavia** (☎ 800/548–5960) and **Borton Overseas** (☎ 800/843–0602).

All flights within Scandinavia are no-smoking, as are all airports in Norway, except in designated areas.

➤ CARRIERS: **SAS** (☎ 810/03–300) serves most major cities, including Svalbard. **Braathens SAFE** (☎ 67/59–70–00) is the major domestic airline, serving cities throughout the country and along the coast as far north as Tromsø and Svalbard. It also has international routes from Oslo to Billund, Denmark; Malmö, Sweden; and Newcastle, England. **Widerøe** (☎ 67/11–14–60) serves smaller airports (with smaller planes), mostly along the coast, and in northern Norway. **Norsk Air** (☎ 33/46–90–00), a subsidiary of Widerøe, provides similar services in the southern part of the country. **Coast Air** (☎ 52/83–41–10) and **Norlink** (☎ 77/67–57–80), an SAS subsidiary, are commuter systems linking both smaller and larger airports.

AIRPORTS

The major gateway to Norway is **Fornebu Airport** in Oslo. Fornebu became such a busy airport that its own air traffic has surpassed its capacity, and therefore a new airport, **Gardermoen**, is scheduled to open in 1998. Other international airports are Bergen, Kristiansand, Sandefjord, Stavanger, and Trondheim. Flying time from New York to Oslo is 7½ hours; a nonstop flight from London to Oslo is about 1¾ hours and about 1½ hours to Stavanger.

➤ AIRPORT INFORMATION: **Fornebu Airport** (☎ 011–47–224/97598).

B

BOAT TRAVEL

Norway's most renowned boat trip is **Hurtigruten**, or the *Coastal Steamer,* which departs from Bergen and stops at 36 ports in six days, ending with Kirkenes, near the Russian border, before turning back. Tickets can be purchased for the entire journey or for individual legs. Shore excursions are arranged at all ports. Tickets are available through **Bergen Line travel agents** (✉ 405 Park Ave., New York, NY 10022, ☎ 800/323–7436), or directly from the companies that run the service: **FFR** (✉ 9600 Hammerfest, ☎ 78/41–10–00), **OVDS** (✉ 8501 Narvik, ☎ 76/92–37–00), **Hurtigruten Booking** (✉ Kjøpmannsgt. 52, 7011 Trondheim, ☎ 73/51–51–20, FAX 73/51–51–46), and **TFDS** (✉ 9000 Tromsø, ☎ 77/68–60–88).

BUS TRAVEL

Every end station of the railroad is supported by a number of bus routes, some of which are operated by NSB, others by local companies. Long-distance buses usually take longer than the railroad, and fares are only slightly lower. Virtually every settlement on the mainland is served by bus, and for anyone with a desire to get off the beaten track, a pay-as-you-go open-ended bus trip is the best way to see Norway.

Most long-distance buses leave from **Bussterminalen** (✉ Galleri Oslo, Schweigaardsgt., 10, ☎ 22/17–01–66), close to Oslo Central Station. **Nor-Way Bussekspress** (✉ Bussterminalen, ☎ 22/17–52–90, FAX 22/17–59–22) has more than 40 different bus services, covering 10,000 km (6,200 mi) and 500 destinations, and can arrange any journey. One of its participating services, **Feriebussen** (✉ Østerdal Billag A/S, 2560 Alvdal, ☎ 62/48–74–00), offers five package tours with English-speaking guides.

C

CAMERAS, CAMCORDERS, & COMPUTERS

Always **keep your film, tape, or computer disks out of the sun.** Carry an extra supply of batteries, and **be prepared to turn on your camera, camcorder, or laptop** to prove to security personnel that the device is real. Always **ask for hand inspection of film,** which becomes clouded after successive exposure to airport x-ray machines, and **keep videotapes and computer disks away from metal detectors.**

➤ PHOTO HELP: **Kodak Information Center** (☎ 800/242–2424).

CUSTOMS

Before departing, **register your foreign-made camera or laptop with U.S. Customs** (☞ Customs & Duties, *below*). If your equipment is U.S.-made, call the consulate of the country you'll be visiting to find out whether the device should be registered with local customs upon arrival.

CAR RENTAL

Rates in Oslo begin at $111 a day and $284 a week. This does not include tax on car rentals, which is 23% in Norway.

Avis (☎ 800/331–1084, 800/879–2847 in Canada). **Budget** (☎ 800/527–0700, 0800/181181 in the U.K.). **Dollar** (☎ 800/800–4000; 0990/565656 in the U.K., where it is known as Eurodollar). **Hertz** (☎ 800/654–

3001, 800/263–0600 in Canada, 0345/555888 in the U.K.). **National InterRent** (☎ 800/227–3876; 01345/222525 in the U.K., where it is known as Europcar InterRent).

CUT COSTS

To get the best deal, **book through a travel agent who is willing to shop around.**

Be sure to **look into wholesalers,** companies that do not own fleets but rent in bulk from those that do and often offer better rates than traditional car-rental operations. Prices are best during off-peak periods. Rentals booked through wholesalers must be paid for before you leave the United States.

➤ RENTAL WHOLESALERS: **Auto Europe** (☎ 207/842–2000 or 800/223–5555, FAX 800–235–6321). **DER Travel Services** (✉ 9501 W. Devon Ave., Rosemont, IL 60018, ☎ 800/782–2424, FAX 800/282–7474 for information or 800/860–9944 for brochures).

NEED INSURANCE?

When driving a rented car you are generally responsible for any damage to or loss of the vehicle. Before you rent, **see what coverage you already have** under the terms of your personal auto-insurance policy and credit cards.

Collision policies that car-rental companies sell for European rentals typically do not cover stolen vehicles. Before you buy additional coverage for theft, find out if your credit card or personal auto insurance will cover the loss.

BEWARE SURCHARGES

Before you pick up a car in one city and leave it in another, **ask about drop-off charges or one-way service fees,** which can be substantial. Note, too, that some rental agencies charge extra if you return the car before the time specified on your contract. To avoid a hefty refueling fee, **fill the tank just before you turn in the car,** but be aware that gas stations near the rental outlet may overcharge.

MEET THE REQUIREMENTS

Ask about age requirements: Several countries require drivers to be over 20 years old, but some car-rental companies require that drivers be at least 25. In Norway your own driver's license is acceptable for a limited time; check with the country's tourist board before you go. An International Driver's Permit is a good idea; it's available from the American or Canadian automobile association, or, in the United Kingdom, from the Automobile Association or Royal Automobile Club.

CHILDREN & TRAVEL

CHILDREN IN NORWAY

In Norway children are to be seen *and* heard and are genuinely welcome in most public places.

Be sure to plan ahead and **involve your youngsters** as you outline your trip. When packing, include things to keep them busy en route. On sightseeing days try to schedule activities of special interest to your children. If you are renting a car don't forget to **arrange for a car seat** when you reserve. Most hotels in Norway allow children under a certain age to stay in their parents' room at no extra charge, but others charge them as extra adults; be sure to **ask about the cutoff age for children's discounts.** Many youth hostels offer special facilities (including multiple-bed rooms and separate kitchens) for families with children. Family hostels also provide an excellent opportunity for children to meet youngsters from other countries. Contact the AYH (☞ Students, *below*).

DISCOUNTS

Children are entitled to discount tickets (often as much as 50% off) on buses, trains, and ferries throughout Norway, as well as reductions on special City Cards. Children under 12 pay half-price and children under 2 pay 10% on SAS and Linjeflyg round-trips. The only restriction on this discount is that the family travel together and return to the originating city in Scandinavia at least two days later. With the ScanRail Pass—good for rail journeys throughout Scandinavia—children under 4 (on lap) travel free; those 4–11 pay half-fare and those 12–25 pay 75% of the adult fare.

FLYING

As a general rule, infants under two not occupying a seat fly at greatly reduced fares and occasionally for free. If your children are two or older **ask about children's airfares.**

In general the adult baggage allowance applies to children paying half or more of the adult fare. When booking, **ask about carry-on allowances for those traveling with infants.** In general, for babies charged 10% of the adult fare you are allowed one carry-on bag and a collapsible stroller, which may have to be checked; you may be limited to less if the flight is full.

According to the FAA it's a good idea to use safety seats aloft for children weighing less than 40 pounds. Airlines, however, can set their own policies: U.S. carriers allow FAA-approved models but usually require that you buy a ticket, even if your child would otherwise ride free, since the seats must be strapped into regular seats. Airline rules vary regarding their use, so it's important to **check your airline's policy about using safety seats during takeoff and landing.** Safety seats cannot obstruct any of the other passengers in the row, so get an appropriate seat assignment as early as possible.

When making your reservation, **request children's meals or a free-standing bassinet** if you need them; the latter are available only to those seated at the bulkhead, where there's enough legroom. Remember, however, that bulkhead seats may not have their own overhead bins, and there's no storage space in front of you—a major inconvenience.

GROUP TRAVEL

➤ FAMILY-FRIENDLY TOUR OPERATORS: **Families Welcome!** (✉ 92 N. Main St., Ashland, OR 97520, ☎ 541/482–6121 or 800/326–0724, FAX 541/482–0660). **Rascals in Paradise** (✉ 650 5th St., Suite 505, San Francisco, CA 94107, ☎ 415/978– 9800 or 800/ 872–7225, FAX 415/442–0289).

CONSUMER PROTECTION

Whenever possible, **pay with a major credit card** so you can cancel payment if there's a problem, provided that you can provide documentation. This is a good practice whether you're buying travel arrangements before your trip or shopping at your destination.

If you're doing business with a particular company for the first time, **contact your local Better Business Bureau and the attorney general's offices** in your state and the company's home state, as well. Have any complaints been filed?

Finally, if you're buying a package or tour, always **consider travel insurance** that includes default coverage (☞ Insurance, *below*).

➤ LOCAL BBBS: **Council of Better Business Bureaus** (✉ 4200 Wilson Blvd., Suite 800, Arlington, VA 22203, ☎ 703/276–0100, FAX 703/525–8277).

CUSTOMS & DUTIES

When shopping, **keep receipts** for all of your purchases. Upon reentering the country, **be ready to show customs officials what you've bought.** If you feel a duty is incorrect, appeal the assessment. If you object to the way your clearance was handled, get the inspector's badge number. In either case, first ask to see a supervisor, then write to the port director at the address listed on your receipt. Send a copy of the receipt and other appropriate documentation.

ENTERING NORWAY

Residents of non-European countries who are over 18 may import duty-free into Norway 200 cigarettes or 500 grams of other tobacco goods, and souvenirs and gifts to the value of Nkr1,200. Residents of European countries who are over 18 may import 200 cigarettes or 250 grams of tobacco or cigars, a small amount of perfume or eau de cologne, and other goods to the value of Nkr1,200. Anyone over 20 may bring in 1 liter of wine and 1 liter of liquor or 2 liters of wine or beer.

ENTERING THE U.S.

You may bring home $400 worth of foreign goods duty-free if you've been out of the country for at least 48 hours and haven't already used the $400 allowance or any part of it in the past 30 days.

Travelers 21 and older may bring back 1 liter of alcohol duty-free. In addition, regardless of your age, you are allowed 200 cigarettes and 100 non-Cuban cigars. (At press time, a federal rule restricting tobacco access to persons 18 years and older did not apply to importation.) Antiques, which the U.S. Customs Service defines as objects more than 100 years old, enter duty-free, as do original works of art done entirely by hand, including paintings, drawings, and sculptures.

You may also send packages home duty-free: up to $200 worth of goods for personal use, with a limit of one parcel per addressee per day (and no alcohol or tobacco products or perfume worth more than $5); label the package PERSONAL USE, and attach a list of its contents and their retail value. Do not label the package UNSOLICITED GIFT, or your duty-free exemption will drop to $100. Mailed items do not affect your duty-free allowance on your return.

➤ INFORMATION: **U.S. Customs Service** (Inquiries, ✉ Box 7407, Washington, DC 20044, ☎ 202/927–6724; complaints, ✉ Office of Regulations and Rulings, 1301 Constitution Ave. NW, Washington, DC 20229; registration of equipment, ✉ Resource Management, 1301 Constitution Ave. NW, Washington DC, 20229, ☎ 202/927–0540).

ENTERING CANADA

If you've been out of Canada for at least seven days you may bring in C$500 worth of goods duty-free. If you've been away for fewer than seven days but more than 48 hours, the duty-free allowance drops to C$200; if your trip lasts 24–48 hours, the allowance is C$50. You may not pool allowances with family members. Goods claimed under the C$500 exemption may follow you by mail; those claimed under the lesser exemptions must accompany you.

Alcohol and tobacco products may be included in the seven-day and 48-hour exemptions but not in the 24-hour exemption. If you meet the age requirements of the province or territory through which you reenter Canada you may bring in, duty-free, 1.14 liters (40 imperial ounces) of wine or liquor *or* 24 12-ounce cans or bottles of beer or ale. If you are 16 or older you may bring in, duty-free, 200 cigarettes and 50 cigars; these items must accompany you.

You may send an unlimited number of gifts worth up to C$60 each duty-free to Canada. Label the package UNSO-LICITED GIFT—VALUE UNDER $60. Alcohol and tobacco are excluded.

➤ INFORMATION: **Revenue Canada** (✉ 2265 St. Laurent Blvd. S, Ottawa, Ontario K1G 4K3, ☎ 613/993–0534, 800/461–9999 in Canada).

ENTERING THE U.K.

From countries outside the EU, including Norway, you may import, duty-free, 200 cigarettes or 50 cigars; 1 liter of spirits or 2 liters of fortified or sparkling wine or liqueurs; 2 liters of still table wine; 60 milliliters of perfume; 250 milliliters of toilet water; plus £136 worth of other goods, including gifts and souvenirs.

➤ INFORMATION: **HM Customs and Excise** (✉ Dorset House, Stamford St., London SE1 9NG, ☎ 0171/202–4227).

D

DINING

Although restaurants in Norway's major cities offer the full range of dining experiences, eating out in any of the smaller towns will probably be limited to traditional local fare. Some particular northern tastes can seem very different, such as the fondness for pickled and fermented fish—to be sampled carefully at first—and a universal obsession with sweet pastries, ice cream, and chocolate. Other novelties for the visitor might be the use of fruit in main dishes and soups, or sour milk on breakfast cereal, or preserved fish paste as a spread for crackers, or the prevalence of crackers and complete absence of sliced bread. The Swedish *smörgåsbord* and its Scandinavian cousins are often the traveling diner's best bet, since they include fresh fish and vegetables alongside meat and starches; they are also among the lower-priced menu choices.

Restaurant meals are a big-ticket item in Norway, but there are ways to keep the cost of eating down. Take full advantage of the large, buffet breakfast usually included in the cost of a hotel room. At lunch, look for the "menu" that offers a set two- or three-course meal for a set price, or limit yourself to a hearty appetizer. At dinner, pay careful attention to the price of wine and drinks, since the high tax on alcohol raises these costs considerably. For more information on affordable eating, *see* Costs *in* Money, *below.*

DISABILITIES & ACCESSIBILITY

ACCESS IN NORWAY

Facilities for travelers with disabilities in Norway are generally good, and the tourist office offers special booklets and brochures on travel and accommodations.

LODGING

The **Best Western** chain (☎ 800/528–1234) offers properties with wheelchair-accessible rooms in Oslo. If wheelchair-accessible rooms are not available, ground-floor rooms are provided.

TIPS AND HINTS

When discussing accessibility with an operator or reservationist, **ask hard questions.** Are there any stairs, inside *or* out? Are there grab bars next to the toilet *and* in the shower/tub? How wide is the doorway to the room? To the bathroom? For the most extensive facilities meeting the latest legal specifications, **opt for newer accommodations,** which are more likely to have been designed with access in mind. Older buildings or ships may offer more limited facilities. Be sure to **discuss your needs before booking.**

➤ COMPLAINTS: **Disability Rights Section** (✉ U.S. Department of Justice, Box 66738, Washington, DC 20035–6738, ☎ 202/514–0301 or 800/514–0301, FAX 202/307–1198, TTY 202/514–0383 or 800/514–0383) for general complaints. **Aviation Consumer Protection Division** (☞ Air Travel, *above*) for airline-related problems. **Civil Rights Office** (✉ U.S. Department of Transportation, Departmental Office of Civil Rights, S-30, 400 7th St. SW, Room 10215, Washington, DC, 20590, ☎ 202/366–4648) for problems with surface transportation.

TRAVEL AGENCIES & TOUR OPERATORS

➤ TRAVELERS WITH MOBILITY PROBLEMS: **Access Adventures** (✉ 206 Chestnut Ridge Rd., Rochester, NY 14624, ☎ 716/889–9096), run by a former physical-rehabilitation counselor. **Hinsdale Travel Service** (✉ 201 E. Ogden Ave., Suite 100, Hinsdale, IL 60521, ☎ 630/325–1335), a travel agency that benefits from the advice of wheelchair traveler Janice Perkins. **Wheelchair Journeys** (✉ 16979 Redmond Way, Redmond, WA 98052, ☎ 425/885–2210 or 800/313–4751), for general travel arrangements.

DISCOUNTS & DEALS

Be a smart shopper and **compare all your options before making a choice.** A plane ticket bought with a promotional coupon may not be cheaper than the least expensive fare from a discount ticket agency. For high-price travel purchases, such as packages or tours, keep in mind that what you get is just as important as what you save. Just because something is cheap doesn't mean it's a bargain.

LOOK IN YOUR WALLET

When you use your credit card to make travel purchases you may get free travel-accident insurance, collision-damage insurance, and medical or legal assistance, depending on the card and the bank that issued it. American Express, MasterCard, and Visa provide one or more of these services, so **get a copy of your credit card's travel-benefits policy.** If you are a member of the American Automobile Association (AAA) or an oil-company-sponsored road-assistance plan, always **ask hotel or car-rental reservationists about auto-club discounts.** And don't forget that auto-club membership entitles you to free maps and trip-planning services.

DIAL FOR DOLLARS

To save money, **look into "1-800" discount reservations services,** which use their buying power to get a better price on hotels, airline tickets, even car rentals. When booking a room, always **call the hotel's local toll-free number** (if one is available) rather than the central reservations number—you'll often get a better price. Always ask about special packages or corporate rates.

When shopping for the best deal on hotels and car rentals **look for guaranteed exchange rates,** which protect you against a falling dollar. With your rate locked in you won't pay more even if the price goes up in the local currency.

➤ AIRLINE TICKETS: ☎ 800/FLY–4–LESS.

➤ HOTEL ROOMS: **Travel Interlink** (☎ 800/888–5898).

SAVE ON COMBOS

Packages and guided tours can both save you money, but don't confuse the two. When you buy a package your travel remains independent, just as though you had planned and booked the trip yourself. Fly/drive packages, which combine airfare and car rental, are often a good deal. If you **buy a rail/drive pass** you'll save on train tickets and car rentals. All Eurail- and Europass holders get a discount on Eurostar fares through the Channel Tunnel.

JOIN A CLUB?

Many companies sell discounts in the form of travel clubs and coupon books, but these cost money. You must use participating advertisers to get a deal, and only after you recoup the initial membership cost or book price do you begin to save. If you plan to use the club or coupons frequently you may save considerably. Before signing up, find out what discounts you get for free.

➤ DISCOUNT CLUBS: **Entertainment Travel Editions** (✉ 2125 Butterfield Rd., Troy, MI 48084, ☎ 800/445–4137; $23–$48, depending on destination). **Great American Traveler** (✉ Box 27965, Salt Lake City, UT 84127, ☎ 800/548–2812; $49.95 per year). **Moment's Notice Discount Travel Club** (✉ 7301 New Utrecht Ave., Brooklyn, NY 11204, ☎ 718/234–6295; $25 per year, single or family). **Privilege Card International** (✉ 237 E. Front St., Youngstown, OH 44503, ☎ 330/746–5211 or 800/236–9732; $74.95 per year). **Sears's Mature Outlook** (✉ Box 9390, Des Moines, IA 50306, ☎ 800/336–6330; $14.95 per year). **Travelers Advantage** (✉ CUC Travel Service, 3033 S. Parker Rd., Suite 1000, Aurora, CO 80014, ☎ 800/548–1116 or 800/648–4037; $49 per year, single or family). **Worldwide Discount Travel Club** (✉ 1674 Meridian Ave., Miami Beach, FL 33139, ☎ 305/534–2082; $50 per year family, $40 single).

THE GOLD GUIDE / SMART TRAVEL TIPS

DRIVING

It's easy enough to explore Norway by car—but beware that gasoline costs over $1.00 per liter of lead-free gas, ferry costs are steep, and reservations are vital. Tolls on some major roads add to the expense, as do the high fees for city parking; tickets for illegal parking are painfully costly.

Norwegian roads are well marked with directional, distance, and informational signs. Even so, double-check all directions and have an up-to-date map before you venture out, because some highway numbers have changed in the past few years, particularly routes beginning with "E." You may come across construction in and around Oslo and other major cities.

Four-lane highways are the exception and are found only around cities. Outside of main routes, roads tend to be narrow and sharply twisting, with only token guardrails, and during the summer roads are always crowded. Along the west coast, waits for ferries and passage through tunnels can be significant. The southern part of Norway can be considered fairly compact—all major cities are about a day's drive from each other. The distances make themselves felt on the way north, where Norway becomes narrower as it inches up to and beyond the Arctic Circle and hooks over Sweden and Finland to touch Russia. Because distances are so great, it is virtually impossible to visit the entire country from one base. Don't expect to cover more than 240 km (150 mi) in a day, especially in fjord country.

Gas stations are plentiful, and *blyfri bensin* (unleaded gasoline) and diesel fuel are sold virtually everywhere from self-service gas pumps. Those marked *kort* are 24-hour pumps, which take oil-company credit cards or bank cards, either of which is inserted directly into the pump. Gas costs roughly four times the typical U.S. price—approximately NKr8.50 per liter.

INSURANCE

All vehicles registered abroad are required to carry international liability insurance and an international accident report form, which can be obtained from automobile clubs. Collision insurance is recommended.

RULES OF THE ROAD

Driving is on the right and you must yield to vehicles approaching from the right. Dimmed headlights are mandatory at all times, as is the use of seat belts and children's seats (when appropriate) in both front and rear seats. All cars must carry red reflecting warning triangles to be placed a safe distance from a disabled vehicle.

The maximum speed limit is 90 kph (55 mph) on major motorways. On other highways, the limit is 80 kph (50 mph). The speed limit in cities and towns is 50 kph (30 mph), and 30 kph (18 mph) in residential areas.

Norway has strict drinking-and-driving laws, and routine roadside checks, especially on Friday and Saturday nights, are common. The legal limit is a blood-alcohol percentage of 0.05%, which corresponds to a glass of wine or a bottle of low-alcohol beer and is a much lower limit than in the United States. If you are stopped for a routine check, you may be required to take a breath test. If that result is positive, you must submit to a blood test. No exceptions are made for foreigners, who can lose their licenses on the spot. You can also be fined or be imprisoned. In addition, an accident involving a driver with an illegal blood-alcohol level usually voids all insurance agreements, so the driver becomes responsible for his own medical bills and damage to the cars.

Speeding is also punished severely. Most roads are monitored by radar and cameras in gray metal boxes. Signs warning of *Automatisk Trafikkontroll* (Automatic Traffic Monitoring) are posted periodically along appropriate roads. Radar controls are frequent on weekends, especially along major highways.

WINTER DRIVING

Some roads, particularly those over mountains, can close for all or part of the winter. If you drive outside major roads, make sure the car is equipped with studded tires for improved traction. Roads are not salted but are left with a hard-packed layer of snow on top of the asphalt. If you're renting, **choose a small car with front-wheel drive.** Also bring an ice scraper, snow brush, small shovel, and heavy clothes for emergencies. Although the weather along the coast is sunny, a few hours inland, temperatures may be 15°F colder, and snowfall is the rule rather than the exception.

➤ EMERGENCY ASSISTANCE:

Norsk Automobil Forbund (✉ NAF, ☎ 22/34–16–00 for 24-hour service) patrols main roads and has emergency telephones on mountain roads.

➤ AUTO CLUBS: In the U.S., **American Automobile Association** (☎ 800/564–6222). In the U.K., **Automobile Association** (AA, ☎ 0990/500–600), **Royal Automobile Club** (RAC, membership ☎ 0990/722–722; insurance 0345/121–345).

E

ELECTRICITY

To use your U.S.-purchased electric-powered equipment, **bring a converter and adapter.** The electrical current in Norway is 220 volts, 50 cycles alternating current (AC); wall outlets take Continental-type plugs, with two round prongs.

If your appliances are dual-voltage, you'll need only an adapter. Don't use 110-volt outlets, marked FOR SHAVERS ONLY, for high-wattage appliances such as blow-dryers. Most laptops operate equally well on 110 and 220 volts and so require only an adapter.

F

FERRIES

Taking a ferry isn't only fun, it's often necessary. Many companies arrange package trips, some offering a rental car and hotel accommodations as part of the deal.

Ferry crossings often last overnight. The trip between Copenhagen and Oslo, for example, takes approximately 16 hours, most lines leaving at about 5 PM and arriving about 9 the next morning.

Ferries and passenger ships remain important means of transportation. Along west-coast fjords, car ferries are a way of life. More specialized boat service includes hydrofoil-catamaran trips between Stavanger, Haugesund, and Bergen. There are also fjord cruises out of these cities and others in the north. **Color Line** (✉ Box 1422, Vika 0115, Oslo, ☎ 22/94–44–00, FAX 22/83– 07–76) is a major carrier in Norwegian waters.

FROM THE U.K.

Only one ferry line serves Norway from the United Kingdom, **Color Line** (✉ Tyne Commission Quay, North Shields [near Newcastle], LEN29 6EA, ☎ 091/296–1313; ✉ Skolte-grunnskaien, 5000 Bergen, ☎ 55/32–27–80; or ✉ 405 Park Ave., New York, NY 10022, ☎ 800/323–7436), which has three departures a week between Bergen, Stavanger, and Newcastle during the summer season (May 22–Sept. 10) and two during the rest of the year. Crossings take about 22 hours. Monday sailings stop first in Stavanger and arrive in Bergen six hours later, whereas the other trips stop first in Bergen.

➤ FERRY LINES: The main ferry operators running within Scandinavian waters are **Color Line** (✉ Box 30, DK–9850 Hirsthals, Denmark, ☎ 45/99–56–19–66, FAX 45/98–94–50–92; ✉ Hjortneskaia, Box 1422 Vika, N–0115 Oslo, Norway, ☎ 47/22–94–44–00, FAX 47/22–83–07–71; ✉ c/o Bergen Line, Inc., 505 5th Ave., New York, NY 10017, ☎ 800/323–7436, FAX 212/983–1275; ✉ Tyne Commission Quay, North Shields NE29 6EA, Newcastle, England, ☎ 0191/296–1313, FAX 091/296–1540), and **ScandLines** (✉ Box 1, DK–3000 Helsingør, Denmark, ☎ 45/49–26–26–83, FAX 45/49–26–11–24; ✉ Knutpunkten 44, S–252 78 Helsingborg, Sweden, ☎ 46/42–186100, FAX 46/42–187410).

Connections from Denmark to Norway and Sweden are available through DFDS and the **Stena Line** (✉ Trafikhamnen, DK–9900 Frederikshavn, Denmark, ☎ 45/96–20–02–00, FAX 45/96–20–02–81; ✉ Jernbanetorget 2, N–0154 Oslo 1, Norway, ☎ 47/23–17–90–00, FAX 47/22–41–44–40; ✉ Scandinavia AB, S–405 19 Göteborg, Sweden, ☎ 46/31–775–0000, FAX 46/31–858595).

You can sail along the magnificent west coast of Norway with the **Fjord Line** (✉ Slottsgatan 1, N–5003 Bergen, Norway, ☎ 47/55–32–37–70, FAX 47/55–32–38–15).

Connections to the Faroe Islands from Norway and Denmark are available through the **Smyril Line** (DFDS—☞ *above*—or ⊠ J. Bronksgøøta 37, Box 370, FR–110 Tórshavn, Faroe Islands, ☎ 298/15–900, FAX 298/15–707; ⊠ Bergen, Norway, ☎ 47/55–32–09–70, FAX 47/55–96–02–72).

G

GAY & LESBIAN TRAVEL

➤ GAY- AND LESBIAN-FRIENDLY TRAVEL AGENCIES: **Advance Damron** (⊠ 1 Greenway Plaza, Suite 800, Houston, TX 77046, ☎ 713/850–1140 or 800/695–0880, FAX 713/888–1010). **Club Travel** (⊠ 8739 Santa Monica Blvd., West Hollywood, CA 90069, ☎ 310/358–2200 or 800/429–8747, FAX 310/358–2222). **Islanders/Kennedy Travel** (⊠ 183 W. 10th St., New York, NY 10014, ☎ 212/242–3222 or 800/988–1181, FAX 212/929–8530). **Now Voyager** (⊠ 4406 18th St., San Francisco, CA 94114, ☎ 415/626–1169 or 800/255–6951, FAX 415/626–8626). **Yellowbrick Road** (⊠ 1500 W. Balmoral Ave., Chicago, IL 60640, ☎ 773/561–1800 or 800/642–2488, FAX 773/561–4497). **Skylink Women's Travel** (⊠ 3577 Moorland Ave., Santa Rosa, CA 95407, ☎ 707/585–8355 or 800/225–5759, FAX 707/584–5637), serving lesbian travelers.

H

HEALTH

MEDICAL PLANS

No one plans to get sick while traveling, but it happens, so **consider signing up with a medical-assistance company.** Members get doctor referrals, emergency evacuation or repatriation, 24-hour telephone hot lines for medical consultation, cash for emergencies, and other personal and legal assistance. Coverage varies by plan, so **review the benefits carefully.**

➤ MEDICAL-ASSISTANCE COMPANIES: **International SOS Assistance** (⊠ Box 11568, Philadelphia, PA 19116, ☎ 215/244–1500 or 800/523–8930; ⊠ 1255 University St., Suite 420, Montréal, Québec H3B 3B6, ☎ 514/874–7674 or 800/363–0263; ⊠ 7 Old Lodge Pl., St. Margarets, Twickenham TW1 1RQ, England, ☎ 0181/744–0033). **MEDEX Assistance**

Corporation (⊠ Box 5375, Timonium, MD 21094-5375, ☎ 410/453–6300 or 800/537–2029). **Traveler's Emergency Network** (⊠ 3100 Tower Blvd., Suite 1000B, Durham, NC 27707, ☎ 919/490–6055 or 800/275–4836, FAX 919/493–8262). **TravMed** (⊠ Box 5375, Timonium, MD 21094, ☎ 410/453–6380 or 800/732–5309). **Worldwide Assistance Services** (⊠ 1133 15th St. NW, Suite 400, Washington, DC 20005, ☎ 202/331–1609 or 800/821–2828, FAX 202/828–5896).

I

INSURANCE

Without insurance you will lose all or most of your money if you cancel your trip, regardless of the reason. It's essential that you **buy trip-cancellation-and-interruption insurance,** particularly if your airline ticket, cruise, or package tour is nonrefundable and cannot be changed. When considering how much coverage you need, look for a policy that will cover the cost of your trip plus the nondiscounted price of a one-way airline ticket, should you need to return home early. Also **consider default or bankruptcy insurance,** which protects you against a supplier's failure to deliver.

Medicare generally does not cover health-care costs outside the United States, nor do many privately issued policies. If your own policy does not cover you outside the United States, **consider buying supplemental medical coverage.** Remember that travel health insurance is different from a medical-assistance plan (☞ Health, *above*).

Citizens of the United Kingdom can buy an annual travel-insurance policy valid for most vacations during the year in which it's purchased. If you are pregnant or have a preexisting medical condition, make sure you're covered.

If you have purchased an expensive vacation, particularly one that involves travel abroad, comprehensive insurance is a must. **Look for comprehensive policies that include trip-delay insurance,** which will protect you in the event that weather problems cause you to miss your flight, tour, or cruise. A few insurers sell waivers for preexisting medical conditions. Companies that offer both features include Access America, Carefree Travel, Travel Insured International, and Travel Guard (☞ *below*).

Always **buy travel insurance directly from the insurance company**; if you buy it from a travel agency or tour operator that goes out of business you probably will not be covered for the agency or operator's default, a major risk. Before you make any purchase, **review your existing health and home-owner's policies** to find out whether they cover expenses incurred while traveling.

➤ TRAVEL INSURERS: In the U.S., **Access America** (✉ 6600 W. Broad St., Richmond, VA 23230, ☎ 804/285–3300 or 800/284–8300), **Carefree Travel Insurance** (✉ Box 9366, 100 Garden City Plaza, Garden City, NY 11530, ☎ 516/294–0220 or 800/323–3149), **Near Travel Services** (✉ Box 1339, Calumet City, IL 60409, ☎ 708/868–6700 or 800/654–6700), **Travel Guard International** (✉ 1145 Clark St., Stevens Point, WI 54481, ☎ 715/345–0505 or 800/826–1300), **Travel Insured International** (✉ Box 280568, East Hartford, CT 06128–0568, ☎ 860/528–7663 or 800/243–3174), **Travelex Insurance Services** (✉ 11717 Burt St., Suite 202, Omaha, NE 68154-1500, ☎ 402/445–8637 or 800/228–9792, ℻ 800/867–9531), **Wallach & Company** (✉ 107 W. Federal St., Box 480, Middleburg, VA 20118, ☎ 540/687–3166 or 800/237–6615). In Canada, **Mutual of Omaha** (✉ Travel Division, 500 University Ave., Toronto, Ontario M5G 1V8, ☎ 416/598–4083, 800/268–8825 in Canada). In the U.K., **Association of British Insurers** (✉ 51 Gresham St., London EC2V 7HQ, ☎ 0171/600–3333).

L

LANGUAGE

Despite the fact that four of the five Scandinavian tongues are in the Germanic family of languages, it is a myth that someone who speaks German can understand Norwegian. Danish, Norwegian, and Swedish are similar, and fluent speakers can generally understand each other.

Norwegian has three additional vowels: æ, ø, and å. Æ is pronounced as a short "a." The ø, sometimes printed as *oe*, is the same as ö in German and Swedish, pronounced very much like a short "u." The å is a contraction of the archaic "aa" and sounds like long "o." These three letters appear at the end of alphabetical listings.

There are two officially sanctioned Norwegian languages, Bokmål and Nynorsk. Bokmål is used by 84% of the population and is the main written form of Norwegian, the language of books, as the first half of its name indicates. Nynorsk, which translates as "new Norwegian," is actually a compilation of older dialect forms from rural Norway, which evolved during the national romantic period around the turn of this century. All Norwegians are required to study both languages, and 25% of all state (NRK) television and radio broadcasting is required to be in Nynorsk. Every Norwegian also receives at least seven years of English instruction, starting in the second grade. Outside major cities, English becomes rarer, and it's a good idea to **take along a dictionary or phrase book.**

The Sami (incorrectly called Lapp) people have their own language, which is distantly related to Finnish.

LODGING

In the larger cities, lodging ranges from first-class business hotels run by SAS, Sheraton, and Scandic to good-quality tourist-class hotels, such as RESO, Best Western, and Scandic Budget, to a wide variety of single-entrepreneur hotels. In the countryside, look for independently run inns and motels. In in Norway they're called *fjellstuer* or *pensjonat*. Before you leave home, **ask your travel agent about discounts** (☞ Hotels, *below*), including summer hotel checks for Best Western, Scandic, and Inter Nor hotels, a summer Fjord pass in Norway, and enormous year-round rebates at SAS hotels for travelers over 65. All EuroClass (business class) passengers can get discounts of at least 10% at SAS hotels when they book through SAS.

Two things about hotels usually surprise North Americans: the relatively limited dimensions of Scandinavian beds and the generous size of Scandinavian breakfasts. Scandinavian double beds are often about 60 inches wide or slightly less, close in size to the U.S. queen size. King-size beds (72 inches wide) are difficult to find and, if available, require special reservations.

Scandinavian breakfasts resemble what many people would call lunch, usually including breads, cheeses, marmalade, hams, lunch meats, eggs, juice, cereal, milk, and coffee. Generally, the farther north you go, the larger the breakfasts become. Breakfast is often included in the price of the hotel.

Older hotels may have some rooms described as "double," which in fact have one double bed plus one foldout sofa big enough for two people. This arrangement is occasionally called a combi-room but is being phased out.

Many older hotels, particularly the country inns and independently run smaller hotels in the cities, do not have private bathrooms. Ask ahead if this is important to you.

Make reservations whenever possible. Even countryside inns, which usually have space, are sometimes packed with vacationing Europeans.

Ask about high and low seasons when making reservations, since different countries define their tourist seasons differently. Some hotels lower prices during tourist season, whereas others raise them during the same period.

CAMPING

For camping information and a list of sites, contact local tourist offices or the **Norwegian Automobile Federation** (✉ Storgt. 2, 0155, Oslo 1, ☎ 22/34–14–00). For a list of vandrerhjem (hostels) in Norway, contact **Norske Vandrerhjem** (✉ Dronningensgt. 26, 0154 Oslo, ☎ 22/42–14–10, FAX 22/42–44–76).

HOTELS

Norway offers Inn Checks, or prepaid hotel vouchers, for accommodations ranging from first-class hotels to country cottages. These vouchers, which must be purchased from travel agents or from the Scandinavian Tourist Board (☞ Visitor Information, *below*) before departure, are sold individually and in packets for as many nights as needed and offer savings of up to 50%. They may also offer summer bargains for foreign tourists. For further information about hotel vouchers, contact the Scandinavian Tourist Board.

M

MAIL

The letter rate for Norway is NKr3.50, NKr4 for the other Nordic countries, NKr4.50 for Europe, and NKr5.50 for outside Europe for a letter weighing up to 20 grams (¾ ounce).

MONEY

The unit of currency in Norway is the *krone* (plural: *kroner*), which translates as "crown," written officially as NOK. Price tags are seldom marked this way, but instead read "Kr" followed by the amount, such as Kr10. (In this book, the Norwegian krone is abbreviated NKr.) One krone is divided into 100 *øre,* and coins of 10 and 50 øre and 1, 5, 10, and 20 kroner are in circulation, although 10 øre are no longer in production. Bills are issued in denominations of 50, 100, 200, 500, and 1,000 kroner. In winter 1998, the exchange rate was NKr7.49 to U.S.$1, NKr12.3 to £1, and NKr5.17 to C$1. These rates fluctuate, so be sure to **check them when planning a trip.**

SAMPLE PRICES

Cup of coffee, from NKr12 in a cafeteria to NKr25 or more in a restaurant; a 20-pack of cigarettes, NKr50; a half-liter of beer, NKr30–NKr50; the smallest hot dog (with bun plus *lompe*—a flat Norwegian potato bread—mustard, ketchup, and fried onions) at a convenience store, NKr15; cheapest bottle of wine from a government store, NKr60; the same bottle at a restaurant, NKr120–NKr200; urban transit fare in Oslo, NKr15; soft drink, from NKr20 in a cafeteria to NKr35 in a better restaurant; one adult movie ticket, NKr45; shrimp or roast beef sandwich at a cafeteria, NKr40; 1½-km (1-mi) taxi ride, NKr30–NKr50 depending on time of day.

ATMS

Before leaving home, **make sure that your credit cards have been programmed for ATM use in Norway.** Note that Discover is accepted mostly in the United States. Local bank cards often do not work overseas or may access only your checking account; **ask your bank about a MasterCard/ Cirrus or Visa debit card,** which works like a bank card but can be used at any ATM displaying a MasterCard/ Cirrus or Visa logo. These cards, too, may tap only your checking account; check with your bank about their policy.

➤ ATM LOCATIONS: **Cirrus** (☎ 800/ 424–7787). A list of **Plus** locations is available at your local bank.

COSTS

Costs are high in Norway. Be aware that sales taxes can be very high, but foreigners can get some refunds by shopping at tax-free stores (☞ Taxes, *below*). City cards can save you transportation and entrance fees in many of the larger cities.

You can **reduce the cost of food by planning.** Breakfast is often included in your hotel bill; if not, you may wish to buy fruit, sweet rolls, and a beverage for a picnic breakfast. Electrical devices for hot coffee or tea should be bought abroad, though, to conform to the local current. **Opt for a restaurant lunch instead of dinner,** since the latter tends to be significantly more expensive. If you order water, specify tap water if that's what you mean, as the term "water" can refer to soft drinks and bottled water, which are also expensive. In Norway, the tip is included in the cost of your meal.

Liquor and strong beer (over 3% alcohol) can be purchased only in state-owned shops, at very high prices, during weekday business hours, usually 9:30 to 6. (When you visit relatives in Scandinavia, a bottle of liquor or fine wine bought duty-free on the trip over is often a much-appreciated gift.)

CURRENCY EXCHANGE

For the most favorable rates, **change money at banks.** Although fees charged for ATM transactions may be higher abroad than at home, Cirrus and Plus exchange rates are excellent, because they are based on wholesale rates offered only by major banks. You won't do as well at exchange booths in airports or rail and bus stations, in hotels, in restaurants, or in stores, although you may find their hours more convenient. To avoid lines at airport exchange booths, **get a small amount of local currency before you leave home.**

➤ EXCHANGE SERVICES: **International Currency Express** (☎ 888/842–0880 on the East Coast or 888/278–6628 on the West Coast for telephone orders). **Thomas Cook Currency Services** (☎ 800/287–7362 for telephone orders and retail locations).

TIPPING

Tipping is kept to a minimum in Norway because service charges are added to most bills. It is, however, handy to have a supply of NKr5 or 10 coins for less formal service. Tip only in local currency.

Airport and railroad porters (if you can find them) have fixed rates per bag, so they will tell you how much they should be paid. Tips to doormen vary according to the type of bag and the distance carried—NKr5–NKr10 each, with similar tips for porters carrying bags to the room. Room service usually has a service charge included already, so tipping is discretionary.

Round off a taxi fare to the next round digit, or tip anywhere from NKr5 to NKr10, a little more if the driver has been particularly helpful with luggage.

All restaurants include a service charge, ranging from 12% to 15%, in the bill. It is customary to add an additional 5% for exceptional service, but it is not obligatory. Maître d's are not tipped, and coat checks have flat rates, ranging from NKr5 to NKr10 per person.

TRAVELER'S CHECKS

Whether or not to buy traveler's checks depends on where you are headed. **Take cash if your trip includes rural areas** and small towns, traveler's checks to cities. If your checks are lost or stolen, they can usually be replaced within 24 hours. To ensure a speedy refund, buy your checks yourself (don't ask someone else to make the purchase). When making a claim for stolen or lost checks, the person who bought the checks should make the call.

O

OPENING AND CLOSING TIMES

Banks are open weekdays 9 to 4, Thursday until 5. Most shops are open 9 or 10 to 5 weekdays, Thursday until 7, Saturday 9 to 2, and are closed Sunday. In some areas, especially in larger cities, stores stay open later on weekdays. Large shopping centers, for example, are usually open until 8 weekdays and 6 on Saturdays. Supermarkets are open until 8 or 10 weekdays and until 6 on Saturdays. During the summer, most shops close weekdays at 4 and at 1 on Saturday; banks open at 8:15 and close at 3, with a Thursday closing at 5. Most post offices are open weekdays 8 to 5, Saturday 9 to 2. In small towns, post offices are often closed on Saturdays.

OUTDOOR ACTIVITIES AND SPORTS

Norway is a sports lover's paradise. Outdoor sports have always been popular, although indoor facilities have been built nationwide. Close to 100 recreational and competitive sports are recognized in Norway, each with its own national association, 57 of which are affiliated with the **Norges Idrettsforbund** (Norwegian Confederation of Sports, ⊠ Hauger Skolevei 1, 1351 Rud, ☎ 67/15–46–00). The tourist board's Norway brochure, which lists sporting- and active-holiday resources and contacts, is a more helpful starting point for visitors.

BIKING

Most cities have marked bike and ski routes and paths. Bicycling on country roads away from traffic is a favorite national pastime, but as most routes are hilly, this demands good physical condition. All cyclists are required to wear protective helmets and use lights at night. You can rent a bike and get local maps through any local tourist board.

Den Norske Turistforening (DNT, ⊠ Box 1963 Vika, 0125 Oslo 1, ☎ 22/ 82–28–00, ℻ 22/83–24–78) provides inexpensive lodging for cyclists planning overnight trips. You can also contact the helpful **Syklistenes Landsforening** (⊠ Maridalsvn. 60, 0458 Oslo 4, ☎ 22/71–92–93) for general information and maps, as well as the latest weather conditions.

BIRD-WATCHING

Northern Norway contains some of northern Europe's largest bird sanctuaries and teems with fantastic numbers of seabirds, including cormorants, razorbills, auks, guillemots, eider ducks, puffins, and even eagles. For organized tours, contact **Borton Overseas** (☎ 800/843–0602) or the Norwegian Tourist Board.

CANOEING

There are plenty of lakes and streams for canoeing in Norway, as well as rental facilities. Contact **Norges Padlerforbund** (⊠ Hauger Skolevei 1, 1351 Bærum, ☎ 67/15–46–00) for a list of rental companies and regional canoeing centers.

DIVING

There are few restrictions regarding diving sites in Norway—special permission is required to dive in a harbor, and diving near army installations is restricted. Contact **Norges Dykkforbund** (⊠ Hauger Skolevei 1, 1351 Baerum, ☎ 67/15–46–00) for a list of diving centers.

FISHING

To fish, you'll have to buy an annual fishing tax card at the post office and a local license from the sporting-goods store nearest the fishing site. Live bait is prohibited, and imported tackle must be disinfected before use.

HANG GLIDING

The mountains and hills of Norway provide excellent take-off spots. However, winds and weather conspire to make conditions unpredictable. For details on local clubs, regulations, and equipment rental, contact **Norsk Aeroklubb** (⊠ Moellesvingen 2, 0854 Oslo, ☎ 22/93–03–00).

RAFTING

Rafting excursions are offered throughout Norway. For more information, contact **Flåteopplevelser** (⊠ Postboks 227, 2051 Jessheim,

☎ 63/97–29–04) or **Norwegian Wildlife and Rafting** (✉ 2254 Lundersæter, ☎ 62/82–97–24).

SAILING

Contact **Norges Seilforbund** (✉ Hauger Skolevei 1, 1351 Bærum, ☎ 67/56–85–75) about facilities around the country.

SKIING

The **Skiforeningen** (✉ Kongevn. 5, 0390 Oslo 3, ☎ 22/92–32–00) provides national snow-condition reports.

SPORTS FOR PEOPLE WITH DISABILITIES

Beitostølen Helsesportsenter (✉ 2953 Beitostølen, ☎ 61/34–12–00) has sports facilities for the blind and other physically challenged people as well as training programs for instructors. Sports offered include skiing, hiking, running, and horseback riding.

P

PACKING FOR NORWAY

Bring a folding umbrella and a lightweight raincoat, as it is common for the sky to be clear at 9 AM, rainy at 11 AM, and clear again in time for lunch. **Pack casual clothes,** as Norwegians tend to dress more casually than their Continental brethren. If you have trouble sleeping when it is light or are sensitive to strong sun, **bring an eye mask and dark sunglasses;** the sun rises as early as 4 AM in some areas, and the far-northern latitude causes it to slant at angles unseen elsewhere on the globe. **Bring bug repellent** if you plan to venture away from the major cities; large mosquitoes can be a real nuisance in the far-northern reaches of Norway.

Bring an extra pair of eyeglasses or contact lenses in your carry-on luggage, and if you have a health problem, **pack enough medication** to last the entire trip or have your doctor write you a prescription using the drug's generic name, because brand names vary from country to country. It's important that you **don't put prescription drugs or valuables in luggage to be checked**: it might go astray. To avoid problems with customs officials, carry medications in the original packaging. Also, don't forget the addresses of offices that handle refunds of lost traveler's checks.

LUGGAGE

In general, you are entitled to check two bags on flights within the United States and on international flights leaving the United States. A third piece may be brought on board, but it must fit easily under the seat in front of you or in the overhead compartment.

If you are flying between two foreign destinations, note that baggage allowances may be determined not by piece but by weight—generally 88 pounds (40 kilograms) in first class, 66 pounds (30 kilograms) in business class, and 44 pounds (20 kilograms) in economy. If your flight between two cities abroad *connects* with your transatlantic or transpacific flight, the piece method still applies.

Airline liability for baggage is limited to $1,250 per person on flights within the United States. On international flights it amounts to $9.07 per pound or $20 per kilogram for checked baggage (roughly $640 per 70-pound bag) and $400 per passenger for unchecked baggage. Insurance for losses exceeding these amounts can be bought from the airline at check-in for about $10 per $1,000 of coverage; note that this coverage excludes a rather extensive list of items, which is shown on your airline ticket.

Before departure, **itemize your bags' contents** and their worth, and label the bags with your name, address, and phone number. (If you use your home address, cover it so that potential thieves can't see it readily.) Inside each bag, **pack a copy of your itinerary.** At check-in, **make sure that each bag is correctly tagged** with the destination airport's three-letter code. If your bags arrive damaged or fail to arrive at all, file a written report with the airline before leaving the airport.

PASSPORTS & VISAS

Once your travel plans are confirmed, **check the expiration date of your passport.** It's also a good idea to **make photocopies of the data page;** leave one copy with someone at home and keep another with you, separated from your passport. If you lose your passport, promptly call the nearest embassy or consulate and the local police; having a copy of the data page can speed replacement.

U.S. CITIZENS

All U.S. citizens, even infants, need only a valid passport to enter Norway for stays of up to three months.

➤ INFORMATION: **Office of Passport Services** (☎ 202/647–0518).

CANADIAN CITIZENS

You need only a valid passport to enter Norway for stays of up to three months.

➤ INFORMATION: **Passport Office** (☎ 819/994–3500 or 800/567–6868).

U.K. CITIZENS

Citizens of the United Kingdom need only a valid passport to enter Norway for stays of up to three months.

➤ INFORMATION: **London Passport Office** (☎ 0990/21010) for fees and documentation requirements and to request an emergency passport.

S

SENIOR-CITIZEN TRAVEL

To qualify for age-related discounts, **mention your senior-citizen status up front** when booking hotel reservations (not when checking out) and before you're seated in restaurants (not when paying the bill). Note that discounts may be limited to certain menus, days, or hours. When renting a car, **ask about promotional car-rental discounts,** which can be cheaper than senior-citizen rates.

➤ EDUCATIONAL TRAVEL PROGRAMS: **Elderhostel** (✉ 75 Federal St., 3rd floor, Boston, MA 02110, ☎ 617/426–8056). **Interhostel** (✉ University of New Hampshire, 6 Garrison Ave., Durham, NH 03824, ☎ 603/862–1147 or 800/733–9753, FAX 603/862–1113).

TRAIN TRAVEL

Travelers over 60 can buy a **SeniorRail Card** for about $27 in Norway. It gives 30% discounts on train travel in 21 European countries for a whole year from purchase.

STUDENTS

To save money, **look into deals available through student-oriented travel agencies.** To qualify you'll need a bona fide student ID card. Members of international student groups are also eligible.

➤ STUDENT IDS AND SERVICES: **Council on International Educational Exchange** (✉ CIEE, 205 E. 42nd St., 14th floor, New York, NY 10017, ☎ 212/822–2600 or 888/268–6245, FAX 212/822–2699), for mail orders only, in the United States. **Travel Cuts** (✉ 187 College St., Toronto, Ontario M5T 1P7, ☎ 416/979–2406 or 800/667–2887) in Canada.

➤ HOSTELING: **Hostelling International—American Youth Hostels** (✉ 733 15th St. NW, Suite 840, Washington, DC 20005, ☎ 202/783–6161, FAX 202/783–6171). **Hostelling International—Canada** (✉ 400-205 Catherine St., Ottawa, Ontario K2P 1C3, ☎ 613/237–7884, FAX 613/237–7868). **Youth Hostel Association of England and Wales** (✉ Trevelyan House, 8 St. Stephen's Hill, St. Albans, Hertfordshire AL1 2DY, ☎ 01727/855215 or 01727/845047, FAX 01727/844126). Membership in the U.S., $25; in Canada, C$26.75; in the U.K., £9.30).

T

TAXES

VALUE-ADDED TAX (V.A.T.)

Value-added tax, VAT for short but called *moms* all over Scandinavia, is a hefty 23% on all purchases except books; it is included in the prices of goods. All purchases of consumer goods totaling more than NKr300 (approximately $45) for export by nonresidents are eligible for value-added tax refunds.

Shops subscribing to "Norway Tax-Free Shopping" provide customers with vouchers, which they must present together with their purchases on departure to receive an on-the-spot refund of 16.25% of the tax.

Shops that do not subscribe to this program have slightly more detailed forms, which must be presented to the Norwegian Customs Office along with the goods to obtain a refund by mail. This refund is closer to the actual amount of the tax.

It's essential to have both the forms and the goods available for inspection upon departure. Make sure the appropriate stamps are on the voucher or other forms before leaving the country.

One way to beat high prices is to **take advantage of tax-free shopping.** Throughout Scandinavia, you can make major purchases free of tax if you have a foreign passport. Ask about tax-free shopping when you make a purchase for $50 (about £32) or more. When your purchases exceed a specified limit (which varies from country to country), you receive a special export receipt. Keep the parcels intact and take them out of the country within 30 days of purchase. When you leave, you can obtain a refund of the tax in cash from a special office at the airport, or, upon arriving home, you can send your receipts to an office in the country of purchase to receive your refund by mail. Be aware that limits for EU tourists are higher than for those coming from outside the EU. In Norway, for non-EU tourists, the refund is 23% for purchases over NKr308.

TAXIS

Even the smallest villages have some form of taxi service. Towns on the railroad normally have taxi stands just outside the station. All city taxis are connected with a central dispatching office, so there is only one main telephone number, the taxi central. Look in the telephone book under "Taxi" or "Drosje."

TELEPHONES

The country code for Norway is 47. There are no area or city codes, except in that numbers in each city start with the same two-digit prefix, such as 22 (Oslo) and 55 (Bergen). You have to dial all eight digits whether or not you're in the city. Telephone numbers starting with the prefix 82 cost extra.

Local calls cost NKr2 or NKr3 from a pay phone and about NKr3 from hotel phones. Long distance rates vary according to distance and time of day. Toll-free numbers beginning with "800" or "810" are also becoming more common, although this is mostly among large corporations.

Public telephones are of two types. Push-button phones, which accept NKr1, 5, and 10 coins (some accept NKr20 coins), are easy to use: lift the receiver, listen for the dial tone, insert the coins, dial the number, and wait for a connection. The digital screen at the top of the box indicates the amount of money in your "account."

Older rotary telephones sometimes have a grooved slope at the top for NKr1 coins, allowing them to drop into the phone as needed. Place several in the slope, lift the receiver, listen for the dial tone, dial the number, and wait for a connection. When the call is connected, the telephone will emit a series of beeps, allowing coins to drop into the telephone.

Both types of telephones have warning signals (short pips) indicating that the purchased time is almost over.

DIRECTORY ASSISTANCE AND OPERATOR INFORMATION

Dial 180 for information for Norway and the other Scandinavian countries, 181 for other international telephone numbers.

For operator-assisted calls, dial 117 for national calls and 115 for international calls. All international operators speak English.

CALLING HOME

The telephone system in Norway is modern and efficient and international direct service is available throughout the country. Before you go, **find out the local access codes** for your destinations. AT&T, MCI, and Sprint long-distance services make calling home relatively convenient, but you may find the local access number blocked in many hotel rooms. First ask the hotel operator to connect you. If the hotel operator balks, ask for an international operator, or dial the international operator yourself. One way to improve your odds of getting connected to your long-distance carrier is to travel with more than one company's calling card (a hotel may block Sprint, for example, but not MCI). If all else fails, call your phone company collect in the United States or call from a pay phone in the hotel lobby.

➤ To Obtain Access Codes: AT&T USADirect (☎ 800/874–4000). MCI Call USA (☎ 800/444–4444). Sprint Express (☎ 800/793–1153).

TOUR OPERATORS

Buying a prepackaged tour or independent vacation can make your trip to Norway less expensive and more hassle-free. Because everything is prearranged you'll spend less time planning.

Operators that handle several hundred thousand travelers per year can use their purchasing power to give you a good price. Their high volume may also indicate financial stability. But some small companies provide more personalized service; because they tend to specialize, they may also be more knowledgeable about a given area.

A GOOD DEAL?

The more your package or tour includes, the better you can predict the ultimate cost of your vacation. Make sure you know exactly what is covered, and **beware of hidden costs.** Are taxes, tips, and service charges included? Transfers and baggage handling? Entertainment and excursions? These can add up.

If the package or tour you are considering is priced lower than in your wildest dreams, **be skeptical.** Also, **make sure your travel agent knows the accommodations** and other services. Ask about the hotel's location, room size, beds, and whether it has a pool, room service, or programs for children, if you care about these. Has your agent been there in person or sent others you can contact?

BUYER BEWARE

Each year consumers are stranded or lose their money when tour operators—even very large ones with excellent reputations—go out of business. So **check out the operator.** Find out how long the company has been in business, and ask several agents about its reputation. **Don't book unless the firm has a consumer-protection program.**

Members of the National Tour Association and United States Tour Operators Association are required to set aside funds to cover your payments and travel arrangements in case the company defaults. Nonmembers may carry insurance instead. Look for the details, and for the name of an underwriter with a solid reputation, in the operator's brochure. Note: When it comes to tour operators, **don't trust escrow accounts.** Although the Department of Transportation watches over charter-flight operators, no regulatory body prevents tour operators from raiding the till. You may want to protect yourself by buying travel insurance that includes a tour-operator default provision. For more information, *see* Consumer Protection, *above.*

It's also a good idea to choose a company that participates in the American Society of Travel Agent's Tour Operator Program (TOP). This gives you a forum if there are any disputes between you and your tour operator; ASTA will act as mediator.

➤ TOUR-OPERATOR RECOMMENDATIONS: **American Society of Travel Agents** (☞ Travel Agencies, *below*). **National Tour Association** (✉ NTA, 546 E. Main St., Lexington, KY 40508, ☎ 606/226–4444 or 800/755–8687). **United States Tour Operators Association** (✉ USTOA, 342 Madison Ave., Suite 1522, New York, NY 10173, ☎ 212/599–6599, FAX 212/599–6744).

USING AN AGENT

Travel agents are excellent resources. In fact, large operators accept bookings made only through travel agents. But it's a good idea to **collect brochures from several agencies,** because some agents' suggestions may be influenced by relationships with tour and package firms that reward them for volume sales. If you have a special interest, **find an agent with expertise in that area;** ASTA (☞ Travel Agencies, *below*) has a database of specialists worldwide. Do some homework on your own, too: Local tourism boards can provide information about lesser-known and small-niche operators, some of which may sell only direct.

GROUP TOURS

Among companies that sell tours to Norway, the following are nationally known, have a proven reputation, and offer plenty of options. The classifications used below represent different price categories, and you'll probably encounter these terms when talking to a travel agent or tour operator. The key difference is usually in accommodations, which run from budget to better, and better-yet to best.

➤ SUPER-DELUXE: **Abercrombie & Kent** (⊠ 1520 Kensington Rd., Oak Brook, IL 60521-2141, ☎ 630/954–2944 or 800/323–7308, FAX 630/954–3324). **Travcoa** (⊠ Box 2630, 2350 S.E. Bristol St., Newport Beach, CA 92660, ☎ 714/476–2800 or 800/992–2003, FAX 714/476–2538).

➤ DELUXE: **Globus** (⊠ 5301 S. Federal Circle, Littleton, CO 80123-2980, ☎ 303/797–2800 or 800/221–0090, FAX 303/347–2080). **Maupintour** (⊠ 1515 St. Andrews Dr., Lawrence, KS 66047, ☎ 913/843–1211 or 800/255–4266, FAX 913/843–8351). **Tauck Tours** (⊠ Box 5027, 276 Post Rd. W, Westport, CT 06881-5027, ☎ 203/226–6911 or 800/468–2825, FAX 203/221–6828).

➤ FIRST-CLASS: **Bennett Tours** (⊠ 270 Madison Ave., New York, NY 10016-0658, ☎ 212/532–5060 or 800/221–2420, FAX 212/779–8944). **Brendan Tours** (⊠ 15137 Califa St., Van Nuys, CA 91411, ☎ 818/785–9696 or 800/421–8446, FAX 818/902–9876). **Brekke Tours** (⊠ 802 N. 43rd St., Ste. D, Grand Forks, ND 58203, ☎ 701/772–8999 or 800/437–5302, FAX 701/780–9352). **Caravan Tours** (⊠ 401 N. Michigan Ave., Chicago, IL 60611, ☎ 312/321–9800 or 800/227–2826, FAX 312/321–9845). **Collette Tours** (⊠ 162 Middle St., Pawtucket, RI 02860, ☎ 401/728–3805 or 800/832–4656, FAX 401/728–1380). **Finnair** (☎ 800/950–5000). **KITT Holidays** (⊠ 2 Appletree Sq., #150, 8011 34th Ave. S, Minneapolis, MN 55425, ☎ 612/854–8005 or 800/262–8728, FAX 612/854–6948). **Scantours** (⊠ 1535 6th St., #205, Santa Monica, CA 90401-2533, ☎ 310/451–0911 or 800/223–7226, FAX 310/395–2013). **Scan Travel Center** (⊠ 66 Edgewood Ave., Larchmont, NY 10538, ☎ 803/671–6758 or 800/759–7226). **Trafalgar Tours** (⊠ 11 E. 26th St., New York, NY 10010, ☎ 212/689–8977 or 800/854–0103, FAX 800/457–6644).

➤ BUDGET: **Cosmos** (☞ Globus, *above*). **Trafalgar** (☞ *above*).

PACKAGES

Like group tours, independent vacation packages are available from major tour operators and airlines. The companies listed below offer vacation packages in a broad price range.

➤ AIR/HOTEL/SIGHTSEEING: **DER Tours** (⊠ 9501 W. Devon St., Rosemont, IL 60018, ☎ 800/937–1235; FAX 800/282–7474, 800/860–9944 for brochures). **Icelandair** (☎ 800/757–3876).

THEME TRIPS

➤ ADVENTURE: **Borton Overseas** (⊠ 1621 E. 79th St., Bloomington, MN 55425, ☎ 612/883–0704 or 800/843–0602, FAX 612/883–0221). **Scandinavian Special Interest Network** (⊠ Box 313, Sparta, NJ 07871, ☎ 201/729–8961, FAX 201/729–6565).

➤ BICYCLING: **Backroads** (⊠ 801 Cedar St., Berkeley, CA 94710-1800, ☎ 510/527–1555 or 800/462–2848, FAX 510/527–1444).

➤ CROSS-COUNTRY SKIING: **Above the Clouds Trekking** (⊠ Box 398, Worcester, MA 01602, ☎ 508/799–4499 or 800/233–4499, FAX 508/797–4779).

➤ CRUISING: **Bergen Line** (⊠ 405 Park Ave., New York, NY 10022, ☎ 212/319–1300 or 800/323–7436, FAX 212/319–1390). **EuroCruises** (⊠ 303 W. 13th St., New York, NY 10014, ☎ 212/691–2099 or 800/688–3876). **Swan Hellenic/Classical Cruises & Tours** (⊠ 132 E. 70th St., New York, NY 10021, ☎ 800/252–7745, FAX 212/774–1545).

➤ CUSTOMIZED PACKAGES: **Scandinavian Special Interest Network** (☞ Adventure, *above*).

➤ FISHING: **Scandinavian Special Interest Network** (☞ Adventure, *above*).

➤ GENEALOGY: **Brekke Tours** (☞ Group Tours, *above*). **Scan Travel Center** (⊠ 66 Edgewood Ave., Larchmont, NY 10538, ☎ 803/671–6758 or 800/759–7226).

➤ HIKING/WALKING: **Above the Clouds Trekking** (☞ Cross-Country Skiing, *above*). **Backroads** (☞ Bicycling, *above*).

TRAIN TRAVEL

NSB, the Norwegian State Railway System, has five main lines originating from the **Oslo S Station.** Train tickets can be purchased in railway stations or from travel agencies. NSB has its own travel agency in Oslo (⊠ Stortingsgt. 28, ☎ 22/83–88–50). The longest train runs north to Trondheim, then extends onward as far as Fauske and Bodø. The southern line hugs the coast to Stavanger, whereas the western line crosses some famous scenic territory on the way to Bergen. An eastern line through Kongsvinger to Stockholm links Norway with Sweden, while another southern line through Gothenburg, Sweden, is the main connection with continental Europe. Narvik, north of Bodø, is the last stop on Sweden's Ofot line, the world's northernmost rail system, which runs from Stockholm via Kiruna. It is possible to take a five-hour bus trip between Bodø and Narvik to connect with the other train.

NSB trains are clean, comfortable, and punctual. Most have special compartments for travelers with disabilities and for families with children younger than two years of age. First- and second-class tickets are available. Both seat and sleeper reservations are required on express and overnight trains. Prices vary according to one-, two-, or three-bunk cabins. Reserve a few days ahead in the summer, during major holidays, and for Friday and Sunday trains.

To save money, **look into rail passes,** but be aware that if you don't plan to cover many miles, you may come out ahead by buying individual tickets.

DISCOUNT PASSES

Discounted fares include family, senior-citizen (including not-yet-senior spouses), and off-peak "mini" fares, which must be purchased a day in advance. NSB gives student discounts only to foreigners studying at Norwegian institutions.

Norway participates in the following rail programs: **EurailPass** (and its flexipass variations), **Eurail Drive, ScanRail Pass, Scanrail 'n Drive, InterRail,** and **Nordturist Card.** A **Norway Rail Pass** is available for one or two weeks of unlimited rail travel within Norway. The ticket is sold in the United States through **ScanAm** (⊠ 933 Hwy. 23, Pompton Plains, NJ

07444, ☎ 800/545–2204). Prices are approximately $190 for one week in second class; $255 for two weeks in second class. First-class rail passes are about 30% higher. Low-season prices are offered October through April. Rail passes do not guarantee that you will get seats on the trains you want to ride, and seat reservations are sometimes required, particularly on express trains. You will also need reservations for overnight sleeping accommodations.

Norway is one of 17 countries in which you can **use EurailPasses,** which provide unlimited first-class rail travel, in all of the participating countries, for the duration of the pass. If you plan to rack up the miles, get a standard pass. These are available for 15 days ($522), 21 days ($678), one month ($838), two months ($1,188), and three months ($1,468).

In addition to standard EurailPasses, **ask about special rail-pass plans.** Among these are the Eurail Youthpass (for those under age 26), the Eurail Saverpass (which gives a discount for two or more people traveling together), a Eurail Flexipass (which allows a certain number of travel days within a set period), the Euraildrive Pass, and the Europass Drive (which combines travel by train and rental car).

Whichever pass you choose, remember that you must **purchase your pass before you leave** for Europe.

Many travelers assume that rail passes guarantee them seats on the trains they wish to ride. Not so. You need to **book seats ahead even if you are using a rail pass**; seat reservations are required on some European trains, particularly high-speed trains, and are a good idea on trains that may be crowded—particularly in summer on popular routes. You will also need a reservation if you purchase sleeping accommodations.

➤ RAIL PASSES: Norwegian rail passes are sold by travel agents as well as **Rail Europe** (⊠ 226–230 Westchester Ave., White Plains, NY 10604, ☎ 914/682–5172 or 800/438–7245; ⊠ 2087 Dundas East, Suite 105, Mississauga, Ontario L4X 1M2, ☎ 416/602–4195).

Eurail and EuroPasses are available through travel agents and **Rail Europe** (⊠ 226-230 Westchester Ave., White Plains, NY 10604, ☎ 914/682–5172 or 800/438–7245; ⊠ 2087 Dundas East, Suite 105, Mississauga, Ontario L4X 1M2, ☎ 416/602–4195), **DER Tours** (⊠ Box 1606, Des Plaines, IL 60017, ☎ 800/782–2424, FAX 800/ 282–7474), or **CIT Tours Corp.** (⊠ 342 Madison Ave., Suite 207, New York, NY 10173, ☎ 212/697– 2100 or 800/248–8687, or 800/248– 7245 in western U.S.).

FROM THE U.K.

Traveling from Britain to Norway by train is not difficult, but it is time-consuming. The best connection leaves London's Victoria Station (☎ 0171/928–5100) at noon and connects at Dover with a boat to Oostende, Belgium. From Oostende there is a sleeping-car-only connection to Copenhagen that arrives the next morning at 8:25. The train to Oslo leaves at 9:45 AM and arrives at 7:42 PM. A number of special discounted trips are available, including the **InterRail Pass,** which is available for European residents of all ages, and the **EurailPass,** sold in the United States only.

A good travel agent puts your needs first. Look for an agency that has been in business at least five years, emphasizes customer service, and has someone on staff who specializes in your destination. In addition, **make sure the agency belongs to the American Society of Travel Agents** (ASTA). If your travel agency is also acting as your tour operator, *see* Buyer Beware in Tour Operators, *above*).

➤ LOCAL AGENT REFERRALS: **American Society of Travel Agents** (ASTA, ☎ 800/965–2782 24-hr hot line, FAX 703/684–8319). **Alliance of Canadian Travel Associations** (⊠ Suite 201, 1729 Bank St., Ottawa, Ontario K1V 7Z5, ☎ 613/521–0474, FAX 613/ 521–0805). **Association of British Travel Agents** (⊠ 55–57 Newman St., London W1P 4AH, ☎ 0171/637– 2444, FAX 0171/637–0713).

Travel catalogs specialize in useful items, such as compact alarm clocks and travel irons, that can **save space**

when packing. They also offer dual-voltage appliances, currency converters, and foreign-language phrase books.

➤ MAIL-ORDER CATALOGS: **Magellan's** (☎ 800/962–4943, FAX 805/568–5406). **Orvis Travel** (☎ 800/541–3541, FAX 540/343–7053). **TravelSmith** (☎ 800/ 950–1600, FAX 800/950–1656).

U

The U.S. government can be an excellent source of inexpensive travel information. When planning your trip, **find out what government materials are available.**

➤ ADVISORIES: **U.S. Department of State** (⊠ Overseas Citizens Services Office, Room 4811 N.S., Washington, DC 20520); enclose a self-addresses, stamped envelope. Interactive hot line (☎ 202/647–5225, FAX 202/ 647–3000). Computer bulletin board (☎ 301/946–4400).

➤ PAMPHLETS: **Consumer Information Center** (⊠ Consumer Information Catalogue, Pueblo, CO 81009, ☎ 719/948–3334) for a free catalog that includes travel titles.

Before you go, call or write to the tourist board for general information. From the U.K., contact the individual countries' tourist boards.

➤ SCANDINAVIAN TOURIST BOARD: U.S. and Canada: (⊠ Box 4649, Grand Central Station, New York, NY 10163–4649, ☎ 212/885–9700, FAX 212/885–9710). U.K.: London: (⊠ 55 Sloan St., London SW1X 9SY, ☎ 071/259–5959, FAX 071/259– 5955).

➤ NORWEGIAN TOURIST BOARD: U.K.: (⊠ 5 Lower Regent St., London SW1Y 4LR ☎ 0171/839–6255, FAX 0171/839–6014).

W

The Norwegian tourist season peaks in June, July, and August, when daytime temperatures are often in the 70s (21°C to 26°C) and sometimes rise into the 80s (27°C to 32°C). A temperature chart for Oslo appears below. In general, the weather is not overly warm, and a brisk breeze and brief rainstorms are possible anytime. Nights can be chilly, even in summer.

Visit in summer if you want to experience the delightfully long summer days. In June, the sun rises in Oslo at 4 AM and sets at 11 PM and daylight lasts even longer farther north, making it possible to extend your sightseeing into the balmy evenings. Many attractions extend their hours during the summer, and many shut down altogether when summer ends. Fall, spring, and even winter are pleasant, despite the area's reputation for gloom. The days become shorter quickly, but

the sun casts a golden light one does not see farther south. On dark days, fires and candlelight will warm you indoors.

The Gulf Stream warms the western coast of Norway, making winters in there similar to those in London. Even the harbor of Narvik, far to the north in Norway, remains ice-free year-round. Away from the protection of the Gulf Stream, however, northern Norway experiences very cold, clear weather that attracts skiers.

CLIMATE

Following are average daily maximum and minumum temperatures for Oslo.

OSLO

Jan.	28F	– 2C	May	61F	16C	Sept.	60F	16C
	19	– 7		43	6		46	8
Feb.	30F	– 1C	June	68F	20C	Oct.	48F	9C
	19	– 7		50	10		38	3
Mar.	39F	4C	July	72F	22C	Nov.	38F	3C
	25	– 4		55	13		31	– 1
Apr.	50F	10C	Aug.	70F	21C	Dec.	32F	0C
	34	1		54	12		25	– 4

➤ FORECASTS: **Weather Channel Connection** (☎ 900/932–8437), 95¢ per minute from a Touch-Tone phone.

1 Destination: Norway

NORWEGIAN LANDSCAPES

JUST NORTH OF LILLEHAMMER lives a Norwegian family on the banks of Mjøsa Lake. Every year they pack their bags and drive to their holiday retreat, where they bask in the warmth of the long, northern sun for four full weeks—then they pack up and drive the 300 ft back home again.

Although most Norwegians vacation a bit farther from home, their sentiments—attachment to, pride in, and reverence for their great outdoors—remain the same as the feelings of those who only journey across the street. Whether in the verdant dales of the interior, the brooding mountains of the north, or the carved fjords and archipelagoes of the coast, their ubiquitous *hytter* (cabins or cottages) dot even the most violent landscapes. It's a question of perspective: to a Norwegian, it's not a matter of whether to enjoy the land but how to enjoy it at this very moment.

In any kind of weather, blasting or balmy, inordinate numbers are out of doors, to fish, bike, ski, hike, and, intentionally or not, strike the pose many foreigners regard as larger-than-life Norwegian: ruddy-faced, athletic, reindeer-sweatered. And all—from cherubic children to decorous senior citizens—are bundled up for just one more swoosh down the slopes, one more walk through the forest.

Although Norway is a modern, highly industrialized nation, vast areas of the country (up to 95%) remain forested or fallow, and Norwegians intend to keep them that way—in part by making it extremely difficult for foreigners, who may feel differently about the land, to purchase property.

When discussing the size of their country, Norwegians like to say that if Oslo remained fixed and the northern part of the country were swung south, it would reach all the way to Rome. Perched at the very top of the globe, this northern land is long and rangy, 2,750 km (1,705 mi) in length, with only 4 million people scattered over it—making it the least densely populated land in Europe except for Iceland.

Thanks to the Gulf Stream, the coastal regions enjoy a moderate, temperate climate in winter, keeping the country green, whereas the interior has a more typical northern climate. Of course, throughout the land, winter temperatures can dip far below zero, but that doesn't thwart the activities of the Norwegians. As one North Caper put it, "We don't have good weather or bad weather, only a lot of weather."

Norwegians are justifiably proud of their native land and of their ability to survive the elements and foreign invasions. The first people to appear on the land were reindeer hunters and fisherfolk who were migrating north, following the path of the retreating ice. By the Bronze Age, settlements began to appear, and, as rock carvings show (and modern school children are proud to announce), the first Norwegians began to ski—purely as a form of locomotion—some 4,000 years ago.

The Viking Age has perhaps left the most indelible mark on the country. The Vikings' travels and conquests took them to Iceland, England, Ireland (they founded Dublin in the 840s), and North America. Though they were famed as plunderers, their craftsmanship and fearlessness are revered by modern Norwegians, who place ancient Viking ships in museums, cast copies of thousand-year-old silver designs into jewelry, and adventure across the seas in sailboats to prove the abilities of their forefathers.

Harald I, better known as Harald the Fairhaired, swore he would not cut his hair until he united Norway, and in the 9th century he succeeded in doing both. But a millennium passed between that great era and Norwegian independence. Between the Middle Ages and 1905, Norway remained under the rule of either Denmark or Sweden, even after the constitution was written in 1814.

The 19th century saw the establishment of the Norwegian identity and a blossoming of culture. This romantic period produced some of the nation's most famous individuals, among them composer Edvard Grieg, dramatist Henrik Ibsen, expressionist painter Edvard Munch, polar explorer Roald Amundsen, and explorer-humanitarian Fridtjof Nansen. Vestiges of nationalist lyricism spangle the buildings of the era with Viking dragonheads and scrollwork, all of which symbolize the rebirth of the Viking spirit.

Faithful to their democratic nature, Norwegians held a referendum to choose a king in 1905, when independence from Sweden became reality. Prince Carl of Denmark became King Haakon VII. His baby's name was changed from Alexander to Olav, and he, and later his son, presided over the kingdom for more than 85 years. When King Olav V died in January 1991, the normally reserved Norwegians stood in line for hours to write in the condolence book at the Royal Palace. Rather than simply sign their names, they wrote personal letters of devotion to the man they called the "people's king." Thousands set candles in the snow outside the palace, transforming the winter darkness into a cathedral of ice and flame.

Harald V, Olav's son, is now king, with continuity assured by his own young-adult son, Crown Prince Haakon. Norwegians continue to salute the royal family with flag-waving and parades on May 17, Constitution Day, a spirited holiday of independence that transforms Oslo's main boulevard, Karl Johans Gate, into a massive street party as people of all ages, many in national costume, make a beeline to the palace.

During both world wars, Norway tried to maintain neutrality. World War I brought not only casualties and a considerable loss to the country's merchant fleet but also financial gain through the repurchase of major companies, sovereignty over Svalbard (the islands near the North Pole), and the reaffirmation of Norway's prominence in international shipping. At the onset of World War II, Norway once again proclaimed neutrality and appeared more concerned with Allied mine-laying on the west coast than with national security. A country of mostly fisherfolk, lumber workers, and farmers, it was just beginning to realize its industrial potential when the Nazis invaded. Five years of German occupation and a burn-and-retreat strategy in the north finally left the nation ravaged. True to form, however, the people who had been evacuated returned to the embers of the north to rebuild their homes and villages.

In 1968 oil was discovered in the North Sea, and Norway was transformed from a fishing and shipping outpost to a highly developed industrial nation. Though still committed to a far-reaching social system, Norway developed in the next 20 years into a wealthy country, with a per capita income and standard of living among the world's highest, as well as long life expectancy.

Stand on a street corner with a map, and a curious Norwegian will show you the way. Visit a neighborhood, and within moments you'll be the talk of the town. As a native of Bergen quipped, "Next to skiing, gossip is a national sport." With one foot in modern, liberal Scandinavia and the other in the provincial and often self-righteous countryside, Norway, unlike its Nordic siblings, is clinging steadfastly to its separate and distinct identity within Europe. Famous for its social restrictiveness—smoking is frowned on, liquor may not be served before 3 PM (and never on Sunday), and violence, even among cartoon characters, is closely monitored—Norway is determined to repel outside interference, so much so that a national referendum in November 1994 chose to reject membership in the European Union. Thanks to Norway's oil supply—which has resulted in a major economic boom—no tragic repercussions to its isolation have occured, and none are expected to before the end of the millenium.

— Updated by Shelley Pannill
and Marius Meland

NEW AND NOTEWORTHY

At the end of 1997, Norway's economic boom was in full swing. Despite Norway's Euroskepticism—and some say because of it—the country's economy has never looked better. The rate of unemployment sunk so low in 1997 that companies feared a labor shortage and slowly started enlisting immigrants to do many jobs. The boom is thanks in large part to the discovery, between 1995 and 1997, of at least 20 new oil and gas fields in the Norwegian sector of the North Sea. What the booming economy means for travellers is more museums to visit and better services since the government tends to invest in tourism and educational projects. Hotels and restaurants remain expensive, but Norway's membership in the European Economic Area helps in exerting a downward pressure on prices.

At the end of 1996, Norway's longtime Prime Minister, Gro Harlem Brundtland, surprised everyone by quitting her job. Brundtland had been a supporter of joining the EU, and saw Norway's 1994 rejection as a major political defeat. The Labor Party's Thorbjorn Jagland replaced Brundtland.

Ever nostalgic, Lillehammer will inaugurate Norway's new Olympic Museum in 1998. A series of life-sized multimedia exhibits will celebrate the history of the Olympics, starting with the 1896 Athens Games and recapping its own 1994 Winter Games.

North Americans just can't get enough of the fjords, according to the Norwegian Tourist Board. It reported a 20% increase in fjord cruise traffic in 1996 and thanked Americans and Canadians for being the third most frequent cruise takers. One of those fjord towns, Alesund, is celebrating its 150th birthday in 1998, with festivities planned througout the year.

WHAT'S WHERE

Norway, roughly 400,000 square km (155,000 square mi), is about the same size as California. Approximately 30% of this long, narrow country is covered with clear lakes, lush forests, and rugged mountains. Western Norway, bordered by the Norwegian Sea and the Atlantic Ocean, is the fabled land of the fjords—few places on earth can match the power and splendor of this land. The magnificent Sognefjord, the longest inlet in western Norway, is only one of many fjords found here, including the Hardangerfjord, Geirangerfjord, Lysefjord, and Nordfjord.

Bergen, often hailed as the "Fjord Capital of Norway," is the second-largest city in the country. The cobblestone streets, well-preserved buildings at the Bryggen, and seven mountains that surround the city all add to its storybook charm.

Eastern Norway, bordered by Sweden, and by Finland and Russia to the north, is punctuated by rolling hills, abundant valleys, and fresh lakes—much more subdued than the landscape of the west. Near Gudbrandsdalen (Gudbrands Valley) you'll find Lillehammer, the site of the 1994 Winter Olympics. Almost directly south, rising from the shores of the Oslofjord, is the capital of Norway—Oslo. With a population of about a half million, Oslo is a friendly, manageable city.

If you follow the coast south, you'll come to Kristiansand, one of Sørlandet's (the Southland's) leading cities. Sørlandet is known for its long stretches of unspoiled, uncrowded beach. Stavanger, farther west, is one of the most cosmopolitan cities in Scandinavia—its oil and gas industry draws people from around the globe.

Halfway between Oslo and Bergen lies Hardangervidda (Hardanger Plateau), Norway's largest national park. At the foot of the plateau is Geilo, one of the country's most popular ski resorts. Almost directly north is the bustling city of Trondheim.

From here, a thin expanse of land stretches up to the Nordkapp (North Cape). Known as the Land of the Midnight Sun (the display of the northern lights in the winter is pretty amazing, too), this region is marked with exquisite landscapes: glaciers, fjords, and rocky coasts. Narvik, a major Arctic port, is the gateway to the Lofoten Islands, where puffins and penguins march about. Even farther north is one of Norway's major universities, Tromsø, the lifeline to settlements and research centers at the North Pole. At the very top of Norway is the county of Finnmark, where many Sami (native Laplanders) live. Access to the area is primarily through Hammerfest, Europe's northernmost city, where the sun is not visible from November 21 to January 21, but is uninterrupted May 17 through July 29.

Pleasures and Pastimes

Beaches

Many Norwegians enjoy beaches in the summer, but low water temperatures, from 14°C to 18°C (57°F to 65°F), are enough to deter all but the most hardy visitors from getting into the water. The beaches around Mandal in the south and Jaeren's Ogna, Brusand, and Bore, closer to Stavanger, are the country's best, with fine white sand. However, all along the Oslo Fjord are good beaches too. The western fjords are warmer and calmer than the open beaches of the south—although they have rock, and not sand, beaches—and inland freshwater lakes are chillier still than Gulf Stream–warmed fjords. Topless bathing is common, and there are nude beaches all along the coast.

Dining

Eating is a cultural element of Norwegian society. The Norwegians pride themselves on gracious entertaining and lavish dinner parties using their finest silver and glassware. Dining out in Norway is expensive, so many weekend nights are spent at the houses of friends and relatives enjoying long, candlelit dinners with lively conversation and oftentimes countless glasses of wine. (The BYOB—Bring Your Own Bottle—policy in Norway is common because alcohol prices are so high.) Recently, as Norwegians spend more time in the office and less time at home, eating at restaurants has become more popular, especially in cities like Oslo and Stavanger. In these larger areas, the dining scene is thriving. Until lately, fine restaurants were invariably French, and fine food usually meant meat. Now, in addition to the old reliable restaurants that serve traditional Norwegian dishes, you'll find spots that serve everything from tapas to Thai cuisine.

Norwegians are beginning to feel competition from foreign foods and are taking greater pride in their native cuisine. Today seafood and game have replaced beef and veal. Fish, from common cod and skate to the noble salmon, have a prominent place in the new Norwegian kitchen, and local capelin roe, golden caviar, is served instead of the imported variety. Norwegian lamb, full of flavor, is now in the spotlight, and game, from birds to moose, is prepared with sauces made from the wild berries that are part of their diet.

Desserts, too, often feature fruit and berries. Norwegian strawberries and raspberries ripen in the long, early summer days and are sweeter and more intense than those grown farther south. Red and black currants are also used. Two berries native to Norway are *tyttebær* (lingonberries), which taste similar to cranberries but are much smaller, and *multer* (cloudberries), which look like orange raspberries but have

an indescribable taste. These wild berries grow above the tree line and are a real delicacy. Multe are often served as *multekrem* (in whipped cream) as a dessert, whereas tyttebær preserves often accompany traditional meat dishes.

For centuries, Norwegians regarded food as fuel, and their dining habits still bear traces of this. *Frokost* (breakfast) is a fairly big meal, usually with a selection of crusty bread, jams, herring, cold meat, and cheese. *Geitost* (a sweet, caramel-flavored whey cheese made wholly or in part from goats' milk) and Norvegia (a Norwegian Gouda-type cheese) are on virtually every table. They are eaten in thin slices, cut with a cheese plane or slicer, a Norwegian invention, on buttered wheat or rye bread.

Lunsj (lunch) is simple and usually consists of *smørbrød* (open-faced sandwiches). Most businesses have only a 30-minute lunch break, so unless there's a company cafeteria, most people bring their lunch from home. Big lunchtime buffet tables, *koldtbord*, where one can sample most of Norway's special dishes all at once, are primarily for special occasions and visitors.

Middag (dinner), the only hot meal of the day, is early—from 1 to 4 in the country, 3 to 7 in the city—so many cafeterias serving home-style food close by 6 or 7 in the evening. In Oslo it's possible to get dinner as late as midnight at certain dining establishments, especially in summertime. You'll probably find that most restaurants in Oslo usually stop serving dinner around 10 PM.

Traditional, home-style Norwegian food is stick-to-the-ribs fare, served in generous portions and blanketed with gravy. One of the most popular meals is *kjøttkaker* (meat cakes), which resemble small Salisbury steaks, served with boiled potatoes, stewed cabbage, and brown gravy. Almost as popular are *medisterkaker* (mild pork sausage patties), served with brown gravy and caraway-seasoned sauerkraut, and *reinsdyrkaker* (reindeer meatballs), served with cream sauce and lingonberry jam. Other typical meat dishes include *fårikål*, a great-tasting lamb and cabbage stew, and *steik* (roast meat), always served well done. Fish dishes include poached *torsk* (cod) or *laks* (salmon), served with a creamy sauce called Sandefjord butter; *seibiff*, fried pollack and onions; and *fiskegrateng*, something between a fish soufflé and a casserole, usually served with carrot slaw.

Norway is known for several eccentric, often pungent fish dishes, but these are not representative—both *rakørret* and *raklaks* (fermented trout and salmon) and *lutefisk* (dried cod soaked in lye and then boiled) are acquired tastes, even for natives. These dishes are often served at holidays, accompanied by the national drink, *akevitt* (sometimes spelled aquavit), a schnapps-like liquor that is made from potatoes and caraway seeds.

Traditional desserts include the ubiquitous *karamellpudding* (crème caramel) and *rømmegrøt* (sour-cream porridge served with cinnamon sugar) and a glass of *saft* (raspberry juice). Rømmrgrøt—a typical farm dish—tastes very much like warm cheesecake batter. It's often served with *fenalår* (dried leg of mutton) and *lefsekling,* a thin tortilla-like pancake made with sour cream and potatoes, buttered and coated with sugar. Christmastime brings with it a delectable array of light, sweet, and buttery pastries. The *bløtkake* (layered cream cake with custard, fruit, and marzipan) is a favorite for Christmas and special occasions but can be purchased in bakeries year-round.

Fishing

Whether it's fly-fishing in western rivers or deep-sea fishing off the northern coast, Norway has all kinds of angling possibilities.

Hiking

Seemingly, one of the most common expressions in the Norwegian language is *gå på tur,* or go for a walk. Every city has surrounding trails where Norwegians usually spend a good part of their weekends hiking and strolling. Many of the trails have cabins where guests can rest, eat, and even spend the night. Den Norske Turistforening (☞ Outdoor Activities and Sports *in* the Gold Guide) and affiliated organizations administer cabins and tourist facilities in the central and northern mountainous areas of the country and will arrange group hikes.

Lodging

Norway is a land of hard beds and hearty breakfasts. Hotel standards are high, and even the simplest youth hostels provide good mattresses with fluffy down comforters and clean showers or baths. Breakfast, usually served buffet style, is almost always included in the room price at ho-

tels, whereas hostels often charge extra for the morning meal.

Norway has several hotel chains. SAS, which is a division of the airline, has a number of luxury hotels designed for the business traveler. Many are above the Arctic Circle and are the "only game in town." Rica and Reso hotels, also luxury chains, have expanded extensively in the past few years. Best Western, Rainbow, and Choice Hotels International are moderate chains, found in most major towns. The most interesting and distinctive hotel chain is Home Hotels (Swedish owned), which has successfully converted existing historic buildings into modern functional establishments in the middle price range. All Home Hotels provide an evening meal, jogging suits, free beer, and other amenities designed to appeal to the single, usually business, traveler. As far as value for money is concerned, they are Norway's best buy. The Farmer's Association operates simple hotels in most towns and cities. These reasonably priced accommodations usually have "-heimen" as part of the name, such as Bondeheimen in Oslo. The same organization also runs cafeterias serving traditional Norwegian food, usually called Kaffistova. All of these hotels and restaurants are alcohol-free.

At times it seems as though the SAS and Rica hotel chains are the only ones in northern Norway, and often that is true. These are always top-rate, usually the most expensive hotels in town, with the best restaurant and the most extensive facilities. Rustic cabins and campsites are also available everywhere, as well as some independent hotels.

In the Lofoten and Vesterålen islands, *rorbuer,* fishing cottages that have been converted into lodgings or modern versions of these simple dwellings, are the most popular form of accommodation. These rustic quayside cabins, with minikitchens, bunk beds, living rooms, and showers, are reasonably priced, and they give a unique experience of the region. *Sjøhus* (sea houses) are larger, usually two- or three-storied buildings similar to rorbuer.

Norway has 90 youth hostels, but in an effort to appeal to vacationers of all ages, the name has been changed to *vandrerhjem* (travelers' home). Norwegian hostels are among the best in the world, squeaky clean and with excellent facilities. Rooms sleep from two to six, and many have private showers. You don't have to be a member, but members get reductions, so it's worth joining. Membership can be arranged at any vandrerhjem, or you can buy a coupon book good for seven nights, which includes the membership fee. Linens are usually rented per night, so it's a good idea to bring your own—if you haven't, you can buy a *lakenpose* (sheet sleeping bag) at specialty stores, or one at the vandrerhjem.

Norway has more than 900 inspected and classified campsites, many with showers, bathrooms, and hookups for electricity. Most also have cabins or chalets to rent by the night or longer.

Orienteering

One of Norway's most popular mass-participation sports is based on running or hiking over territory with a map and compass to find control points marked on a map. Special cards can be purchased at sports shops to be punched at control points found during a season. It's an enjoyable, inexpensive family sport.

Shopping

Almost no one leaves Norway without buying a hand-knit sweater. Although the prices for these sweaters may seem high, the quality is outstanding. The classic knitting designs, with snowflakes and reindeer, are still bestsellers and can be bought at most *Husfliden* (homecraft) outlets and specialty stores, whereas more modern sweaters, made of combinations of brightly colored yarns, can be purchased from yarn shops.

Given the Norwegians' affection for the outdoors, an abundance of high-quality sportsgear and outerwear is available. Good buys include Helly-Hansen rain gear, insulated boots, and the *supertrøye*, a gossamer-thin, insulated undershirt.

Handicraft lovers will marvel at Norway's goods. You'll find handmade pewter and wrought-iron candlesticks, hand-dipped candles, handblown glass, and hand-turned wood bowls, spoons, and platters made of birch roots, decorated with rosemaling (intricate painted or carved floral folk-art designs). Although your visit may be in June, this is a great place to stock up on your Christmas goods. All Husfliden stores and many gift shops sell Christmas ornaments handmade from straw and wood shavings. *Juleduk* (Christmas tablecloths) with typical Norwegian themes are for sale year-round at embroidery shops. Other, more offbeat, items include *ostehøvler* (cheese slicers) and *kransekakeformer*, graduated forms for making almond ring cakes. If you're looking for Norwegian recipes, you may want to seek out Arne Brimi's cookbook—*A Taste of Norwegian Nature*. It's sold in most bookstores.

Silver is a good buy in Norway, especially with the value-added tax refund (☞ Taxes *in* the Gold Guide). Norwegian silver companies produce a wide range of patterns. Although the price of Norwegian silver is competitive, at 830 parts to 1,000 (compared with 925 parts in sterling), it's not as pure as English or American silver. However, some will argue that it's stronger.

Unfortunately, Norwegian rustic antiques may not be exported. Even the simplest corner shelf or dish rack valued at $50 is considered a national treasure if it is known to be more than 100 years old. However, you'll find that there are some really good replicas of old Norwegian farm furniture available.

Skiing

The ski is Norway's contribution to the world of sports. In 1994 the Winter Olympics were held in Lillehammer, which, along with other Norwegian resorts, regularly hosts World Cup competitions and world skiing championships. In addition to downhill and cross-country, the 100-year-old Telemark style is enjoying a revival across the country. It involves a characteristic deep-knee bend in the turns and traditional garb, including heavy boots attached to the skis only at the toe. Cross-country skiing is a great way to see Norway's nature; it requires only basic equipment, and rentals are readily available. Most every city has lit trails for evening skiing. Norway's skiing season lasts from November to Easter. But winter's not the only time for skiing in Norway—you may want to try summer skiing on a glacier.

FODOR'S CHOICE

Dining

★ **Bagatelle, Oslo.** One of the best restaurants in Europe features the Franco-

Norwegian cuisine of internationally known owner-chef Eyvind Hellstrøm. *$$$$*

✴ **Refsnes Gods, Moss.** Chef Erwin Stocker adds a French touch to traditional Norwegian seafood to create what some call the best fare in Norway. *$$$*

Lodging

✴ **Ambassadeur, Oslo.** Hand-picked antiques, china tea sets, and tapestries in the salon only hint at the sweet, individual styles of the rooms with monikers like "Roma" and "Osa." *$$$–$$$$*

✴ **Frogner House, Oslo.** Sitting inconspicuously amid rows of other turn-of-the-century townhouses, Frogner is cozily dressed in pastels and abundant lace coverings. *$$$–$$$$.*

✴ **Clarion Admiral Hotel, Bergen.** Right on the water across the harbor from Bryggen, this former dockside warehouse–cum geometric Art Nouveau hotel dates from 1906. *$$–$$$*

✴ **Kvikne's Hotel, Balestrand.** This huge wooden gingerbread house at the edge of the Sognefjord has been a landmark since 1915. *$$*

Castles and Churches

✴ **Akershus Slott, Oslo.** Parts of this historic fortress, on the brow of the fjord, date from the 1300s.

Museums

✴ **Munchmuseet, Oslo.** Edvard Munch, who painted *The Scream*, bequeathed thousands of his works to Oslo when he died in 1944.

✴ **Norsk Folkemuseum, Bygdøy, Oslo.** Some 140 structures from all over the country have been reconstructed on the museum grounds.

Special Moments

✴ Eating dinner in a Sami tent, with your reindeer parked outside

✴ People-watching along Oslo's Karl Johans Gate during the 17th of May (Constitution Day) celebrations

✴ Admiring the monumental sculptures in Oslo's Vigeland Park

BOOKS AND VIDEOS

One of the greatest influences on 20th-century drama is the Norwegian poet and dramatist Henrik Ibsen, best known for his works *A Doll's House* (1879) and *Hedda Gabler* (1890).

In the 20th century, three Norwegian novelists have won the Nobel Prize in Literature: Bjørnstjerne Bjørnson in 1903; Knut Hamsun in 1920 for his novel *Another Growth Of The Soil* (Vintage), a story of elemental existence in rural Norway; and Sigrid Undset in 1928 for her masterpiece *Kristin Lavransdatter.* This trilogy, a landmark among historical novels, gives a rich insight into 14th-century Scandinavia. In 1995, Liv Ullmann directed the epic film *Kristin Lavransdatter,* an adaptation of Sigrid Undset's trilogy set in 14th-century Norway. Try and find it on video before your trip for a sneak preview of the Norwegian landscape.

Jostein Gaarder is one of Norway's modern-day novelists. His book *Sophie's World* (Berkeley Publishing, 1997) explores the history of philosophy through a young Norwegian's eyes.

Living in Norway (Abbeville Press, 1993) is a glossy depiction of Norwegian interior design.

Junk Mail, a film about a disillusioned Norwegian mailman who becomes involved with a woman on his route, was well received at the 1997 Cannes Film Festival.

FESTIVALS AND SEASONAL EVENTS

WINTER

JAN.➤ In Tromsø, the **Northern Lights Festival** celebrates the return of daylight with performances by notable Norwegian and international musicians.

FEB.➤ Lillehammer's **Winter Festival** is a cultural affair including music, theater, and art exhibitions. The **Røros Fair** in the town of Røros (designated as Cultural Heritage Landmark by UNESCO) has been an annual tradition since 1854.

FEB. 20–MAR. 2➤ The **Nordic World Ski Championships** in Trondheim is the biggest event celebrating Trondheim's 1,000th-year anniversary.

MAR.➤ Europe's largest dogsledding competition, the **Finnmark Race,** follows old mail routes across Finnmarksvidda. The **Birkebeiner Race** commemorates a centuries-old cross-country ski race from Lillehammer to Rena. At the **Voss Jazz Festival,** European and American jazz and folk artists appear at Voss, a major ski resort in western Norway.

SPRING

MAR.–APR.➤ The **Karasjok Easter Festival** features a variety of concerts, theater performances, art exhibits, snowmobile rallies, and reindeer races.

MAY 17➤ **Constitution Day** brings out every Norwegian flag and crowds of marchers for parades and celebrations throughout the country.

MAY.➤ The **Grete Waitz Race** is a 5-km (3-mi), women-only race in Oslo. The festivities of the annual **Bergen International Festival,** customarily opened by the king, include dance, music, and theater performances.

MAY 30–JUNE 8➤ Trondheim's 1,000-year anniversary is in full swing during the city's **Festival Week.**

SUMMER

JUNE 23➤ **Midsummer Night,** called *Sankt Hans Afton,* is celebrated nationwide with bonfires, fireworks, and outdoor dancing. Meet fellow Norwegian Americans and Norwegians at the annual **Emigration Festival** in Stavanger.

JULY➤ The plays, exhibitions, concerts, and historic walking tours of the **Kristin Festival** pay tribute to *Kristin Lavransdatter,* the Nobel prize–winning novel by Sigrid Undset; they are held at Jorund Farm, the site of Liv Ullmann's movie based on the same novel. More than 400 jazz musicians participate in the extremely popular **Molde International Jazz Festival.**

JULY 23–26➤ Boats and crews of the **Cutty Sark Regatta** will be in Trondheim.

AUG.➤ You'll find none other than folk music, folk dancing, and folk songs at the **Telemark International Folk Music Festival** in the town of Bø in Telemark. The **Peer Gynt Festival** in Lillehammer brings art exhibits, processions with national costumes, and open-air theater performances of Henrik Ibsen's *Peer Gynt*—as well as Edvard Grieg's music. The **Oslo Chamber Music Festival** draws participants from around the world.

LATE AUG.➤ The **Norwegian Food Festival** awards the Norwegian Championship in cooking, seminars, and lectures.

AUTUMN

SEPT.➤ The **Oslo Marathon** stretches 42 km (26 mi) through the streets of Oslo.

DEC. 10➤ The **Nobel peace prize** is awarded—by invitation only—in Oslo.

2 Oslo

What sets Oslo apart from other European cities is not so much its cultural tradition or its internationally renowned museums as its simply stunning natural beauty. What other world capital has subway service to the forest, or lakes and hiking trails within city limits? But Norwegians will be quick to remind you that Oslo—with thriving theaters, vibrant nightlife, and more—is as cosmopolitan as any world capital. And like other major metropolises, Oslo also has modern architectural monstrosities, traffic problems, and even a bit of urban sprawl.

ALTHOUGH IT IS ONE OF THE WORLD'S largest capital cities in area, Oslo has only 480,000 inhabitants. Nevertheless, in recent years the city has taken off: shops are open later, cafés and restaurants are crowded at all hours, and theaters play to full houses every night of the week.

Even without nightlife, Oslo has a lot to offer—parks, water, trees, hiking and skiing trails (2,600 km/1,600 mi in greater Oslo), and above all, spectacular views. Starting at the docks opposite City Hall, right at the edge of the Oslo Fjord, the city sprawls up the sides of the mountains that surround it, providing panoramic vistas from almost any vantage point but no definable downtown skyline. A building spree in the late 1980s and early '90s has added a number of modern towers, particularly in the area around the Central Railway Station, which clash painfully with the neoclassical architecture in the rest of the city.

Oslo has been Norway's center of commerce for about 500 years, and most major Norwegian companies are based in the capital. The sea has always been Norway's lifeline to the rest of the world: the Oslo Fjord teems with activity, from summer sailors and shrimpers to merchant ships and passenger ferries heading for Denmark and Germany.

Oslo is an old city, dating from the mid-11th century. The city has actually burned down 14 times since its creation, and was all but destroyed by a fire in 1624, when it was redesigned and renamed Christiania by Denmark's royal builder, King Christian IV. During the mid-19th century, and under the influence of the Swedish king, Karl Johan, who ruled the newly united Kingdom of Norway and Sweden, the grand axis—named after himself—was constructed. A definite product of the European city planning trends, Karl Johans Gate has been at the center of city life ever since. An act of Parliament finally changed the city's name back to Oslo, its original Viking name, in 1925.

EXPLORING OSLO

Karl Johans Gate, starting at Oslo Sentralstasjon (Oslo Central Station, also called Oslo S Station) and ending at the Royal Palace, forms the backbone of downtown Oslo. Many of Oslo's museums and historic buildings lie between the parallel streets of Grensen and Rådhusgata. Just north of the center of town is a historic area with a medieval church and old buildings. West of downtown is Frogner, the residential area closest to town, with embassies, fine restaurants, antiques shops, galleries, and the Vigeland sculpture park. Farther west is the Bygdøy Peninsula, with five interesting museums and a castle. Northwest of town is Holmenkollen, with beautiful houses, a famous ski jump, and a restaurant. On the east side, where many new immigrants live, are the Munch Museum and the botanical gardens.

Downtown: The Royal Palace to City Hall

Although the city is huge (454 square km/175 square mi), downtown Oslo is compact, with shops, museums, historic sights, restaurants, and clubs concentrated in a small, walkable center—brightly illuminated at night.

A Good Walk

Oslo's main promenade, Karl Johans Gate, runs from **Slottet** ① through town. Walk down the incline, and to your left you will see three yellow buildings of the old **Universitet** ②—today they are used only by the law school. Murals painted by Edvard Munch decorate the interior walls of these buildings. Around the corner from the university on Universitetsgata is the **Nasjonalgalleriet** ③, which contains hundreds of Norwegian, Scandinavian, and European works, including Munch's famous painting *The Scream*. Back-to-back with the National Gallery, across a parking lot, is a big cream-brick Art Nouveau–style building housing the **Historisk Museum** ④, whose collection of Viking artifacts is impressive. Continue along Frederiksgate to the university and cross Karl Johans Gate to the **Nationalteatret** ⑤ and Studenterlunden Park. This impressive building is not only the national theater, but a popular meeting place—many buses stop out front, and the T-bane (subway) is right beside it.

Walk past the Lille Grensen shopping area and once again cross Karl Johans Gate to see **Stortinget** ⑥, the Norwegian Parliament. Then go back to Stortingsgata. From here, turn left on Universitetsgata, and walk through a cul-de-sac–type area toward the water to reach the redbrick **Rådhuset** ⑦, a familiar landmark with its two block towers, dedicated during Oslo's 900th-year jubilee celebrations in 1950. After visiting Rådhuset, end your tour with an *øl* (beer) or mineral water at one of the many outdoor cafés at Aker Brygge (☞ *Dining, below*).

TIMING

The walk alone should take no more than two hours, even if you take time to wander around in Royal Palace park. If you happen to be at the Royal Palace midday, you might catch the changing of the guard, which happens every day at 1:30. When you are planning your tour, take note that many museums are closed on Mondays.

Sights to See

④ **Historisk Museum** (Historical Museum). Intricately carved *stav kirke* (wood church) portals and other Viking and medieval artifacts are on display here. There's an exhibition about the Arctic, as well as Asian and African ethnographic exhibits. ⊠ *Frederiksgt. 2,* ☎ *22/85–99–12.* ☞ *Free.* ☉ *Mid-May–mid-Sept., Tues.–Sun. 11–3; late Sept.–early May, Tues.–Sun. noon–3.*

③ **Nasjonalgalleriet** (The National Gallery). Many Scandinavian impressionists, who have recently been discovered by the rest of the world, are represented here in Norway's official art museum. Some impressive fjord and moonlight scenes by Norwegian artists such as Christian Krogh and J.C. Dahl fill the walls of the 19th- and early 20th-century Norwegian rooms. The gallery also has an extensive Munch collection. ⊠ *Universitetsgt. 13,* ☎ *22/20–04–04.* ☞ *Free.* ☉ *Mon., Wed., Fri., and Sat. 10–6; Thurs. 10–8; Sun. 11–4.*

⑤ **Nationalteatret** (National Theater). In front of this neoclassical theater, built in 1899, are statues of Norway's great playwrights, Bjørnstjerne Bjørnson (who wrote the words to the national anthem and won a Nobel Prize for his plays) and Henrik Ibsen, author of *A Doll's House, Hedda Gabler,* and *The Wild Duck*. Most performances are in Norwegian, so you may just want to take a guided tour of the interior. Call for details. ⊠ *Stortingsgt. 15,* ☎ *22/41–27–10.*

★ ⑦ **Rådhuset** (City Hall). The redbrick exterior of Oslo's City Hall may seem dull compared with the marble-floored interior, whose murals and frescoes are bursting with color. Many sculptures outside, as well as murals inside, reflect the artistic climate in Norway in the 1930s—socialist modernism in its highest form. Much of the adornment depicts not only daily life but also Viking gods and Norwegian literary figures. This may be the only City Hall in the world with a sculpture of a prostitute; it's on the east side of the building facing the fjord. The Nobel Peace Prize has been handed out in the Main Hall since 1990. ⊠ *Råd-*

huspl., ☎ *22/86–16–00.* 🎟 *NKr 15.* ☉ *May–Aug., Mon.–Sat. 9–5, Sun. noon–5; Sept.–Apr., Mon.–Sat. 9–3:30, Sun. noon–5. Guided tours year-round, weekdays 10, noon, and 2.*

★ ❶ **Slottet** (The Royal Palace). The neoclassical palace, completed in 1848, is closed to visitors, but the garden is open to the public. An equestrian statue of Karl Johan, king of Sweden and Norway from 1818 to 1844, stands in the square in front of the palace.

❻ **Stortinget** (The Norwegian Parliament). Built in the middle of the 19th century, this classic building is perched on the top of a small hill. At night, the steps here become a great spot for people-watching. When Parliament is in session, the public gallery is open to curious onlookers. ⊠ *Karl Johans Gt. 22,* ☎ *22/31–30–50.* 🎟 *Free.* ☉ *Guided tours on weekdays in July and Aug.; tours Sat. only Sept.–June.*

❷ **Universitetet** (The University). The great hall of the center building is decorated with murals by Edvard Munch, such as *The Sun,* whose penetrating rays over a fjord give a whole new meaning to the notion of daylight. It was the site of the Nobel Peace Prize award ceremony until 1989. The hall still receives other notable visitors, such as Salman Rushdie, who showed up almost unannounced in 1995. ⊠ *Aulaen, Karl Johans Gt. 47,* ☎ *22/85–97–11* 🎟 *Free.* ☉ *July, weekdays 10:45–2.*

Kvadraturen and Akershus Castle

The Kvadraturen is the oldest part of Oslo still standing. In 1624, after the town of Oslo burned down for the 14th time, King Christian IV renamed the city Christiania and moved it from the area that is today south of Oslo S Station, called Gamlebyen (☞ *below*), and rebuilt it adjacent to the Akershus fortress. The king decreed that houses were to be built in stone or brick instead of wood—in order to prevent future fires. He also built a stone wall around the newly rebuilt city to protect it from his enemies, the Swedes.

A Good Walk

The Kvadraturen area, which includes Akershus Slott, is bound on the east side of the fortress by Skippergata and on the north side by Karl Johans Gate between Oslo Domkirke and Stortorvet. The boundary follows Øvre Vollgata around to the other side of the fortress. Kvadraturen translates roughly as "square township," which refers to the area's geometrically ordered streets. Be aware that the streets around Skippergata and Myntgata are known as a mini–red-light district, so you may see some unsavory characters. The area, however, is not dangerous, especially if you go during daylight.

Start at Stortorvet, Oslo's main square. On the right of the square is **Oslo Domkirke** ⑧, completed in 1697. Take a look inside—artists have been contributing to the cathedral's richly decorated interior since the 18th century. Behind the cathedral is a semicircular arcade called Kirkeristen, or **Basarhallene,** housing many artisans' small shops.

From the cathedral, follow Kirkegata left past Karl Johan to the **Museet for Samtidskunst** ⑨, which is housed in the 1902 Bank of Norway building. Take some time to view the museum's contemporary works, especially the ones by Norwegian artists. From the museum, take the side street Revierstredet to Dronningensgate, where you'll come across a building that does not seem to fit in with its 17th-century neighbors. Designed and built in the early 1990s, this brick and steel office building houses the **Astrup Fearnley Museet for Moderne Kunst** ⑩. This stop is a must for modern-art lovers.

14

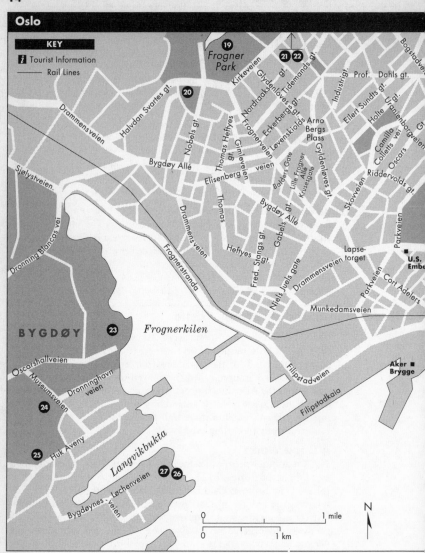

KEY

ℹ️ Tourist Information

—— Rail Lines

Akershus Slott og Festning, **11**

Astrup Fearnley Museet for Moderne Kunst, **10**

Fram-Museet, **26**

Gamle Aker Kirke, **14**

Gamlebyen, **16**

Historisk Museum, **4**

Holmenkollbakken, **22**

Kon-Tiki Museum, **27**

Kunstindustri-museet, **15**

Munchmuseet, **13**

Museet for Samtidskunst, **9**

Nasjonalgalleriet, **3**

Nationalteatret, **5**

Norges Hjemmefront Museum, **12**

Norsk Folkemuseum, **24**

Oscarshall Slott, **23**

Oslo Domkirke, **8**

Oslo Ladegård, **18**

Rådhuset, **7**

St. Halvards Kirke, **17**

Slottet, **1**

Stortinget, **6**

Tryvannstårnet, **21**

Universitet, **2**

Vigelandsmuseet, **20**

Vigelandsparken, **19**

Vikingskiphuset, **25**

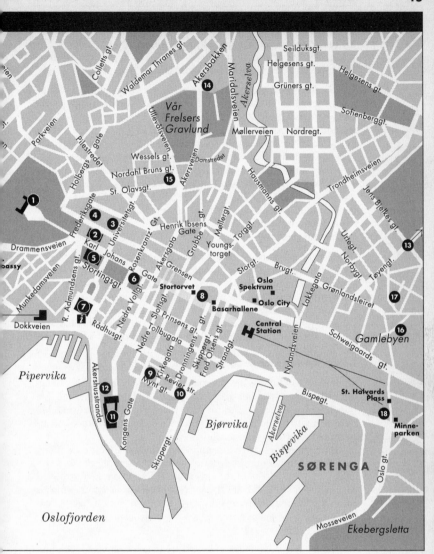

Take Dronningensgate back to Rådhusgata and turn left. As you go up the street, notice the 17th-century building at 11 Rådhusgata. It houses the celebrated restaurant Statholdergaarden (☞ Dining, *below*). This was the home of the "statholder," the official representative from Copenhagen when Norway was under Danish rule.

Continue on Rådhusgata until you reach the corner of Nedre Slottsgate. The yellow building you see was the old city hall; now it's the 141-year-old Gamle Raadhus (☞ Dining, *below*) restaurant. This structure, first built in 1641, has also served as a courthouse, prison, and wine cellar. It became a restaurant in 1856. The revered dining spot closed down in 1996 after an unexplained fire, but the management hopes to reopen it sometime in the next few years. Diagonally across Rådhusgata in the two 17th-century buildings are an art gallery and an artsy café. The building that houses Kafé Celcius was one of the first buildings erected in Christian IV's town. The building has had many functions, starting as a schoolhouse and eventually serving as a military hospital and the living quarters of a mayor.

Turn left on Akersgata and walk alongside the grassy hill to the entrance of **Akershus Slott og Festning** ⑪, the central element of Christian IV's Kvadraturen. It's a slight climb, but the views from the top are worth it. The castle became the German headquarters during the occupation of Norway in World War II, and many members of the Resistance were executed on the castle grounds. Their memorial has been erected at the site, across the bridge at the harbor end of the castle precinct. In a building next to the castle, at the top of the hill, is the **Norges Hjemmefront Museum** ⑫.

Walk back to Rådhusgata to see another interesting building, **Skogbrand Insurance** (Rådhusgt. 23B). Architects Jan Digerud and Jon Lundberg have won awards for their innovative 1985 vertical addition to this 1917 building. Once you have your fill of history and architecture, you can get in touch with something a bit more corporeal at the Emanuel Vigeland Museum, which displays artistic erotica created by the brother of the celebrated sculptor Gustav Vigeland. To get here, turn right on any of the streets along Rådhusgata back to Karl Johans and take the T-bane (T-bane is short for *tunnelbane,* which is an underground railway, or subway) line 1 from Nationalteatret station direction Frognerseteren and get off at Slemdal.

TIMING

The walk alone should take at least three hours. Combined with museum visits and breaks, the itinerary could take up more than half a day. Akershus Festning will take at least half an hour. Many museums are closed Mondays. Astrup Fearnley is open afternoons only; and the Teatermuseet is open only a few days a week—plan your tour accordingly. Try to do this tour during daylight hours, catching late-afternoon sun from atop the Akershus grounds. Also note that the T-bane ride to the Emanuel Vigeland Museet in Slemdal takes about 15 minutes and that the museum is open only a few hours on Sunday afternoons.

Sights to See

⑪ Akershus Slott og Festning (Akershus Castle and Fortress). The oldest part of the castle was built around 1300 and includes an "escape-proof" room built four centuries later for a thief named Ole Pedersen Høyland. In fact he broke out of this cell, robbed the Bank of Norway, was caught, and brought back to jail. With no possibility of a second escape, he killed himself here. Today some of the building is used for state occasions, but a few rooms, including the chapel, are open to the public. ⊠ *Akershus Slott, Festningspl.,* ☎ *22/41–25–21.* ☞ *Grounds and* concerts free; castle NKr20. ☉ Grounds daily 6 AM–9 PM; concerts, mid-May–mid-Oct., Sun. at 2; castle May–mid-Sept., Mon.–Sat. 10–4. Guided tours May–Sept., Mon.–Sat. 11, 1, and 3; Sun. 1 and 3.

❿ Astrup Fearnley Museet for Moderne Kunst (Astrup Fearnley Museum for Modern Art). Shiny marble floors and white and gray walls (whose colors may change with the exhibitions) provide a neutral and elegant background for a series of fascinating and often disturbing works. Several works by the German artist Anselm Kiefer are part of the museum's permanent collection. Spacious exhibition rooms lead to a glassed-in sculpture garden with Niki de St. Phalle's sparrow and several other oversize 20th-century figures. ⊠ Dronningens Gt. 4, ☎ 22/93–60–60. ⚏ NKr30. ☉ Tues., Wed., and Fri.–Sun. noon–4; Thurs. noon–7. Guided tours weekends at 1.

<table>
<tr><td>OFF THE
BEATEN PATH</td><td>**EMANUEL VIGELANDS MUSEET –** Although he never gained the fame of his brother Gustav, the creator of Vigeland Park, the younger Emanuel is an artist of some notoriety. His alternately saucy, natural, and downright erotic frescoes make even the sexually liberated Norwegians blush. To get here, take T-bane line 1 in the direction of Frognerseteren and get off at Slemdal, one of Oslo's hillside residential neighborhoods. ⊠ Grimelundsvn. 8, ☎ 22/14–93–42. ⚏ Free. ☉ Sun. noon–3.</td></tr>
</table>

❾ Museet for Samtidskunst (The Museum of Contemporary Art). The building, a good example of Norwegian Art Nouveau architecture, houses a fine collection of international and Norwegian contemporary works in small rooms. ⊠ Bankpl. 4, ☎ 22/33–58–20. ⚏ Free. ☉ Tues.–Wed., Fri. 10–5, Thurs. 10–8, Sat. 11–4, Sun. 11–5. Guided tours by appointment only.

⓬ Norges Hjemmefront Museum (Norwegian Resistance Museum). Winding hallways take you through a series of audiovisual displays documenting events that took place during the German occupation (1940–45). ⊠ Norges Hjemmefrontmuseum, Akershus Festning, ☎ 23/09–31–38. ⚏ NKr20. ☉ Mid-Apr.–mid-June and Sept., Mon.–Sat. 10–4, Sun. 11–4; mid-June–Aug., Mon.–Sat. 10–5, Sun. 11–5; Oct.–mid-Apr., Mon.–Sat. 10–3, Sun. 11–4.

❽ Oslo Domkirke (Oslo Cathedral). In the 19th century, the fire department operated a fire lookout point from the bell tower here, which you can visit today. This dark brown brick structure has been Oslo's main church since the 17th century. Inside is an intricately carved Baroque pulpit and a five-story organ. Built in 1697, the church underwent extensive renovations before reopening in the summer of 1997 to celebrate its 300th anniversary. ⊠ Stortorvet 1, ☎ 22/41–27–93. ⚏ Free. ☉ June–Aug., weekdays 10–3, Sat. 10–1; Sept.–May, weekdays 10–3.

<table>
<tr><td>NEED A
BREAK?</td><td>**Pascal** (⊠ Tollbugt. 11, ☎ 22/42–11–19), a Parisian patisserie inside an old-fashioned Norwegian konditori (café), serves enormous croissants and pastries with French coffee. Look for the little angels baking bread—they're painted on the ceiling.</td></tr>
</table>

East, North, and South of Downtown: Munch Museum, Damstredet, and Gamlebyen

The Munch Museum is east of the city center in Tøyen, an area in which Edvard Munch spent many of his years in Oslo. The Tøyen district has a much different feel than Oslo's cushy west side—it's simpler and more industrial. West of Tøyen, just north of the city center, is the quiet, old-fashioned district of Damstredet, its quaint streets lined with artisans' shops. If you're a die-hard history buff, you'll probably enjoy the last half of this tour through Gamlebyen. However, if this is your first time in Oslo and you have a limited amount of time, you may want to end your tour at the Kunstindustrimuseet. Gamlebyen, south of the city center, is somewhat off the beaten track, and although the area is interesting, some of the ruins are barely discernible.

A Good Walk

Start by taking any T-bane from the city center to Tøyen, where **Munchmuseet** ⑬ sits on a hill near the **Botanisk Hage,** a quiet oasis of plants and flowers. Munch's family lived in a house in the neighborhood during part of his life. After visiting the museum, head back toward the city center. Take the T-bane toward Sentrum and get off at Stortinget.

Head down Karl Johans Gate and take a right onto Akersgata. Follow it past the offices of **Aftenposten,** Norway's leading daily paper, which display the day's headlines in the window. As you head up the hill, you will see a huge rotund building, **Deichmanske Bibliotek,** the city's library. When you reach St. Olavs Church, veer gently to the right on Akersveien. You may want to take a detour down **Damstredet** when you come to it—it's one of the city's oldest streets. Afterward, continue back along Akersveien. **Vår Frelsers Gravlund** (Our Savior's Graveyard), where you can seek out the gravestones of many famous Norwegians who are buried here, including Ibsen and Munch, will be on your left. At the graveyard's northeastern corner is **Gamle Aker Kirke** ⑭, the city's only remaining medieval church.

On the other side of the cemetery, follow Ullevålsveien down the hill to the corner of St. Olavs Gate and Akersgata, where you'll find the **Kunstindustrimuseet** ⑮. The museum has a superb furniture collection.

If history and archaeology interest you, visit **Gamlebyen** ⑯, the old town, on the south side of Oslo S Station. South of here on Oslo Gate is St. Halvards Plass. During the 13th century, the area near St. Halvards Plass was the city's ecclesiastical center. Still intact are the foundations of **St. Halvards Kirke** ⑰, dating from the early 12th century. Some other ruins, including Korskirke and Olavs Kloster, lie in **Minneparken.** Nearby on Bispegata is **Oslo Ladegård** ⑱, a restored Baroque-style mansion that sits on the site and foundations of a 13th-century Bishop's Palace. Government construction of the Gardemoebanen (commuter railway) to the new Oslo Airport at Gardemoen has inspired many archaeologists and city historians to mobilize in an effort to preserve the ruins area.

The oldest traces of human habitation in Oslo are the 5,000-year-old carvings on the runic stones near **Ekebergsletta Park.** They are across the road from the park on Karlsborgveien and are marked by a sign reading FORTIDSMINNE. To reach the park, walk south on Oslo Gate until it becomes Mosseveien. The park will be on your right. Here is a good spot to rest your feet and end your tour.

TIMING

The Munchmuseet will take up most of the morning, especially if you take a guided tour. Don't plan your tour for a Monday because the Munchmuseet and Kunstindustrimuseet are closed. The second half of the tour, from Gamlebyen to Ekebergsletta, is a perfect way to spend a summer Sunday afternoon. Things are quiet, and locals tend to stroll around this area when the weather is nice.

Sights to See

⑭ **Gamle Aker Kirke** (Old Aker Church). Oslo's medieval stone basilica has undergone many changes since it was constructed around 1100. ☒ *Akersvn. 26,* ☎ *22/69–35–82.* ☜ *Free.* ◷ *Mon.–Sat. noon–2, Sun. 9–1.*

⑯ Gamlebyen (The Old City). This area contains the last remains of medieval Oslo. Because of repeated fires, Christian IV moved Oslo from this site (after the fire of 1624) to a safer area near Akershus Festning (Akershus Fort). Today it's the largest homogeneous archaeological site found in any capital city in Scandinavia. To get here, go back to Stortorvet and take *trikk* (as the Norwegians fondly call the streetcars) 18, marked "Ljabru," from Stortorvet to St. Halvards Plass (you can also take trikk 19 from Nationalteatret). Contact Oslo Byantikvar (☎ 22/20–85–80) for information on guided tours of the area, or for a self-guided tour ask the Norway Information Center where you can get a copy of *Guide to Gamlebyen* by Morten Krogstad and Erik Schia.

⑮ Kunstindustrimuseet (Museum of Applied Art). Clothes worthy of any fairy tale, including Queen Maud's jewel-encrusted coronation gown from 1904, are displayed here in the museum's Royal Norwegian Costume Gallery. Extensive collections of industrial designs and arts and crafts include more than 35,000 objects. ⊠ *St. Olavs Gt. 1,* ☎ *22/20–35–78.* ⊠ *NKr25.* ⊙ *Tues.–Fri. 11–3, weekends noon–4.*

Minneparken. Oslo was founded by Harald Hårdråde ("Hard Ruler") in 1048, and the earliest settlements were near what is now Bispegata, a few blocks behind Oslo S Station. Ruins are all that are left of the city's former spiritual center: the **Korskirke** (Cross Church, ⊠ Egedes Gate 2), a small stone church dating from the end of the 13th century; and **Olavs Kloster** (Olav's Cloister, ⊠ St. Halvards Plass 3), built around 1240 by Dominican monks (⊠ Entrance at Oslo Gt. and Bispegt). Call the Oslo Bymuseum (☎ 22/42–06–45) for guided tours.

★ ⑬ Munchmuseet (Munch Museum). Edvard Munch, one of Scandinavia's leading artists, bequeathed an enormous collection of his work (about 1,100 paintings, 4,500 drawings, and 18,000 graphic works) to the city when he died in 1944. It languished in warehouses for nearly 20 years, until the city built a museum to house it in 1963. For much of his life Munch was a troubled man, and his major works, dating from the 1890s, with such titles as *The Scream* and *Vampire,* reveal his angst, but he was not without humor. His extraordinary talent as a graphic artist emerges in the print room, with its displays of lithograph stones and woodblocks. ⊠ *Tøyengt. 53,* ☎ *22/67–37–74.* ⊠ *NKr40.* ⊙ *June–mid-Sept., daily 10–6; mid-Sept.–May, Tues.–Sat. 10–4, Thurs. and Sun. 10–6.*

⑱ Oslo Ladegård. The original building, a 13th-century Bispegård (Bishop's Palace), burned down in the 1624 fire, but its old vaulted cellar was not destroyed. The building was restored and rebuilt in 1725; it now belongs to the city council and contains scale models of 16th- to 18th-century Oslo. ⊠ *St. Halvards Pl., Oslogt. 13,* ☎ *22/19–44–68.* ⊠ *NKr20.* ⊙ *May–Sept.; guided tours on Wed. at 6, Sun. at 1.*

⑰ St. Halvards Kirke (St. Halvard's Church). This medieval church, named for the patron saint of Oslo, remained the city's cathedral until 1660. St. Halvard became the city's patron saint when his murdered body was found floating in the Drammensfjord, despite the presence of a heavy stone around his neck. He had been trying to save a pregnant woman from three violent pursuers when they caught and murdered him along with her. ⊠ *Minneparken, entrance at Oslogt. and Bispegt.*

Frogner, Majorsturen, and Holmenkollen

One of the city's most stylish neighborhoods, Frogner combines old-world Scandinavian elegance with contemporary European chic. Most of the pastel-and-white buildings in the area were constructed in the early years of this century. Many have interesting wrought-iron work and sculptural detail. Terribly hip boutiques and galleries coexist with embassies and ambassadors' residences on the streets near and around Bygdøy Allé. Holmenkollen, the hill past Frogner Park, features miles of ski trails—and more beautiful homes of the affluent.

A Good Walk

Catch the No. 12 "Majorstuen" trikk from Nationalteatret on the Drammensveien side of the Royal Palace. You can also take the No. 15 from Aker Brygge.

Opposite the southwest end of the palace grounds is the triangular **U.S. Embassy,** designed by Finnish-American architect Eero Saarinen and built in 1959. Look to the right at the corner of Drammensveien and Parkveien for a glimpse of the venerable **Nobel Institute.** Since 1905 these stately yellow buildings have been the secluded setting where the five-member Nobel Committee decides who will win the Nobel Peace Prize. The 15,000-volume library is open to the public.

Stay on the trikk and ride to Frogner Park or walk the seven short blocks. To walk, follow Balders Gate to Arno Bergs Plass, with its central fountain. Turn left on Gyldenløves Gate until you reach Kirkeveien. Turn right past the Dutch Embassy, and cross the street at the light. Frogner Park, also called Vigelandspark interchangeably, is just ahead.

Walk through the front gates of the park and toward the monolith ahead: you are entering **Vigelandsparken** ⑲. There's nothing anywhere else in the world quite like this stunning sculpture garden designed by one of Norway's greatest artists; who is, ironically, virtually unknown to the rest of the world. Across from the park, you can study the method to his madness at **Vigelandsmuseet** ⑳.

After you leave the park, continue on Kirkeveien to the Majorstuen underground station. Here you have two options: you can take a walk down Bogstadveien, look at the shops, and explore the Majorstuen area and then take the Holmenkollen line of the T-bane to Frognerseteren; or you can skip the stroll down Bogstadveien and head right up to Holmenkollen. The train ride up the mountain passes some stunning scenery. If you have brought your children, you may want to make a detour at the first T-bane stop, Frøen, and visit the **Barnekunstmuseet.**

Continue on the T-bane to the end of the line. This is Frognerseteren—where city dwellers disappear to on winter weekends. The view of the city here is spectacular. The **Tryvannstårnet** ㉑ has an even better panoramic view of Oslo. Downhill is **Holmenkollbakken** ㉒, where Norway's most intrepid skiers prove themselves every February during the Holmenkollen Ski Festival.

TIMING

This is a good tour for Monday, since the museums mentioned are open, unlike most others in Oslo. You will need a whole day for both neighborhoods since there is some travel time involved. The trikk ride from the city center to Frogner Park is about 15 minutes; the T-bane to Frognerseteren is about 20. You're no longer in the compact city center, so distances between sights are greater. The walk from Frognerseteren is about 15 minutes and is indicated with signposts. Try to save Holmenkollen with its magnificent views for a clear day. Summer hours for museums and lookout points are extended because the days are so long. In the spring, though, go before the sun starts to set.

If you want to see Norwegians younger than two years old on skis, a winter Sunday in Frognerseteren is your best bet. Frogner Park has some skiers and sledders, and families flock to Holmenkollen for Sunday ski school.

Sights to See

Barnekunstmuseet (Children's Art Museum). The museum was the brain-child of Rafael Goldin, a Russian immigrant who has collected children's drawings from more than 150 countries. ⊠ *Lille Frøensvn. 4,* ☎ *22/46–85–73.* ▣ *NKr30.* ☉ *Mid-June–mid-Aug., Tues.–Thurs. and Sun. 11–4; mid-Aug.–mid-Dec. and late Jan.–mid-June, Tues.–Thurs. 9:30–2, Sun. 11–4.*

★ ㉒ **Holmenkollbakken** (Holmenkollen Ski Museum and Ski Jump). Oslo's ski jump holds a special place in the hearts of Norwegians, who contend they invented the sport. The 1892 jump was rebuilt for the 1952 Winter Olympics and is still used for international competitions. At the base of the jump, turn right, past the statue of the late King Olav V on skis, to enter the museum. It displays equipment from the Fritjof Nansen and Roald Amundsen polar voyages and a model of a ski maker's workshop, in addition to a collection of skis, the oldest dating from pre-Viking times. You can also climb (or ride the elevator) to the top of the jump tower. ⊠ *Kongevn. 5,* ☎ *22/92–32–64.* ▣ *NKr50.* ☉ *July–Aug., daily 9 AM–10 PM; June, daily 9–8; Apr.–May and Sept., daily 10–5; Oct.–Mar., daily 10–4.*

㉑ **Tryvannstårnet** (Tryvann's Tower). The view from Oslo's TV tower encompasses 36,000 square ft of hills, forests, cities, and several bodies of water. You can see as far as the Swedish border to the east and nearly as far as Moss to the south. ⊠ *Voksenkollen,* ☎ *22/14–67–11.* ▣ *NKr30.* ☉ *May and Sept., daily 10–5; June, daily 10–8; July, daily 9 AM–10 PM; Aug., daily 9–8; Oct.–Apr., daily 10–4*

㉒ **Vigelandsmuseet.** This small museum displays many of the plaster models for the Vigeland Park sculptures, the artist's woodcuts and drawings, and mementos of his life. ⊠ *Nobelsgt. 32,* ☎ *22/44–11–36.* ▣ *NKr20.* ☉ *May–Sept., Tues.–Sat. 10–6, Sun. noon–7; Oct.–Apr., Tues.–Sat. noon–4, Sun. noon–6.*

★ ⑲ **Vigelandsparken** (Frogner Park). This park, formally called Frogner Park, contains more than 50 copper statues by sculptor Gustav Vigeland, hence the moniker Vigelandspark. Vigeland began his career as a wood-carver, and his talent was quickly appreciated and supported by the townspeople of Oslo. In 1921 they provided him with a free house and studio, in exchange for which he began to chip away at his life's work, which he would ultimately donate to the city. He worked through World War II and the German occupation, and after the war the work was unveiled to the combined enchantment and horror of the townsfolk. Included was the 470-ton monolith that is now the highlight of the park, as well as hundreds of writhing, fighting, and loving sculptures representing the varied forms and stages of human life. The figures are nude, but they're more monumental than erotic—bullet-headed, muscular men and healthy, solid women with flowing hair. Look for the park's most beloved sculpture—an enraged baby boy stamping his foot and scrunching his face in fury. Known as *Sinnataggen* (The Really Angry One), this ball of rage has been filmed, parodied, painted red, and even stolen from the park.

The grassy grounds of Vigelandspark are a living part of the city—people walk dogs on the green and bathe chubby babies in the fountains, and they jog, ski, and sunbathe throughout. The park complex also includes the City Museum, a swimming pool (☞ Outdoor Activities and Sports, *below*) an ice rink and skating museum (☎ 22/43–49–20), several playgrounds, and an outdoor restaurant, Herregårdskroen, where you can have anything from a buffet lunch to a three-course dinner. ⊠ *Middlethunsgt.* ▣ *Park entrance free.*

Bygdøy

Oslo's most important historic sights are concentrated on Bygdøy Peninsula, as are several beaches, jogging paths, and the royal family's summer residence.

A Good Walk

The most pleasant way to get to Bygdøy, from May to September, is to catch a ferry from the Rådhuset. Times vary, so check with NORTRA (☞ Visitor Information *in* Oslo A to Z, *below*) for schedules. Another alternative is to take Bus 30, marked "Bygdøy," from Stortingsgata at Nationalteatret along Drammensveien to Bygdøy Allé, a wide avenue lined with chestnut trees. The bus passes Frogner Church and several embassies on its way to Olav Kyrres Plass, where it turns left, and soon left again, onto the peninsula. If you see some horses on the left, they come from the king's stables (the dark red building with the monogram); the royal family's current summer residence, actually just a big white frame house, is on the right. Get off at the next stop, Norsk Folkemuseum. The pink castle nestled in the trees is **Oscarshall Slott** ㉓, once a royal summer palace.

Next is the **Norsk Folkemuseum** ㉔, which consists of some 150 structures from all over the country that have been reconstructed on site. Around the corner to the right is the **Vikingskiphuset** ㉕, one of Norway's most famous attractions, which houses some of the best-preserved remains of the Viking era found yet.

Follow signs on the road to the **Fram-Museet** ㉖, an A-frame structure in the shape of a traditional Viking boathouse, which houses the famed *Fram* polar ship as well as artifacts from various expeditions. Across the parking lot from the Fram-Museet is the older **Kon-Tiki Museum** ㉗ with Thor Heyerdahl's famous raft, along with the papyrus boat *Ra II.* You can get a ferry back to the City Hall docks from the dock in front of the Fram-Museet. Before heading back to Oslo, you may want to have a snack at **Lanternen Kro,** which overlooks the entire harbor.

If your kids are squirming to break out of the museum circuit, entertain the thought of a trip to **VikingLandet,** an attraction park that stages the more peaceful aspects of the Vikings' existence, from farming to burial mounds. You can combine the excursion with a trip to Tusen-Fryd, an amusement park next door.

TIMING

Block out a day for Bygdøy. You could spend at least half a day at the Folkemuseum alone. Note that the museums on Bygdøy tend to be open daily but close earlier than their counterparts that close Mondays.

The HMK trip to VikingLandet is an afternoon trip, so count on spending half a day. It takes between 10 and 20 minutes to reach the park from downtown Oslo by bus. If you decide to go on your own from Oslo S Station, you might want to spend the whole day playing in both parks.

Sights to See

★ ◌ ㉖ **Fram-Museet.** The *Fram* polar ship takes up almost every inch of this museum, which was constructed around it. Matter-of-fact displays of life on board ship vividly depict the history of polar exploration. The *Fram* was constructed in 1892 by Scottish-Norwegian shipbuilder Colin Archer. Fridtjof Nansen led the first *Fram* expedition, across the ice surrounding the North Pole; the ship's most famous voyage took Roald Amundsen to Antarctica, the first leg of his successful expedition to the South Pole in 1911. ⊠ *Bygdøynes,* ☎ 22/43–83–70. 🎟 *NKr20.* ☉ *June–Aug., daily 9–6:45; May and Sept., daily 10–4:45; Mar.– Apr. and Oct.–Nov., weekdays 11–2:45, weekends 11–3:45; Dec.–Feb., weekends 11–3:45.*

★ ◌ ㉗ **Kon-Tiki Museum.** The museum celebrates Norway's most famous 20th-century explorer. Thor Heyerdahl continued the Norwegian tradition of exploration in his 1947 voyage from Peru to Polynesia on the *Kon-Tiki,* a balsa raft, to confirm his theory that the first Polynesians originally came from Peru. The *Kon-Tiki,* now showing its age, is suspended on a plastic sea. The *Ra II* sailed from Morocco to the Caribbean in 1970. ⊠ *Bygdøynesvn. 36,* ☎ 22/43–80–50. 🎟 *NKr 25.* ☉ *Apr.–May and Sept., daily 10:30–5; June–Aug., daily 9:30–5:45; Oct.– Mar., daily 10:30–4.*

★ ◌ ㉔ **Norsk Folkemuseum** (Norway's Folk Museum). You'll get a bird's-eye view of the entire country with imaginative exhibitions, 153 authentic houses, and tour guides in traditional garb. The **Gol Stavkirke** (Gol Stave Church), constructed around 1200, is one of the most important buildings here. In summer and on weekends year-round, guides in the buildings demonstrate various home crafts, such as weaving tapestries, sewing national costumes, and baking flatbread. Indoor collections in the main building include toys, dolls and dollhouses, a Sami (Lapp) collection, national costumes, and Ibsen's actual study. On one side of this museum is a reconstructed 19th-century village, with shops and houses. The museum puts on a summer calendar of special events, including daily activities from folk dancing to concerts. ⊠ *Museumsvn. 10,* ☎ 22/12–37–00. 🎟 *NKr 50.* ☉ *May and Sept. daily 10–5; June–Aug., daily 9–6; Oct.–Apr., weekdays 11–3, Sun. 11–4.*

㉓ **Oscarshall Slott.** This eccentric neo-Gothic palace, built in 1852 for King Oscar I, served as a site for picnics and other summer pursuits. It now houses Norwegian art, including works by Tidemand and Gude. ⊠ *Oscarshallvn.,* ☎ 22/43–77–49. 🎟 *NKr15.* ☉ *Mid-May–mid-Sept., Tues., Thurs., and Sun. noon–4.*

◌ **VikingLandet.** Norway's first and only theme park on the Viking Age takes you back 1,000 years to experience daily life as a Viking. You encounter Viking warriors and nobles throughout the park, which is built on the idea of an early Viking community's farms and marketplaces. You can combine the trip with a visit to **Norgesparken Tusenfryd,** Oslo's amusement park. There are carnival rides, such as a merry-go-round, a Ferris wheel, and a roller coaster with a loop, and a water slide. There's a separate entrance fee, but both parks are under the same management. HMK provides an afternoon bus excursion from Norway Information Center (☞ Guided Tours *in* Oslo A to Z, *below*). There's also a free shuttle bus that departs from the south side of Oslo S Station. ⊠ *Both parks: Vinterbro,* ☎ 64/94–63–63. 🎟 *Combined ticket NKr180.* ☉ *May and late Aug.–Sept., weekends noon–6; early June, weekdays 10:30–3; mid-June–late Aug., daily noon–6.*

★ ㉕ **Vikingskiphuset.** Norway's claim to fame centers on its incorrigible Viking explorers, and this museum celebrates their fascinating culture.

The building resembles a cathedral on the outside, and inside the feeling of reverence is very real. It's hard to believe that the three ships on display, all found buried along the Oslo Fjord, are nearly 1,200 years old. Viking elites wanted to make sure their dead were well equipped for life after death, so they buried them in long ships with all the necessities, which sometimes included a servant. The discoverers of the *Oseberg* even found wood, leather, and woolen textiles intact. Burial ships often reflected the social status of the person buried. The richly carved *Oseberg*, thought to have been the burial chamber for Queen Åse, is the most decorative, whereas the *Gokstad* is a functional longboat, devoid of ornament. Items found with the ships, including tools, household goods, and a tapestry, are also on view. ⊠ *Huk Aveny 35,* ☎ *22/43–83–79.* ✉ *NKr30.* ⊙ *May–Aug., daily 9–6; Sept., daily 11–5; Apr. and Oct., daily 11–4; Nov.–Mar., daily 11–3.*

DINING

Food was once an afterthought in Oslo, but not anymore. The city's chefs are winning contests worldwide. Norwegian cuisine, based on products from the country's pristine waters and lush farmland, is now firmly in the culinary spotlight. Menus change daily, weekly, or according to the season in many of Oslo's finer restaurants.

In Oslo, bad food is expensive and good food doesn't necessarily cost more—it's just a matter of knowing where to go. If you visit Oslo in summer, head for Aker Brygge, the wharf turned shopping area. Hundreds of café goers vie for the sun and the view at the fjord-side outdoor tables. Most restaurants here offer a summer menu that is considerably less expensive than the regular one. Aker Brygge is also a good place to buy shrimp, an activity that heralds the coming of summer for many locals. If you don't want to buy them fresh off the boat, order them at one of the floating restaurants. Generally they come on a baguette or in a big bowl with mayonnaise on the side.

A good place to get a meal that won't cost more than your hotel room is the food court at Paléet Shopping Center, which is open daily 10–8. A bit pricier, and a lot snazzier than the fast-food bonanzas of most American malls, this food court has a variety of stands with international fare, ranging from Danish and Greek to American.

Many of the less expensive restaurants listed below are simply cafés, bars, and even sometimes discotheques. These types of establishments are becoming increasingly popular as restaurants as Oslo's twentysomething generation decides it likes to eat out. (Because of high prices, eating out is a huge luxury for most Norwegians.) Meals at these cheaper spots invariably include pasta dishes, shellfish, pizzas, and salads rather than lobsters and lamb chops. For a more exhaustive list of Oslo cafés, pick up a copy of *Café Guiden,* a glossy publication describing more than 100 spots in detail. It is available in most bars and cafés (☞ Cafés *in* Nightlife and the Arts, *below*).

Downtown: Royal Palace to the Parliament

$$$$ ✕ **D'Artagnan.** Diplomas, certificates, and prizes from all over the world
★   line the walls of this downtown *restaurant gastronomique.* Owner Freddie Nielsen, one of Norway's most celebrated restaurateurs, received both his education and inspiration in France, but do not expect nouvelle cuisine here. Only the famished should embark upon the seven-course Grand Menu. The saffron-poached pike with asparagus is a good way to start a meal, and the boned fillet of salmon with dill lobster-cream sauce is delectable. The veal is so tender you can cut it with your

fork. The dessert cart is loaded with jars of fruit preserved in liqueurs, which are served with sorbets and ice creams. ⊠ *Øvre Slottsgt. 16,* ☎ *22/41–50–62. AE, DC, MC, V. Closed Sun. and mid-July–mid-Aug. No lunch Jan.–Aug.*

$$$ ✕ **Babette's Gjestehus.** Chef Ortwin Kulmus and his friendly staff make their guests feel welcome at this tiny restaurant hidden in the shopping arcade by City Hall. Bright blue walls, starched white tablecloths, and lace curtains against paned windows contribute to the rustic, homey feel. The food is Scandinavian with a French twist. Try the garlic-marinated rack of lamb in rosemary sauce or pan-fried breast of duck with creamed spring cabbage. Dishes vary according to season but are always well prepared. ⊠ *Rådhuspassasjen, Roald Amundsensgt. 6,* ☎ *22/41–64–64. Reservations essential. AE, DC, MC, V. Closed Sun. No lunch.*

$$$ ✕ **Theatercafeen.** This Oslo institution, on the ground floor of the Hotel
★ Continental, is *the* place to see and be seen. Built in 1900, the last Viennese-style café in northern Europe retains its Art Nouveau character. The menu is small and jumbled, with starters and main dishes interspersed; the only hint of the serving size is the price column. Pastry chef Robert Bruun's *konfektkake* (a rich chocolate cake) and apple tart served with homemade ice cream are reasons enough to visit. ⊠ *Stortingsgt. 24–26,* ☎ *22/82–40–50. AE, DC, MC, V.*

$$ ✕ **Dinner.** Though its name is not the best for a restaurant specializ-
★ ing in Szechuan-style cuisine, this is the place for Chinese food. Don't bother with the other Chinese restaurants. ⊠ *Stortingsgt. 22,* ☎ *22/ 42–68–90. AE, DC, MC, V. No lunch.*

$$ ✕ **A Touch of France.** Just downstairs from D'Artagnan (☞ *above*), Freddie Nielsen's clean, inviting wine bistro is straight out of Paris. The French ambience is further accented by the waiters' long, white aprons, the Art Nouveau decor, old French posters, and closely packed tables. The tempting menu includes a steaming hot bouillabaisse. ⊠ *Øvre Slottsgt. 16,* ☎ *22/42–56–97. AE, DC, MC, V.*

$ ✕ **Brasserie 45.** Overlooking the fountain on Karl Johans Gate, this brasserie serves a solid meal in an elegant Scandinavian setting, complete with candlelight, red walls, and shiny wooden floors. The idea is simple: 45 dishes for 45 kroner each. There are both meat and fish dishes, often garnished with a tasty Brasserie 45 sauce (a tomato sweet-and-sour sauce) and potatoes or pasta. The portions are small, but a three-course meal at NKr135 is still a bargain in Oslo. ⊠ *Karl Johans Gt. 45 (upstairs),* ☎ *22/41–34–00. AE, DC, MC, V.*

$ ✕ **Café Sjakk Matt.** This popular spot between Vika and Karl Johan is one of the many bars that serve food as well—although they've made it a specialty. However, you do have to order at the bar. A variety of pita sandwiches and melts, ratatouille, quiche, and the house specialty, lasagna, are some of what's on the menu. Hot dishes usually come with salad and nutty Norwegian bread. The place has a modern Scandinavian feel: dozens of candles, potted plants, and shiny floors. ⊠ *Haakon VII's Gt. 5,* ☎ *22/83–41–56. AE, DC, MC, V.*

$ ✕ **Den Grimme Ælling.** Dane Bjarne Hvid Pedersen's smørbrød are the best buy in town: lots of meat, fish, or cheese on a small piece of bread. This popular Copenhagen restaurant in the food court at Paleet also has daily dinner specials, such as homemade *hakkebøf* (Danish Salisbury steak) with gravy, onions, and potatoes. ⊠ *Paleet, Karl Johans Gt. 41B,* ☎ *22/42–47–83. No credit cards.*

$ ✕ **Kaffistova.** Norwegian country cooking is served, cafeteria style, at this downtown restaurant. Everyday specials include soup and a selection of entrées, including a vegetarian dish. Kjøttkaker (meat cakes) served with creamed cabbage is a Norwegian staple, and the steamed salmon with Sandefjord butter is as good here as in places where it costs

26

Oslo Dining and Lodging

KEY

i Tourist Information
—— Rail Lines

Dining
A Touch of France, **31**
Babette's
Gjestehus, **19**
Bagatelle, **10**
Brasserie 45, **25**
Café Sjakk Matt, **16**
Clodion Art Café, **2**
Coco Chalet, **34**
D'Artagnan, **31**
De Fem Stuer, **3**
Den Grimme
Ælling, **26**

Det Gamle
Raadhus, **35**
Dinner, **18**
Dionysos Taverna, **40**
Engebret Café, **37**
Feinschmecker, **6**
Frognerseteren, **4**
Hos Thea, **9**
Kaffistova, **32**
Kastanjen, **7**
Klosteret, **41**

Lofoten
Fiskrestaurant, **15**
Markveien Mat og
Vinhus, **42**
Maud's, **17**
Palace Grill, **11**
Restaurant
Le Canard, **5**
Statholdergaarden, **36**
Theatercafeen, **20**
Vegeta, **23**

Lodging
Ambassadeur, **13**
Bristol, **28**
Frogner House, **12**
Gabelshus, **8**
Grand Hotel, **33**
Haraldsheim, **43**
Holmenkollen Park
Hotel Rica, **3**
Hotell
Bondeheimen, **32**
Hotel Continental, **20**
Hotel Karl Johan, **27**
Munch, **30**

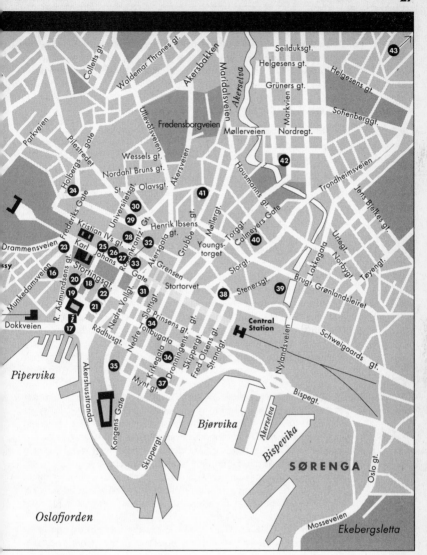

Radisson SAS
Park Royal, **1**

Radisson SAS Plaza
Hotel Oslo, **39**

Radisson SAS
Scandinavia Hotel, **24**

Rainbow Cecil, **22**

Rainbow
Gyldenløve, **14**

Rainbow Hotel
Stefan, **29**

Rica Victoria, **21**

Royal Christiania, **38**

three times as much. Low-alcohol beer is the strongest drink served. ⊠ *Rosenkrantz' Gt. 8,* ☏ *22/42–99–74. AE, DC, MC, V.*

$ ✕ **Vegeta.** Next to the Nationalteatret bus and trikk station, this no-smoking restaurant is a popular spot for hot and cold vegetarian meals and salads. The all-you-can-eat specials offer top value. ⊠ *Munk-edamsvn. 3B,* ☏ *22/83–40–20. AE, DC, MC, V.*

Kvadraturen and Aker Brygge

$$$$ ✕ **Statholdergaarden.** Award-winning chef Bent Stiansen is currently the shining star of Norwegian haute cuisine. As a result, it is hard to get a table here—especially around Christmastime—so plan early. The four-course gastronomic menu changes daily. You can also order directly from the à la carte menu. Try one of the imaginative appetizers, such as smoked duck breast with fried goat cheese and pine nut salad. Specialties include salmon mousse and other fish delicacies. This restaurant, in a building that dates back to 1640, is in the heart of Oslo's oldest standing neighborhood. ⊠ *Rådhusgt. 11,* ☏ *22/41–88–00. Reservations essential. Jacket and tie. AE, DC, MC, V. Closed Sun. and 3 wks in July.*

$$$ ✕ **Engebret Café.** This somber, old-fashioned restaurant at Bankplassen was a haunt for bohemian literati at the turn of the century. Today it draws tourists, especially in summer, for casual fare and drinks at the outdoor café. The more formal dinner menu includes traditional Norwegian staples, such as reindeer and salmon. Food critics give these two dishes rave reviews year after year. This is a good spot for refreshment after visiting the Contemporary Art Museum; try to get an outdoor table and listen to the museum's fountain trickle away in the distance. ⊠ *Bankplassen 1,* ☏ *22/33–66–94. AE, DC, MC, V.*

$$–$$$ ✕ **Lofoten Fiskerestaurant.** With all windows overlooking the water at Aker Brygge, this is Oslo's quintessential fish restaurant. All types of fish, from salmon to cod to monkfish, are served fresh and cooked in a variety of sauces, from house bouillabaisse to classic wine or saffron sauce. The clientele is well-heeled, and the elegant wood-paneled interior brings to mind a vintage Scandinavian cruise ship. Try to get an outdoor table in summer: you take advantage of a cheaper menu as well as late-evening sunlight on the fjord. Service can be slow on busy evenings, but it's definitely worth the wait. ⊠ *Stranden 75, Aker Brygge,* ☏ *22/83–08–08. AE, DC, MC, V.*

$$ ✕ **Det Gamle Raadhus.** This restaurant in the former city hall is famous for its lutefisk, a Scandinavian specialty made from dried fish that has been soaked in lye and then poached. However, the menu here does allow ample choice for the less daring. This is Oslo's oldest restaurant—it celebrated its 350th birthday in 1991. Unfortunately the restaurant suffered extensive fire damage in 1996, but at press time was scheduled to reopen in 1998. Call 22/41–44–41 to be certain. ⊠ *Nedre Slottsgt. 1,* ☏ *22/42–01–07. AE, DC, MC, V. Closed Sun.*

$$ ✕ **Maud's.** In the same building as the Norway Information Center, this restaurant would logically attract tourists. However, it seems to attract more locals. The regional Norwegian dishes are so traditional that they seem exotic to some Norwegian city folk who left the nest long ago. Specialties include potato dumplings and myriad fish and meat dishes served with none other than potatoes boiled to perfection. Lunch plates and open-faced sandwiches are reasonably priced, as are the "everyday meals," served from 1 to 7. ⊠ *Vestbaneplassen. 1,* ☏ *22/83–72–28. AE, DC, MC, V. Closed Sun.*

$ ✕ **Coco Chalet.** Best known for its homemade cakes and pies, Coco Chalet is moving into the world of affordable haute cuisine. The Asian-inspired menu features a delectable chicken breast with vegetables julienne. The dining room of this restaurant in Oslo's oldest neighborhood feels somewhat like a haunted mansion: white tablecloths bedeck the tables at all hours of the day, spooky candelabras sit on the mantle, and the mostly female staff wears black uniforms with white aprons and collars. ⊠ *Øvre Slottsgt. 8,* ☎ *22/33–32–66. AE, DC, MC, V.*

East of Downtown

$$$ ✕ **Klosteret.** This popular east-side eatery's name means "the cloisters." Its not-so-medieval dining room is downstairs in a spacious cellar with a rounded brick ceiling. Wacky iron candelabras sprouting from red walls like thorny branches and stark steel-backed chairs are somehow in perfect harmony with the gold-bedecked saints and Christ childs that adorn the walls. The handwoven menus are sheathed in monastic hymnal pages and offer a variety of meat and fish, as well as a daily vegetarian dish. Main courses are often served atop a bed of sautéed leafy greens, which makes for an innovative presentation as well as a refreshing change from traditional Norwegian *kinakål,* a white lettuce-cabbage usually substituted for greens. Take a taxi. ⊠ *Fredensborgvn. 13,* ☎ *22/20–66–90. AE, DC, MC, V. Closed Sun. and 3–4 wks in July.*

$$$ ✕ **Markveien Mat og Vinhus.** This artsy food and wine house in the heart of the Grunerløkka district serves fresh French-inspired cuisine. The atmosphere is relaxed and the clientele is bohemian. Paintings cover the yellow walls, and the tables are black and somber. As most touristy spots in Oslo lie in the *Vest* (west), a trip to the *Øst* (east) will give you a chance to see how the other side lives. ⊠ *Torvbakkgt. 12 (entrance on Markvn. 57),* ☎ *22/37–22–97. AE, DC, MC, V. Closed Sun.*

$$ ✕ **Dionysos Taverna.** Nicola Murati gives his guests a warm welcome
★ in this unpretentious little Greek restaurant. The hors d'oeuvre platter, which includes stuffed grape leaves, meatballs, feta cheese, tomatoes, and cucumbers, is a meal in itself. The souvlaki and moussaka are authentically prepared, as are the more unusual casserole dishes. A bouzouki duo provides live music on Thursday, Friday, and Saturday. ⊠ *Calmeyersgt. 11,* ☎ *22/60–78–64. AE, MC, V. No lunch.*

Frogner and Majorstuen

$$$$ ✕ **Bagatelle.** One of Oslo's best restaurants is a short walk from
★ downtown. Paintings by contemporary Norwegian artists accent the otherwise subdued interior, but the food is the true show here. Internationally known chef-owner Eyvind Hellstrøm's cuisine is modern Norwegian with French overtones. His grilled scallops with a saffron-parsley sauce and the marinated salmon tartare with an herbed crème fraîche are extraordinary. Bagatelle has a wine cellar to match its food. ⊠ *Bygdøy Allé 3,* ☎ *22/44–63–97. Jacket and tie. AE, DC, MC, V. Closed Sun. No lunch.*

$$$$ ✕ **Feinschmecker.** The name is German, but the food is modern Scandinavian. The atmosphere is friendly and intimate, with green rattan chairs, yellow tablecloths, and floral draperies. Owners Lars Erik Underthun, one of Oslo's foremost chefs, and Bengt Wilson, one of Scandinavia's leading food photographers, make sure the food looks as good as it tastes. The roast rack of lamb with crunchy fried sweetbreads on tagliatelle and the chocolate-caramel teardrop with passion-fruit sauce are two choices on the menu, which makes for fascinating reading. ⊠ *Balchensgt. 5,* ☎ *22/44–17–77. Reservations essential. AE, DC, MC, V. Closed Sun. and last 3 wks of July. No lunch.*

$$$ ✕ **Hos Thea.** An old-fashioned–looking gem with blue-and-beige decor,
★ this restaurant has only 36 seats. It's at the beginning of Embassy Row, a short distance from downtown. Owner Sergio Barcilon, originally from Spain, is one of the pioneers of the new Scandinavian cooking.

The small menu offers four or five choices in each category, but every dish is superbly prepared, from the venison in a sauce of mixed berries to the sherbets and fruitcake. Noise and smoke levels can be high late in the evening. ⊠ *Gabelsgt. 11, entrance on Drammensvn.,* ☎ *22/44–68–74. Reservations essential. AE, DC, MC, V. No lunch.*

$$$ ✕ **Palace Grill.** This tiny dining spot across from the Royal Palace has won its way into the ranks of the hip on the Oslo restaurant scene. You can sip a beer in the adjoining cowboy rock-and-roll bar while you wait for one of about eight tables. Don't let the "grill" part confuse you: it may be relaxed, but it's far from fast food. The Norwegian ingredients of the French-inspired menu, which is written on a hanging chalkboard, change daily. If you've had your fill of reindeer in Norway, you can still take a glimpse at the exotic sauces. Try the chicken leg with eggplant and sweet green shallot sauce if it's on the menu. ⊠ *Solligt. 2 (just off Dramensveien),* ☎ *22/56–14–02. Reservations not accepted. AE, DC, MC, V. Closed Sun. and 1 month in summer.*

$$$ ✕ **Restaurant Le Canard.** Undoubtedly one of Oslo's plushest locales, this oasis in Frogner is brimming with eclectic antiques, Oriental rugs, chandeliers, and Baroque paintings. It is housed in a looming brick mansion with spires and wrought-iron decorations that was built at the turn of the century. The main dining room is spread throughout the first floor's rooms and color-coded salons; upstairs is reserved for private parties. In summer you can dine on the lawn in the garden. The specialty is, of course, duck, from beef with duck-liver in Madeira sauce to sautéed breast of duck with horseradish and cognac sauce. The wine cellar holds more than 2,000 bottles. ⊠ *Pres. Harbitzgt. 4,* ☎ *22/43–40–28. AE, DC, MC, V. Closed Sun. No lunch in winter.*

$$ ✕ **Kastanjen.** This casual Frogner bistro, named after the chestnut trees
★ that line the street, is the kind every neighborhood needs. The style of food is new traditional—modern interpretations of classic Norwegian dishes. Be sure to check out the warmly lit downstairs lounge for before or after-dinner drinks. ⊠ *Bygdøy Allé 18,* ☎ *22/43–44–67. AE, DC, MC, V. Closed Sun. and 2 wks in July.*

$ ✕ **Clodion Art Café.** A bright blue facade and cartoons of the suns, stars, and moon adorn the entrance to this trendy Frogner café. Meals here are light but always tasty: try the spicy shrimp brochette with rice for a nice change from usual café fare. Go for aesthetic reasons instead, and your hunger for creativity will be sated. Not an inch of the place is left unpainted, and the curvy, colorful couches will make you want to stay all day. ⊠ *Bygdøy Allé 63, entrance on Thomas Heftyes Gt.,* ☎ *22/44–97–26. AE, DC, MC, V, DC.*

Holmenkollen

$$$$ ✕ **De Fem Stuer.** Near the famous Holmenkollen ski jump, in the his-
★ toric Holmenkollen Park Hotel, this restaurant has first-rate views and food. Chef Frank Halvorsen's modern Norwegian dishes have strong classic roots. Well worth trying is the three-course "A Taste of Norway" meal. ⊠ *Holmenkollen Park Hotel, Kongevn. 26,* ☎ *22/92–27–34. Jacket and tie. AE, DC, MC, V.*

$$ ✕ **Frognerseteren.** Just above the Holmenkollen ski jump, this restaurant, specializing in fish and venison, looks down on the entire city. Be sure not to miss the house specialty—scrumptious apple cake. The upstairs room has the same view as the more expensive panoramic veranda, and there is also an outdoor café. Take the Holmenkollbanen to the end station and then follow the signs downhill to the restaurant. ⊠ *Hollmenkollvn. 200,* ☎ *22/14–05–50. DC, MC, V.*

LODGING

Most hotels are centrally located, a short walk from Karl Johans Gate, and often between the Royal Palace and the central railway station. The newest hotels are in the area around Oslo S Station, at the bottom end of Karl Johan. For a quiet stay, choose a hotel in Frogner, the elegant residential neighborhood just minutes from downtown.

Oslo usually has enough hotel rooms to go around, but it's always a good idea to reserve a room at least for the first night of your stay, especially if you will be arriving late. Otherwise, the hotel accommodations office at Oslo S Station (☞ Visitor Information *in* Oslo A to Z, *below*) is open from 8 AM to 11 PM and can book you in anything from a luxury hotel to a room in a private home for a fee of NKr20. Usually there are last-minute discount rooms.

Lodging in the capital is expensive. Prices for downtown accommodations are high, even for bed-and-breakfasts, although just about all hotels have weekend, holiday, and summer rates (25% to 50% reductions). Taxes and service charges, unless otherwise noted, are included. Breakfast is usually included also, but be sure to ask before booking your room.

You can cut your lodging costs considerably—and get more for your money than with summer or weekend rates—by buying an Oslo Package in advance. This combines an Oslo Card (☞ Getting Around *in* Oslo A to Z, *below*) with discounted room rates at almost all of Oslo's better hotels. Contact local agents of the Scandinavian Tourist Board for more information and reservations. In the United States or Canada, call **Scanam World Tours** (☎ 201/835–7070, FAX 201/835–3030); in Australia, the **Mansions Travel Service** (☎ 61/7–229–5631, FAX 61/7–221–9731); in the United Kingdom, **Scantours UK** (☎ 0171/839–2927, FAX 0171/839–4327).

If you want to rent an apartment, contact **B&B Oslo Apartments** (✉ Stasjonsvn. 13, Blommenholm, 1300 Sandvika, ☎ 67/54–06–80, FAX 67/54–09–70), which is open weekdays 8:30–4. Most are in Bærum, 15 minutes from downtown Oslo, and about 20 are in Skøyen, a grassy suburban area, closer to both the airport and the center. All are no more than a 10-minute walk from public transport.

Downtown: Royal Palace to the Parliament

$$$$ ★ 🏨 **Grand Hotel.** Right in the center of town on Karl Johans Gate, the Grand has been Oslo's premier hotel since it opened in 1874. Ibsen used to start his mornings with a brisk walk followed by a stiff drink at the Grand Café in the company of journalists. Munch was also a regular guest, and since his time the Grand has hosted many famous people and all recipients of the Nobel Peace Prize. Many Norwegians check in on Constitution Day, May 17, in order to have a room overlooking the parades. The lobby only hints at the style and flair of the rooms. Even standard rooms are large, looking more like guest quarters in an elegant house than hotel rooms. Those in the newer wing are smaller, cheaper, and not as nice. The hotel's restaurant, Julius Fritzner, is considered one of Oslo's most elegant dining establishments. ✉ *Karl Johans Gt. 31, 0159,* ☎ *22/42–93–90,* FAX *22/42–12–25. 287 rooms, 50 suites. 3 restaurants, 3 bars, indoor pool, sauna, health club, meeting rooms. AE, DC, MC, V.*

$$$$ ★ 🏨 **Hotel Continental.** An elegant turn-of-the-century facade has put the Continental on Norway's historic-preservation list. Its location—across from Nationalteatret and next door to a high concentration of cafés,

clubs, and cinemas—is perfect for both vacationers and business travelers. The Brockmann family, owners since 1900, have succeeded in combining the rich elegance of the Old World with modern living. Munch graphics from the family's own collection adorn the walls. Antique furniture and shiny white porcelain fixtures add a distinctive touch to the rooms. Theatercafeen (☞ Dining, *above*) is a landmark, and the newest addition, Lipp, a restaurant-café-bar-nightclub, is among Oslo's "in" places. Dagligstuen (The Sitting Room) is a wonderful place in which to start or end the evening with an appetizer or nightcap. ⊠ *Stortingsgt. 24–26, 0161,* ☎ *22/82–40–00,* FAX *22/42–96–89. 154 rooms, 23 suites. 3 restaurants, 2 bars. AE, DC, MC, V.*

$$$$ 🏨 **Radisson SAS Scandinavia Hotel.** Oslo's established business hotel, built in 1974, has some competition but can still hold its own: there's a business-class airline check-in in the lobby, and the lower-level shopping arcade has stylish clothing and leather-goods shops. The simple, elegant rooms come in four different styles: art deco, Italian, Asian, and predictably, for a hotel run by an airline, high-tech "business class." The SAS is across the street from the palace grounds; downtown is a few blocks downhill. ⊠ *Holbergs Gt. 30, 0166,* ☎ *22/11–30–00,* FAX *22/11–30–17. 496 rooms, 3 large suites. 2 restaurants, 2 bars, pool, health club, nightclub, dance club, business services. AE, DC, MC, V.*

$$$ 🏨 **Bristol.** The Bristol caters to people who want a dignified hotel in the center of town. The immense lobby lounge was decorated in the 1920s with an intricate Moorish theme and feels more like Fez than Scandinavia. Nevertheless, it is a tribute to style, and the piano bar is one of Oslo's best. The rooms do not necessarily reflect the lobby's lushness: small and comfortable, they have all the amenities of modern Scandinavia and are simply decorated with Scandinavian or Regency-style furniture. ⊠ *Kristian IV's Gt. 7, 0164,* ☎ *22/82–60–00,* FAX *22/82–60–01. 141 rooms, 4 suites. 2 restaurants, 2 bars, nightclub, convention center. AE, DC, MC, V.*

$$$ 🏨 **Hotel Karl Johan.** The hundred-year-old Karl Johan, once known as the Nobel, is elegant: one look at the wrought-iron railing and stained-glass windows that line the circular staircase will make you feel you're in 19th-century Paris. The lobby's hardwood floors are shiny and covered with Oriental rugs and velvety navy carpet; fabrics are gold and navy striped; and Old English caricatures hang on the off-white walls. Every room has a different Norwegian treasure, but the feel is sophisticated, not rustic. Its location, next door to the Grand, couldn't be better, and the hotel claims to have a set of regulars who prefer it to its overshadowing neighbor. If you're sensitive to noise, ask for a room away from Rosenkrantz' Gate, where bar hoppers and nightclubbers boogie until the wee hours. ⊠ *Karl Johans Gt. 33 , 0162,* ☎ *22/42–74–80,* FAX *22/42–05–19. 74 rooms, 12 suites. Restaurant, bar. AE, DC, MC, V.*

$$$ 🏨 **Rainbow Hotel Stefan.** This hotel makes every aspect of a stay here a positive experience, from hot drinks for late arrivals to breakfast tables complete with juice boxes and plastic bags for packing a lunch (request this service in advance). The top-floor lounge has books and magazines in English. The Stefan's kitchen is famous for creating the best buffet lunch in town. ⊠ *Rosenkrantz' Gt. 1, 0159,* ☎ *22/42–92–50,* FAX *22/33–70–22. 138 rooms. Restaurant, library, meeting rooms. AE, DC, MC, V.*

$$$ 🏨 **Rica Victoria.** This modern business hotel occupies one of the city center's taller buildings, giving some top-floor rooms glimpses of Oslo's rooftops. The rooms, built around a center atrium, are elegant and very stylish, furnished with Biedermeier reproductions, brass lamps, and paisley-print textiles in bold reds and dark blues. Rooms

with windows on the atrium may be claustrophobic for some but colorful and fun for others. ⊠ *Rosenkrantz' Gt. 13, 0160,* ☎ *22/42–99–40,* ℻ *22/41–06–44. 199 rooms, 5 suites. Restaurant, bar. AE, DC, MC, V.*

$$ 🏨 **Hotell Bondeheimen.** Founded in 1913 for country folk visiting the city, Bondeheimen, which means "farmers' home," still gives discounts to members of Norwegian agricultural associations. The interior is simple, furnished with all the makings of a contemporary Norwegian country home. Cube-shape cushioned chairs, sofas, and solid tables are made of pine, and fabrics and carpets are dyed in farmers' colors: green, blue, yellow, and red. Modern Norwegian graphics hang on the walls, and bathrooms have rustic swigs of hay on the walls. The lobby has a small library of books on Norway, even some in English. Bondeheimen is affiliated with the country kitchen Kaffistova (☞ Dining, *above*). It is a good choice for families, but if you are looking for quiet, ask for a room in back. ⊠ *Rosenkrantz' Gt. 8 (entrance on Kristian IV's Gate), 0159,* ☎ *22/42–95–30,* ℻ *22/41–94–37. 76 rooms. Cafeteria, sauna, library, meeting rooms. AE, DC, MC, V.*

$$ 🏨 **Rainbow Cecil.** This modern hotel, one block from Parliament, is down the road from several other, more expensive hotels and is closer to the main drag than most. The second floor opens onto a plant-filled atrium, the hotel's activity center. In the morning it's a breakfast room, but in the afternoon it becomes a lounge, serving coffee, juice, and fresh fruit, with newspapers available in many languages. Many rooms face the atrium for the sake of peace and quiet, but others have a view of the Stortinget and its many passers-by (where you'll get a better feel for the city). The hotel provides umbrellas for rainy days and claims to have the best air-conditioning in the city for those rare—but beloved—summer heat waves. ⊠ *Stortingsgt. 8, 0130,* ☎ *22/42–70–00,* ℻ *22/42–26–70. 112 rooms, 2 suites. AE, DC, MC, V.*

East of Downtown

$ 🏨 **Haraldsheim.** Oslo's hilltop youth hostel is one of Europe's largest. Most of the rooms have four beds, and those in the new wing have showers. Bring your own sheets or rent them there. It is 6 km (almost 3 mi) from the city center—take trikk 10 or 11 (marked "Kjelsås") to Sinsen. Nonmembers of the International Youth Hostel organization and those older than 25 years pay a surcharge. ⊠ *Haraldsheimvn. 4, 0409,* ☎ *22/15–50–43,* ℻ *22/22–10–25. 264 beds. V.*

$ 🏨 **Munch.** This modern B&B, about a 10-minute walk from Karl Johans Gate, is unpretentious, well run, clean, and functional. The decent-size rooms are painted in pastels or blue with floral curtains. The lobby, with Chinese rugs and leather couches, contrasts with the rest of the hotel. ⊠ *Munchsgt. 5, 0165,* ☎ *22/42–42–75,* ℻ *22/20–64–69. 180 rooms. Breakfast room. AE, DC, MC, V.*

Frogner, Majorstuen, and Holmenkollen

$$$$ 🏨 **Holmenkollen Park Hotel Rica.** The magnificent 1894 building in the national romantic style commands an unequaled panorama of the city in a quiet and natural setting. It is worth a visit even if you don't lodge there, perhaps for a meal at its legendary restaurant, De Fem Stuer (☞ Dining, *above*). The rather ordinary guest rooms are in a newer structure behind it. The ice-covered snowflake sculpture in the lobby is appropriate for a hotel that's a stone's throw from the Holmenkollen ski jump. Ski and walking trails are just outside. ⊠ *Kongevn. 26, 0390,* ☎ *22/92–20–00,* ℻ *22/14–61–92. 221 rooms. 2 restaurants, bar, pool, sauna, cross-country skiing, nightclub, convention center. AE, DC, MC, V.*

$$$–$$$$ ⊞ **Ambassadeur.** Hidden behind a pale pink facade with wrought-iron
★ balconies in a stylish residential area near the Royal Palace, the Am-
bassadeur is a 15-minute walk from both downtown and Frogner
Park. Originally built in 1889 as an apartment hotel, it still has a turn-
of-the-century feel. The owner has hand-picked antiques, china tea sets,
and tapestries for the small downstairs salon. The rooms are individ-
ually furnished according to themes. "Roma" rooms have canopy
beds draped in pale taffeta and maps of old Rome on the walls. "Peer
Gynt" rooms have Scandinavian landscape paintings and a Norwegian
farmhouse feel. If it's a special occasion, request the pricey "Osa" suite.
The painted wooden furniture, carved canopy bed, and exquisite
printed fabrics could easily be on display at the Norwegian Folk Mu-
seum. The hotel's small, professional staff doesn't bother with titles
because everyone does whatever task presents itself, from laundering
a shirt on short notice to delivering room service. ⊠ *Camilla Colletts
vei 15, 0258,* ☎ *22/44–18–35,* ℻ *22/44–47–91. 41 rooms, 8 suites.
Bar, indoor pool, sauna, meeting room. AE, DC, MC, V.*

$$$–$$$$ ⊞ **Frogner House.** This elegant hotel opened in 1992 and receives
mainly business clients, but welcomes independently traveling tourists
looking for a quiet stay. The five-story red-brick and stone building
went up in 1890 as an apartment house and now sits inconspicuously
amid rows of other turn-of-the-century townhouses. Dressed in pas-
tels and abundant lace coverings, the rooms are spacious and insulated.
Some have balconies, and many have views of the boutique-lined res-
idential streets. ⊠ *Skovveien 8, 0257,* ☎ *22/56–00–56,* ℻ *22/56–05–
00. 60 rooms, 8 suites. Meeting room. AE, DC, MC, V.*

$$ ⊞ **Gabelshus.** With only a discreet sign above the door, this ivy-cov-
ered brick house in a posh residential area is one of Oslo's most per-
sonal hotels. It's been owned by the same family for almost 50 years.
The lounges are filled with antiques, some in the national romantic style,
but the rooms are plain. It's a short walk to several of Oslo's best restaurants and a short trikk ride to the center of town. The Ritz Hotel, across
the parking lot, is owned by the same family and takes the overflow.
⊠ *Gabels Gt. 16, 0272,* ☎ *22/55–22–60,* ℻ *22/44–27–30. 50 rooms
(plus 42 rooms in Ritz). Restaurant. AE, DC, MC, V.*

$ ⊞ **Rainbow Gyldenløve.** Nestled among the many shops and cafés on
Bogstadveien, this hotel is one of the city's most reasonable. It is within
walking distance of Vigeland Park, and the trikk stops just outside the
door. ⊞ *Bogstadvn. 20, 0355,* ☎ *22/60–10–90,* ℻ *22/60–33–90. 169
rooms. Coffee shop. AE, DC, MC, V.*

Near Fornebu Airport and Oslo S Station

$$$$ ⊞ **Radisson SAS Plaza Hotel Oslo.** Northern Europe's largest hotel is
a three-minute walk from Karl Johans Gate and just across from Oslo's
central train station. A snazzy 33-story skyscraper in a city that has
few, Oslo Plaza has become a part of the city's skyline. It is favored
by business travelers, who tend toward the pricier deluxe suites in the
tower, where the views of Oslo are worth the price. Below the 27th
floor, the standard rooms are decorated in red and blue tones and have
ample marble baths. ⊠ *Sonja Henies Pl. 3, 0134,* ☎ *22/17–10–00,* ℻
*22/17–73–00. 653 rooms, 20 suites. 2 restaurants, bar, indoor pool,
health club, convention center. AE, DC, MC, V.*

$$$$ ⊞ **Royal Christiania.** It started out as bare-bones housing for 1952
★ Olympians. The original plain exterior has been retained, but inside
it's a whole new luxury hotel, built around a central seven-story atrium.
The emphasis here is on discreet comfort—the large rooms are deco-
rated with soft-colored love seats and armchairs. ⊠ *Biskop Gunnerus'
Gt. 3, 0106,* ☎ *22/42–94–10,* ℻ *22/42–46–22. 451 rooms, 73 suites.*

2 restaurants, 2 bars, indoor pool, health club, nightclub, convention center. AE, DC, MC, V.

$$$ ⊞ **Radisson SAS Park Royal.** Oslo Fornebu Airport's only hotel is somewhat anonymous, with long, narrow corridors and standard American-style hotel rooms. There are excellent business facilities, including a business-class airline check-in, and the airport bus stops right outside. ⊠ *Fornebuparken, Box 185, 1324 Lysaker,* ☎ *67/12–02–20,* FAX *67/12–00–11. 254 rooms, 14 suites. Restaurant, bar, tennis court, health club, business services. AE, DC, MC, V.*

NIGHTLIFE AND THE ARTS

Nightlife

For the past few years Oslo has strived to be the nightlife capital of Scandinavia, although local government factions have talked about toughening laws on noise pollution and drinking. At any time of the day or night, people are out on Karl Johan, and many clubs and restaurants in the central area stay open until the wee hours. Still, strict zoning laws have prohibited the sale of anything harder than "light" beer after 2:30 AM, which means many nightclubs close their doors earlier than one would expect.

Night-lifers can pick up a copy of the free monthly paper *Natt og Dag* at almost any café, bar, or hip-looking shop. It lists rock, pop, and jazz venues and contains an "øl barometer," listing the city's cheapest and most expensive places for a beer—a necessary column in a city where a draft, on average, costs NKr33. The listings are in Norwegian, but some ads are in English.

Many bars and nightclubs in Oslo have a minimum age, which will often give you a sense of who goes there. A minimum age of 18 will generally draw high schoolers, whereas 24 will draw young professionals.

Bars and Lounges

Barbeint (⊠ Drammensvn. 20, ☎ 22/44–59–47) is an ultrahip spot where students, media folk, and local celebrities from the fashionable Frogner district convene on their way in from or out on the town. Avant-garde art adorns the walls, and the loud, cutting-edge music ranges from funk-metal and rock to rap. The trendiest twentysomethings imbibe the night away at **Beach Club** (⊠ Aker Brygge, ☎ 22/83–83–82), a kitschy American hamburger joint with life-size stuffed fish on the walls and diner-style tables and booths. If you're more partial to lounging than drinking, try the English-style bar at the **Bristol Hotel** (⊠ Kristian IV's Gt. 7, ☎ 22/41–58–40). **Børsen Online Café** (⊠ Nedre Vollgt. 19, enter on Stortingsgt., ☎ 22/33–08–00) caters to the cyber crowd and the upwardly mobile. The former can surf the net on one of several monitors that overlook a starry-skied dance floor, while the latter speculate on beer prices, which fluctuate according to supply and demand. For variety, get an outdoor table at **Lorry** (⊠ Parkvn. 12, ☎ 22/69–69–04), just over from the Royal Palace. Filled with a cast of grizzled old artists, the place advertises 204 brews, but don't be surprised if not all of them are in stock. For the serious beer connoisseur, **Oslo Mikrobryggeriet** (⊠ Bogstadvn. 6, ☎ 22/56–97–76) brews eight varieties of beer, including the increasingly popular Oslo Pils, on the premises. **Studenten Bryggeri** (⊠ Karl Johans Gt. 45, ☎ 22/42–56–80), another microbrewery, is often packed with students and loud music as well.

Cafés

Many cafés are open for cappuccino and quiet conversation practically around the clock, and they're the cheapest eateries as well (☞ Dining, *above*). The **Broker Café** (✉ Bogstadvn. 27, ☎ 22/69–36–47) in Majorstuen has great pasta and salads and old, cushiony sofas on which to drink or dine. **Café Bacchus** (✉ Dronningensgt. 27, ☎ 22/42–45–49), in the old railroad offices by Oslo Domkirke, is tiny but serves a mean brownie. Background music is classical during the day, jazz into the night. **Clodion Art Café** (☞ Dining, *above*) is one of Oslo's hippest spots for coffee. Downtown, **Nichol & Son** (✉ Olavs Gt. 1, ☎ 22/83–19–60), a must for Jack Nicholson fans, is an amiable spot to relax with a newspaper. In the trendy area around Frogner and Homansbyen, try **Onkel Oswald** (✉ Hegdehaugsvn. 34, ☎ 22/69–05–35) for a burger or sandwich. The Spanish-inspired **Tapas** (✉ Hegdehaugsvn. 22, ☎ 22/60–38–28) serves bowls of café au lait in the morning and aperitif-size chunks of potatoes, chorizo, and cheese later on.

Gay Bars

For information about gay and lesbian activities in Oslo, you can read *Blikk*, the gay newsletter, or call **LLH** (Landsforening for Lesbisk of Homofil Frigjøring, ☎ 22/36–19–48), the nationwide gay and lesbian liberation association. The main gay bar in town is the all-new **Club Castro** (✉ Kristian IV's Gt. 7, ☎ 22/41–51–08), which caters to a young, energetic crowd. **Andy Capp Pub** (✉ Fr. Nansens Pl. 4, ☎ 22/41–41–65) draws an older crowd of mostly men, and it reeks of old smoke. **Den Sorte Enke** (The Black Widow, ✉ Karl Johans Gt. 10, ☎ 22/33–23–01), Oslo's self-designated "gay-house," attracts a crowd of mainly younger men to dance the night away. **London Bar og Pub** (✉ C.J. Hambros Pl. 5, ☎ 22/41–41–26) is packed on weekends with an over-30 crowd. **Potpurriet** (✉ Øvre Vollgt. 13, ☎ 22/41–14–40) organizes well-attended women's dance nights on the last Friday of each month.

Jazz Clubs

Norwegians love jazz. Every August, the **Oslo Jazz Festival** (✉ Tollbugt. 28, ☎ 22/42–91–20) brings in major international artists and attracts big crowds. Festivities commence with a Dixie-style parade, but all types of jazz are present and explained in free leaflets and newsletters everywhere. **Herr Nilsen** (✉ C.J. Hambros Pl. 5, ☎ 22/33–54–05) features some of Norway's most celebrated jazz artists in a Manhattanesque setting. There is live music three days a week and a jazz café on Saturday afternoons. **Oslo Jazzhus** (✉ Stockholmsgt. 12, ☎ 22/38–59–63) is in an out-of-the-way location and is open only Thursday through Saturday, but the music is worth the journey. **Stortorvets Gjæstgiveri** (✉ Grensen 1, ☎ 22/42–88–63) often presents New Orleans–style and ragtime bands and is known for its swinging dance nights.

Nightclubs

Most dance clubs open late, and the beat doesn't really start until around midnight. There's usually a minimum age, and the cover charge is around NKr50. Oslo's beautiful people congregate at the elegant **Barock** (✉ Universitetsgt. 26, ☎ 22/42–44–20). **Cosmopolite** (✉ Industrigt. 36, ☎ 22/69–16–63) has a big dance floor and music from all over the world, especially Latin America. **Kristiania** (✉ Kristian IV's Gt. 12, ☎ 22/42–56–60), another hot spot, has a live jazz club, a disco, and a bar filling up its three art-bedecked floors. **Lipp** (✉ Olav V's Gt. 2, ☎ 22/41–44–00) is extremely popular as a restaurant, nightclub, and bar. Most of the big hotels have discos that appeal to the over-30 crowd. **Smuget** (✉ Rosenkrantz Gt. 22, ☎ 22/42–52–62) is an institution: live rock and blues every night except Sunday bring crowds who then flock to the in-house discotheque. Thursday is student disco night at **Snorre-Kompagniet** (✉ Rosenkrantz' Gt. 11, ☎ 22/33–52–60), where the hip-hopping clientele is often still teenaged.

Rock Clubs

At Oslo's numerous rock clubs, the cover charges are low, the crowds young and boisterous, and the music loud. If your taste leans toward reggae and calypso, try the **Afro International Night Club** (⊠ Brennerivn. 5, ☎ 22/36–07–53), which has frequent Caribbean evenings. **Blue Monk** (⊠ St. Olavs Gt. 23, ☎ 22/20–22–90) has live music on Wednesdays, Fridays, and Saturdays—and the beer is surprisingly cheap. In the basement you'll find the boisterous Sub Pub, which airs punk and '80s classics. **Rockefeller** (⊠ Torggt. 16, ☎ 22/20–32–32) presents a good mix of musical styles, from avant-garde to salsa. **Sentrum Scene** (⊠ Arbeidersamfunnets Pl. 2, ☎ 22/20–60–40) claims to be Scandinavia's largest live-music venue. It certainly attracts big names, such as Lenny Kravitz and the Neville Brothers.

The Arts

The monthly tourist information brochure *What's on in Oslo* lists cultural events in Norwegian, as does *Aftenposten,* Oslo's (and Norway's) leading newspaper, in its evening "Oslo Puls" section. The Wednesday edition of *Dagbladet,* Oslo's daily liberal tabloid, also gives an exhaustive preview of the week's events. Tickets to virtually all performances in Norway, from classical or rock concerts to hockey games, can be purchased at any post office. You can also call **Billet Service** (☎ 810–33–133) and pick up tickets at the post office later.

Art

Art galleries are cropping up all over town as a generation of young artists comes of age. Although much official Norwegian art is folk art, some of the newer artists take a more postmodern approach to their craft. Pick up a copy of *Listen,* a brochure that lists all current exhibitions.

Film

All films are shown in the original language with subtitles, except for some children's films, which are dubbed. You can buy tickets to any film showing at the box office of any of Oslo's cinemas, and you can reserve tickets by calling any cinema and leaving your phone number. Tickets cost NKr50 and are discounted some days in summer. If you like alternative and classic films, try **Cinemateket** (⊠ Dronningensgt. 16, ☎ 22/47–45–00), the city's only independent cinema.

Music

The **Norwegian Philharmonic Orchestra,** under the direction of Mariss Janssons, is among Europe's leading ensembles. Its house, **Konserthuset** (⊠ Munkedamsvn. 14, ☎ 22/83–32–00), was built in 1977 in marble, metal, and rosewood. In the summer, folkloric dances are staged here twice a week. **Den Norske Opera** (⊠ Storgt. 23, ☎ 22/42–94–75 for information; 22/42–77–24 to order tickets between 10 and 6) and the ballet perform at Youngstorvet. The breathtaking **Gamle Logen** (⊠ Grev Wedels Pl. 2, ☎ 22/33–54–70), Norway's oldest concert hall, often sponsors classical music series, especially piano music.

For a thoroughly Norwegian cultural experience, check out the **Norwegian Masters** (☎ 22/43–34–70), who play character monologues from Ibsen's *Peer Gynt* against a backdrop of Munch paintings and to the music of the beloved Grieg, who originally wrote music to accompany the Norwegian fable. The performance takes place in English, and its venue changes from year to year.

Theater

Nationalteatret (⊠ Stortingsgt. 15, ☎ 22/41–27–10) performances are in Norwegian: bring along a copy of the play in translation, and you're all set. The biennial Ibsen festival, which features plays by the great dramatist in both Norwegian and English, is set for summer 1998 and 2000. **Det Norske Teater** (⊠ Kristian IV's Gt. 8, ☎ 22/42–43–44) is a showcase for pieces in Nynorsk (☞ Language *in* the Gold Guide) and guest artists from abroad.

OUTDOOR ACTIVITIES AND SPORTS

Surrounding Oslo's compact center is a variety of lovely and unspoiled landscapes, including forests, farmland, and, of course, the fjord. Just 15 minutes north of the city center by tram is the **Oslomarka,** where locals ski in winter and hike in summer. The area is dotted with 27 small *hytter* (cabins), which are often available free of charge for backpackers on foot or on ski. These can be reserved through the **Norske Turistforening** (⊠ Stortingsgt. 28, ☎ 22/82–28–00), which has maps of the *marka* (fields and land), surrounding Oslo as well. The **Oslo Archipelago** is also a favorite with sunbathing urbanites, who hop ferries to their favorite isles.

Aerobics

If you need a fitness fix, you can visit one of the many health studios around the city. Most have a "klippekort" system, which means you buy 10 hours' worth of fitness and they "klip," or punch, your card with each entry. The ever-popular **Trim Tram** (⊠ Stranden 55, Aker Brygge, ☎ 22/83–66–50) offers myriad low- and high-intensity aerobics and step classes at reasonable rates. **Friskis & Svettis** (⊠ Munkedamsvn. 17–18, ☎ 22/83–25–40) holds free aerobics classes on the green in Frogner Park. From mid-May to mid-August you can watch or join the hundreds of health-conscious Osloites huffing and puffing and rolling in the dirt. Call for times and intensity levels.

Beaches

Beaches are scattered throughout the archipelago and sun-loving Scandinavians pack every patch of sand during the long summer days to make up for lack of light in winter. The most popular beach is Paradisbukta at Huk (on the Bygdøy peninsula), which devotes one portion of the beach to nude bathers and the other to "clothed." To get there, follow signs along Huk Aveny from the Folk- and Viking Ship museums. You can also take Bus 30A, marked "Bygdøy," to its final stop.

Biking

Oslo is a bike-friendly city. There are many marked paths in and around town meant for bicycles and pedestrians, and cyclists are allowed to use sidewalks. (Note, however, that cars do not have to stop for bicycles the way they do for pedestrians at crosswalks.) One great ride starts at Aker Brygge and takes you along the harbor to the Bygdøy peninsula, where you can visit the museums or cut across the fields next to the royal family's summer house. Ask locals how to get to Huk, the peninsula's popular beach (☞ Beaches, *above*).

Den Rustne Eike (The Rusty Spoke, ⊠ Vestbanepl. 2, ☎ 22/83–72–31), just a few doors down from the Norway Information Center, rents bikes and equipment, including helmets. The store also offers five different sightseeing tours and has maps of the area for those braving it on their own. If you feel like roughing the terrain of the Holmenkollen marka (woods), you can rent mountain bikes from **Tomm Murstad Skiservice** (⊠ Tryvannsvn. 2, ☎ 22/14–41–24) in the summer. Just take T-bane 1 to Frognerseteren and get off at the Voksenkollen station. **Syklistenes Landsforening** (National Organization of Cyclists, ⊠ Stortingsgt.

23C, ☎ 22/41–50–80) sells books and maps for cycling holidays in Norway and abroad and gives friendly, free advice.

Fishing

A national fishing license (NKr90, available in post offices) and a local fee (NKr100 from local sports shops) are required to fish in the Oslo Fjord and the surrounding lakes. You can also fish throughout the Nordmarka woods area in a canoe rented from Tomm Murstad (☞ Biking, *above*). Ice fishing is popular in winter, but you'll have a hard time finding an ice drill—truly, you may want to bring one from home.

Golf

Oslo's international-level golf course, **Oslo Golfklubb** (✉ Bogstad, 0740 Oslo 7, ☎ 22/50–44–02) is private, and heavily booked, but will admit members of other golf clubs (weekdays before 2 PM and weekends after 2 PM) if space is available. Visitors must have a handicap certificate of 20 or lower for men, 28 or lower for women. Fees range from NKr275 to NKr325.

Hiking and Running

Head for the woods surrounding Oslo, the marka, for jogging or walking; there are thousands of kilometers of trails, hundreds of them lit. Frogner Park has many paths, and you can jog or hike along the Aker River, but a few unsavory types may be about late at night or early in the morning. Or you can take the Sognsvann trikk to the end of the line and walk or jog along the Sognsvann stream. For walks or jogs closer to town, explore the stately residential area around Drammensveien west of the Royal Palace, which has paths leading to Bygdøy. The Norske Turistforening (☞ *above*) has many maps of trails around Oslo and can recommend individual routes.

Grete Waitz and Ingrid Kristiansen have put Norway on the marathon runners' map in recent years. The first national marathon championships were held in Norway in 1897, and the Oslo Marathon always attracts a large following. **Norges Friidretts Forbund** (✉ Karl Johans Gt. 2, 0104 Oslo, ☎ 22/42–03–03) has information about local clubs and competitions.

Skiing

The **Skiforeningen** (✉ Kongevn. 5, 0390 Oslo 3, ☎ 22/92–32–00) provides national snow-condition reports and can provide tips on the multitude of cross-country trails. They also offer cross-country classes for young children (3- to 7-year-olds), downhill for older children (7- to 12-year-olds), and both, in addition to Telemark-style and racing techniques, for adults.

Among the floodlit trails in the Oslomarka are the **Bogstad** (3½ km/ 2 mi), marked for the disabled and blind, the **Lillomarka** (about 25 km/15½ mi), and the **Østmarken** (33 km/20½ mi).

For downhill, which usually lasts from mid-December to March, there are 15 local city slopes as well as organized trips to several outside slopes, including **Norefjell** (☎ 32/14–94–00), 100 km (66 mi) north of the city.

You can rent both downhill and cross-country skis from **Tomm Murstad Skiservice** (✉ Tryvannsvn. 2, ☎ 22/14–41–24) at the Tryvann T-bane station. This is a good starting point for skiing; although there are but few downhill slopes in this area, a plethora of cross-country trails for every level of competence exist.

Swimming

Tøyenbadet (⊠ Helgesensgt. 90, ☎ 22/67–18–87) and **Frogner Park** (☎ 22/08–22–50) have large outdoor swimming pools that are open from mid-May through late August, depending on the weather (weekdays 7–7:30, weekends 10–5:30). Tøyenbadet also has an indoor pool that's open year-round. All pools cost NKr37. Pools are free with the Oslo Card (☞ Getting Around, *below*).

SHOPPING

Oslo is the best place for buying anything Norwegian. Prices of handmade articles, such as knitwear, are controlled, making comparison shopping unnecessary. Otherwise shops have both sales and specials—look for the words *salg* and *tilbud*. Sales of seasonal merchandise, combined with the value-added tax refund, can save you more than half the original price. Norwegians do like au courant skiwear, so there are plenty of bargains in last season's winter sportswear.

Stores are generally open from 9 to 5 during the week, but they often close by 3 on Saturdays. Shopping malls and department stores are open later, until 8 during the week and 6 on weekends. Shops also stay open late Thursdays as well as on the first Saturday of the month, known as *super lørdag* (super Saturday) to enthusiastic shoppers. Only during the holiday season are stores open Sunday.

Several shopping districts stand out. From the city center, you can wander up the tree-lined Bygdøy Allé and poke around the fashionable **Frogner** area, which is brimming with modern and antique furniture stores, interior design shops, gourmet food shops, art galleries, haute couture, and a solid majority of Oslo's beautiful people. Stores of every ilk are crammed into the downtown area around **Karl Johans Gate,** where many shoppers flock. The concentration of department stores is especially high in this part of town. **Majorstuen** starts at the T-bane station with the same name and proceeds down Bogstadveien to the Royal Palace. Once you're off the main shopping street, a tiny smattering of independent shops and galleries cater to needs as obscure as your next safari hunt. **Vikaterrassen,** near Aker Brygge (☞ *below*), is a pleasant shopping street with small, exclusive stores. Its glass and concrete facade sits directly underneath a more magnificent building that houses Norway's Ministry of Foreign Affairs.

Department Stores

Christiania GlasMagasin (⊠ Stortorvet 9, ☎ 22/90–89–00) is an amalgamation of shops under one roof rather than a true department store, but it has a much more extensive selection of merchandise than most department stores in town. The best buys are glass and porcelain. Christmas decorations reflecting Norway's rural heritage are easily packed. There is also a wide selection of pewter ware. **Steen & Strøm** (⊠ Kongens Gt. 23, ☎ 22/00–40–01), one of Oslo's first department stores, sells the usual: cosmetics, clothing, books, accessories. It also has a well-stocked outdoors floor.

Shopping Centers

Aker Brygge, Norway's first major shopping center, is right on the water across from the Tourist Information Office at Vestbanen. Shops are open until 8 most days, and some even on Sundays. **Oslo City** (⌧ Stenersgt. 1E, ☎ 22/17–09–92), at the other end of downtown, with access to the street from Oslo S Station, is the largest indoor mall, but the shops are run-of-the-mill, and the food is mostly fast. The elegant **Paleet** (⌧ Karl Johans Gt. 39–41, between Universitetsgt. and Rosenkrantz' Gt., ☎ 22/41–70–86) opens up into a grand atrium lined with supports of various shades of black and gray marble. There's a good bookstore and some high-end clothing shops on the main floor; the basement houses a food court.

Specialty Stores

Antiques

Norwegian rustic antiques cannot be taken out of the country, but just about anything else can with no problem. The Frogner district is dotted with antiques shops, especially Skovveien and Thomas Heftyes Gate between Bygdøy Allé and Frogner Plass. Deeper in the heart of the Majorstua district, Industrigate is famous for its good selection of shops. **Blomqvist Kunsthandel** (⌧ Tordenskiolds Gt. 5, ☎ 22/41–26–31) has a good selection of small items and paintings, with auctions six times a year. The rare volumes at **Damms Antiqvariat** (⌧ Tollbugt. 25, ☎ 22/41–04–02) will catch the eye of any antiquarian book buff, with books in English as well as Norwegian, which could be harder to find back home. **Esaias Solberg** (⌧ Dronningens Gt. 27, ☎ 22/42–41–08), behind Oslo Cathedral, has exceptional small antiques. **Kaare Berntsen** (⌧ Universitetsgt. 12, ☎ 22/20–34–29) sells paintings, furniture, and small items, all very exclusive and priced accordingly. **Marsjandisen** (⌧ Paléet, ☎ 22/42–71–68), nestled in the slickest of shopping centers, carries "merchandise" ranging from discontinued Hadeland glasses to letter openers and authentic war-era postcards, pins, and buttons. **West Sølv og Mynt** (⌧ Niels Juels Gt. 27, ☎ 22/55–75–83) has the largest selection of silver, both old and antique, in town.

Books

Bjørn Ringstrøms Antikvariat (⌧ Ullevålsvn. 1, ☎ 22/20–78–05), across the street from the Museum of Applied Art, has a wide selection of used books and records. **Erik Qvist** (⌧ Drammensvn. 16, ☎ 22/44–52–69), across from the Royal Palace, has an extensive English-language selection. **Pocketboka** (⌧ Ole Vigs Gt. 25, ☎ 22/69–00–18) at Majorstuen sells used paperbacks. **Tanum Libris** (⌧ Karl Johans Gt. 37–41, ☎ 22/41–11–00) has scores of English-language books, ranging from travel guides to contemporary fiction.

Embroidery

Randi Mangen (⌧ Jacob Aalls Gt. 17, ☎ 22/60–50–59), near Majorstuen, sells only embroidery. **Husfliden** (☞ Handicrafts, *below*) sells embroidery kits, including do-it-yourself *bunader* (national costumes); traditional yarn shops also sell embroidery.

Food

Buy a smoked salmon or trout for a special treat. Most grocery stores sell vacuum-packed fish. **W. Køltzow** (⌧ Stranden 3, ☎ 22/83–00–70), at Aker Brygge, can pack fish for export.

Fur

Look for the Saga label for the best-quality farmed Arctic fox and mink. Other popular skins include Persian lamb, beaver, and mink. **Hansson** (⌧ Kirkevn. 54, ☎ 22/69–64–20), near Majorstuen, has an excellent selection of furs. **Studio H. Olesen** (⌧ Karl Johans Gt. 31, enter at Rosenkrantz' Gt., ☎ 22/33–37–50) has the most exclusive designs.

Furniture

Norway is well known for both rustic furniture and orthopedic yet well-designed chairs. **Tannum** (✉ Stortingsgt. 28, ☎ 22/83–42–95) is a good starting point. Drammensveien and Bygdøy Allé have a wide selection of interior-design stores.

Glass, Ceramics, and Pewter

Abelson Brukskunst (✉ Skovvn. 27, ☎ 22/55–55–94), behind the Royal Palace, is crammed with the best modern designs. The shops at **Basarhallene** behind the cathedral also sell glass and ceramics. If there's no time to visit a glass factory (☞ West of the Oslo Fjord *in* Chapter 3), department stores are the best option: **Christiania GlasMagasin** (✉ Stortorvet 9, ☎ 22/90–89–00) stocks both European and Norwegian glass designs. **Lie Antikk & Kunsthandverk** (✉ Hegdehaugsveien 27, ☎ 22/60–98–61) is a tiny shop at the bottom of Hegdehaugsveien that sells colorful wine glasses and claims to have the city's best collection of blown glass. **Norway Designs** (✉ Stortingsgt. 28, ☎ 22/83–11–00) specializes in glass crafted by Norwegian and Scandinavian folk artists.

Handicrafts

Basarhallene, the arcade behind the cathedral, is also worth a browse for handicrafts made in Norway. **Format Kunsthandverk** (✉ Vestbanepl. 1, ☎ 22/83–73–12) has beautiful, yet pricey, individual pieces (but you can buy a postcard to show your friends back home). **Heimen Husflid AS** (✉ Rosenkrantz' Gt. 8, ☎ 22/41–40–50, enter at Kristian IV's Gt.) has small souvenir items and a specialized department for Norwegian national costumes. **Husfliden** (✉ Møllergt. 4, ☎ 22/42–10–75), one of the finest stores with handmade goods in the country, has an even larger selection, including pewter, ceramics, knits, handwoven textiles, furniture, handmade felt boots and slippers, hand-sewn loafers, sweaters, national costumes, wrought-iron accessories, Christmas ornaments, and wooden kitchen accessories—all made in Norway.

Jewelry

Gold and precious stones are no bargain, but silver and enamel jewelry, along with reproductions of Viking pieces, are. Some silver pieces are made with Norwegian stones, particularly pink thulite. **David-Andersen** (✉ Karl Johans Gt. 20, ☎ 22/41–69–55; ✉ Oslo City, ☎ 22/17–09–34) is Norway's best-known goldsmith, with stunning silver and gold designs. **ExpoArte** (✉ Drammensvn. 40, ☎ 22/55–93–90), also a gallery, specializes in custom pieces and displays work of avantgarde Scandinavian jewelers. **Heyerdahl** (✉ Roald Amundsensgt. 6, ☎ 22/41–59–18), near City Hall, is a good, dependable jeweler.

Knitwear and Clothing

Norway is famous for its handmade, multicolored ski sweaters, and even mass-produced (machine-knit) models are of top quality. The prices are regulated, so buy what you like when you see it. **Husfliden** (☞ Handicrafts, *above*) stocks handmade sweaters in the traditional style. **Maurtua** (✉ Fr. Nansens Pl. 9, ☎ 22/41–31–64), near City Hall, has a huge selection of sweaters and blanket coats. **Oslo Sweater Shop** (✉ SAS Scandinavia Hotel, Tullinsgt. 5, ☎ 22/11–29–22) has one of the city's widest selections. **Rein og Rose** (✉ Ruseløkkvn. 3, ☎ 22/83–21–39), in the Vikaterassen strip, has extremely friendly salespeople and a good selection of knitwear, yarn, and textiles. **Siril** (✉ Rosenkrantz' Gt. 23, ☎ 22/41–01–80), near City Hall, is a small shop with attentive staff. **William Schmidt** (✉ Karl Johans Gt. 41, ☎ 22/42–02–88), founded in 1853, is Oslo's oldest shop specializing in sweaters and souvenirs.

Sportswear

Look for the ever-popular Helly-Hansen brand. The company makes everything from insulated underwear to rainwear, snow gear, and great insulated mittens. **Sportshuset** (⊠ Ullevålsvn. 11, ☎ 22/20–11–21; ⊠ Frognervn. 9C, ☎ 22/55–29–57) has the best prices. **Gresvig** (⊠ Storgt. 20, ☎ 22/17–39–80) is a little more expensive but has a good selection. **Sigmund Ruud** (⊠ Kirkevn. 57, ☎ 22/69–43–90) also has a comprehensive stock of quality sportswear.

Watches

For some reason, Swiss watches are much cheaper in Norway than in many other countries. **Bjerke** (⊠ Karl Johans Gt. 31, ☎ 22/42–20–44; ⊠ Prinsensgt. 21, ☎ 22/42–60–50) has a large selection.

Street Markets

Although some discerning locals wonder where it procures its wares, the best flea market is on Saturday at **Vestkanttorvet,** near Frogner Park at Amaldus Nilsens Plass at the intersection of Professor Dahlsgate and Eckerberg Gate. Check the local paper for weekend garage sales, or *loppemarkeder,* held in schools.

OSLO A TO Z

Arriving and Departing

By Boat

Several ferry lines connect Oslo with the United Kingdom, Denmark, Sweden, and Germany. **Color Line** (☎ 22/22–94–44–00) sails to Kiel, Germany, and to Hirtshals, Denmark; **DFDS Scandinavian Seaways** (☎ 22/41–90–90) to Copenhagen via Helsingborg, Sweden; and **Stena Line** (☎ 23/17–90–00) to Frederikshavn, Denmark.

By Bus

The main bus station, **Bussterminalen** (☎ 23/00–24–00), is under Galleri Oslo, across from the Oslo S Station. You can buy local bus tickets at the terminal or on the bus. Tickets for long-distance routes on **Nor-Way Bussekspress** (☎ 22/17–52–90, ☏ 22/17–59–22) can be purchased here or at travel agencies. For local traffic information, call **Trafikanten** (☎ 22/17–70–30 or 177).

By Car

Route E18 connects Oslo with Göteborg, Sweden (by ferry between Sandefjord and Strömstad, Sweden); Copenhagen, Denmark (by ferry between Kristiansand and Hirtshals, Denmark); and Stockholm directly overland. The land route from Oslo to Göteborg is the E6. All streets and roads leading into Oslo have toll booths a certain distance from the city center, forming an "electronic ring." The toll is NKr12 and was implemented to reduce pollution downtown. If you have the correct amount in change, drive through one of the lanes marked "Mynt." If you don't, or if you need a receipt, use the "Manuell" lane.

By Plane

Oslo Fornebu Airport (☎ 67/59–33–40), 20 minutes southwest of the city, will remain Oslo's main international and domestic airport until late 1998. It is a relatively small airport, but walks between international arrivals, baggage claim, and passport control can seem long.

SAS (☎ 810/03–300) is the main carrier, with both international and domestic flights. The main domestic carriers are **Braathens SAFE** (☎ 67/59–70–00) and **Widerøe** (☎ 67/11–14–60).

Other major airlines serving Fornebu include **British Airways** (☎ 22/82–20–00), **Air France** (☎ 22/83–56–30), **Delta Air Lines** (☎ 22/41–56–00), **Finnair** (☎ 67/53–11–97), **Icelandair** (☎ 22/83–35–70), **KLM** (☎ 67/58–38–00), and **Lufthansa** (☎ 22/83–65–65).

Gardermoen Airport (☎ 63/97–84–77), 50 km (30 mi) north of Oslo, is slated to become Oslo's main airport by October 1998. At press time, Gardermoen was served mostly by charter airlines.

Between the Airport and Downtown: Oslo Fornebu Airport is a 15- to 20-minute ride from the center of Oslo at off-peak hours. At rush hour (7:30–9 AM from the airport and 3:30–5 PM to the airport), the trip can take more than twice as long. None of the downtown hotels provide free shuttle service, although some outside the city do. The trip to Gardermoen Airport from the city center takes 19 minutes by express train; there are six trains scheduled per hour. By taxi the trip takes about 40 minutes but is extremely expensive, upwards of $100.

Flybussen (☎ 67/59–62–20; NKr40; *to Oslo* weekdays and Sun. 7:30 AM–11:30 PM, Sat. 7:30 AM–11:00 PM; *to Fornebu* weekdays, 6 AM–9:40 PM, Sat. 6 AM–7:40 PM, Sun. 6 AM–9:50 PM) departs from its terminal under Galleri Oslo shopping center every 10–15 minutes and reaches Fornebu approximately 20 minutes later. Another bus departs from the SAS Scandinavia Hotel. Between the two buses, there are stops at the central train station as well as at Stortinget, Nationaltheatret, and near Aker Brygge. There is also a bus that departs Galleri Oslo for Gardermoen daily; the trip takes about 40 minutes. Call for specific departure times.

Another alternative is Suburban Bus 31, marked "Snarøya," which stops outside the Arrivals terminal. On the trip into town it stops on the main road opposite the entrance to the airport. You can catch this bus at both the central railway station, Jernbanetorget, or at Nationaltheatret. The cost is Nkr21.

There is a taxi line to the right of the Arrivals exit. The fare to town is about NKr130. All taxi reservations should be made through the **Oslo Taxi Central** (☎ 22/38–80–90; dial 1 for direct reservation) no less than 20 minutes before pickup time.

By Train

Long-distance trains arrive at and leave from **Oslo S Station** (☎ 22/17–14–00), whereas most suburban commuter trains use **Nationaltheatret** or **Oslo S.** Commuter cars reserved for monthly pass holders are marked with a large black "M" on a yellow circle. Trains marked "C," or InterCity, offer such upgraded services as breakfast and "office cars" with phones and power outlets, for an added fee.

Getting Around

Most public transportation starts running by 5:30 AM, with the last run just after midnight. On weekends there is night service on certain routes. Tickets on all public transportation within Oslo cost NKr18 with a one-hour transfer, whereas tickets that cross communal boundaries have different rates. It pays to buy a pass or a multiple-travel card, which includes transfers. A one-day "Tourist Ticket" pass costs NKr40, and a seven-day pass costs NKr130. A "Flexikort," purchased at post offices, tourist information offices, T-bane stations, and on some routes, is good for eight trips with free transfer within one hour and costs NKr105. Oslo Sporveier operates most modes of transport in the city, including tram, bus, underground, train, and boat. **Trafikanten** (✉ Jernbanetorget, ☎ 22/17–70–30 or 177), the information office for public transportation, is open weekdays 7 AM–11 PM, weekends 8 AM–11 PM.

The **Oslo Card** offers unlimited travel on all public transport in greater Oslo as well as free admission to museums, sightseeing attractions, and the racetrack, as well as discounts at various stores and cinemas (May–July). A one-day Oslo Card costs NKr130, a two-day card NKr200, and a three-day card NKr240. It can be purchased at tourist information offices, hotels, and central post offices. The Oslo Package, available through the same office, combines a four-day Oslo Card with a discount on accommodations (☞ Lodging, *above*).

By Bus

About 20 bus lines, including six night buses on weekends, serve the city. Most stop at Jernbanetorget opposite Oslo S Station. Tickets can be purchased from the driver.

By Car

If you plan to do any amount of driving in Oslo, buy a copy of the *Stor Oslo* map, available at bookstores and gasoline stations. It may be a small city, but one-way streets and few exit ramps on the expressway make it very easy to get lost.

Oslo Card holders can park for free in city-run street spots or at reduced rates in lots run by the city (P-lots), but pay careful attention to time limits and be sure to ask at the information office exactly where the card is valid. Parking is very difficult in the city—many places have one-hour limits and can cost up to NKr17 per hour. Instead of individual parking meters in P-lots, you'll find one machine that dispenses validated parking tickets to display in your car windshield. Travelers with disabilities with valid parking permits from their home country are allowed to park free and with no time limit in spaces reserved for those with disabilities.

By Ferry

A ferry to Hovedøya and other islands in the harbor basin leaves from Vippetangen, behind Akershus Castle (take Bus 29 from Jernbanetorget or walk along the harbor from Aker Brygge). These are great spots for picnics and short hikes. From April through September, ferries run between Rådhusbrygge 3, in front of City Hall, and Bygdøy, the western peninsula, where many of Oslo's major museums are located. There is also ferry service from Aker Brygge to popular summer beach towns along the fjord's coast, including Drøbak (☞ East of the Oslo Fjord *in* Chapter 3).

By Streetcar/Trikk

Eight trikk lines serve the city. All stop at Jernbanetorget opposite Oslo S Station. Tickets can be purchased from the driver.

By Subway/T-bane

Oslo has seven T-bane lines, which converge at Stortinget station. The four eastern lines all stop at Tøyen before branching off, whereas the four western lines run through Majorstuen before emerging above ground for the rest of their routes to the northwestern suburbs. Tickets can be purchased at the stations. Get a free map, "Sporveiens hovedkart," of Oslo's extensive public transportation system at post offices, Trafikanten, and most centrally located stations. It is undoubtedly the best public transport map of Oslo for tourists.

By Taxi

All city taxis are connected with the central dispatching office (☎ 22/38–80–90), which can take up to 30 minutes to send one during peak hours. Cabs can be ordered from 20 minutes to 24 hours in advance. (If you leave a cab waiting after you've sent for one, there is an additional fee added to your fare.) Special transport, including vans and cabs equipped for people with disabilities, can be ordered (☎ 22/38–80–90; then dial 1 for direct reservations, 2 for advance reservations, 3 for information, and 4 if you have special needs). Taxi stands are located all over town, usually alongside Narvesen kiosks, and are listed in the telephone directory under "Taxi" or "Drosjer."

It is possible to hail a cab on the street, but cabs are not allowed to pick up passengers within 100 yards of a stand. It is not unheard of to wait for more than an hour at a taxi stand in the wee hours of the morning, after everyone has left the bars. A cab with its roof light on is available. Rates start at NKr18 for hailed or rank cabs, NKr55 for ordered taxis, depending on the time of day.

Contacts and Resources

Currency Exchange
After normal banking hours, money can be changed at a few places. The bank at **Oslo S Station** is open June–September, daily 8 AM–11 PM; October–May, weekdays 8 AM–7:30 PM, Saturday 10–5. The bank at **Oslo Fornebu Airport** is open weekdays 6:30 AM–9 PM, Saturday 7–5, Sunday 7 AM–8 PM. All post offices exchange money. **Oslo Central Post Office** (✉ Dronningensgt. 15) is open weekdays 8–6, Saturday 9–3.

Doctors and Dentists
Doctors: Norway's largest private clinic, **Volvat Medisinske Senter** (✉ Borgenvn. 2A, ☎ 22/95–75–00) is near the Borgen or Majorstuen T-bane stations, not far from Frogner Park. It is open weekdays from 8 AM to 10 PM, weekends 10 to 10. **Oslo Akutten** (✉ N. Vollgt. 8, ☎ 22/41–24–40) is an emergency clinic downtown, near Stortinget. **Centrum Legesenter** (✉ Fritjof Nansens Pl., ☎ 22/41–41–20) is a small, friendly clinic across from City Hall.

Dentists: For emergencies only, **Oslo Kommunale Tannlegevakt** (✉ Kolstadgt. 18, ☎ 22/67–30–00) at Tøyen Senter is open evenings and weekends. **Oslo Private Tannlegevakt** (✉ Hansteens Gt. 3, ☎ 22/44–46–36), near the American Embassy, is a private clinic open seven days a week.

Embassies
U.S. (✉ Drammensvn. 18, ☎ 22/44–85–50). **Canada** (✉ Oscars Gt. 20, ☎ 22/46–69–55). **U.K.** (✉ Thomas Heftyes Gt. 8, ☎ 22/55–24–00).

Emergencies
Police: ☎ 112 or 22/66–90–50. **Fire:** ☎ 110 or 22/11–44–55. **Ambulance:** ☎ 113 or 22/11–70–80. **Car Rescue:** ☎ 22/23–20–85. **Emergency Rooms: Oslo Legevakt** (✉ Storgt. 40, ☎ 22/11–70–70), the city's public and thus less expensive, but slower, hospital, is near the Oslo S Station and is open 24 hours. **Volvat Medisinske Senter** (✉ Borgenvn. 2A, ☎ 22/95–75–00) operates an emergency clinic from 8 AM to 10 PM during the week, 10 to 10 on weekends.

Guided Tours
Tickets for all tours are available from Norway Information at Vestbanen (☞ Visitor Information, *below*) and at the Oslo S Station. Tickets for bus tours can be purchased on the buses. All tours, except HMK's Oslo Highlights tour (☞ *below*), operate during summer only.

Dogsled Tours: For a fast and exciting experience, tour the marka by dogsled. Both lunch and evening tours are available. Contact **Norske Sledehundturer** (✉ Einar Kristen Aas, 1514 Moss, ☎ 69/27–56–40, FAX 69/27–37–86).

Forest Tours: Tourist Information at Vestbanen can arrange four- to eight-hour motor safaris through the forests surrounding Oslo (☎ 22/83–00–50).

Orientation: HMK Sightseeing (✉ Hegdehaugsvn. 4, ☎ 22/20–82–06) offers several bus tours in and around Oslo. Tours leave from the Norway Information Center at Vestbanen; combination boat-bus tours depart from Rådhusbrygge 3, the wharf in front of City Hall. **Båtservice Sightseeing** (✉ Rådhusbryggen 3, ☎ 22/20–07–15) has a bus tour, five cruises, and one combination tour.

Personal Guides: Norway Information at Vestbanen can provide an authorized city guide for your own private tour. **OsloTaxi** (✉ Trondheimsvn. 100, ☎ 22/38–80–70) also gives private tours.

Sailing: Norway Yacht Charter (✉ H. Heyerdahls Gt. 1, ☎ 22/42–64–98) arranges sailing or yacht tours and dinner cruises for groups of five people to 600.

Sleigh Rides: Vangen Skistue (✉ Laila and Jon Hamre, Fjell, 1404 Siggerud, ☎ 64/86–54–81) will arrange an old-fashioned sleigh ride through Oslomarka, the wooded area surrounding the city. In summertime, they switch from sleighs to carriages.

Street Train: Starting at noon and continuing at 45-minute intervals until 10 PM, the Oslo Train, which looks like a chain of dune buggies, leaves Aker Brygge for a 30-minute ride around the town center. The train runs daily in summer. Ask at the Norway Information Center (☞ Visitor Information, *below*) for departure times.

Walking: Organized walking tours are listed in *What's on in Oslo,* available from Norway Information and at most hotels.

Late-Night Pharmacies

Jernbanetorgets Apotek (✉ Jernbanetorget 4B, ☎ 22/41–24–82), across from Oslo S Station, is open 24 hours. **Sfinxen Apotek** (✉ Bogstadvn. 51, ☎ 22/46–34–44), near Frogner Park, is open weekdays from 8:30 AM to 9 PM, Saturdays from 8:30 AM to 8 PM, and Sundays from 5 PM to 8 PM.

Travel Agencies

Winge Reisebureau (✉ Karl Johans Gt. 33/35, ☎ 22/00–45–90) is the agent for American Express—here you can cash travelers' checks. An **American Express** office is near the Rådhuset (✉ Fritjof Nansens pl. 6, ☎ 22/98–37–35). **Bennett Reisebureau** (✉ Linstowsgt. 6, ☎ 22/69–71–00) is a business travel agency. **Kilroy Travels Norway** (✉ Universitetssenteret, Blindern, ☎ 22/85–32–40; or ✉ Nedre Slottsgt. 23, ☎ 22/42–01–20) distributes ISIC cards for students and GO cards for people younger than 25.

Visitor Information

The main tourist office, the **Norway Information Center** (☎ 22/83–00–50 from outside Norway; or the local number, ☎ 82/06–01–00, which is a toll call), is in the old Vestbanen railway station. The hours are as follows: spring and fall 9–6; summer 9–8; winter 9–4. The office at the main railway station, **Sentralstasjonen** (✉ Jernbanetorget, ☎ no phone) is open daily 8 AM–11 PM; during winter the office takes a break from 3 PM to 4:30 PM. Look for the big, round blue-and-green signs marked with a white I. Information about the rest of the country can be obtained from **NORTRA** (✉ Nortravel Marketing, Postboks 2893, Solli, 0230 Oslo, ☎ 22/92–52–00, FAX 22/56–05–05).

3 Side Trips from Oslo

If you've got a weakness for the water and things maritime, getting out of Oslo to the windswept fjord beaches might be a good idea. The area northwest of Oslo draws many visitors to its green, hilly countryside. No matter which way you head, you'll find plenty to do.

Henie-Onstad Kunstsenter and Bærums Verk

1 The **Henie-Onstad Kunstsenter** (Henie-Onstad Art Center) is just a short journey from Oslo, about 12 km (7 mi) southwest of the city on E18. This modern art center resulted from a union between Norway's famous skater Sonja Henie and Norwegian shipping magnate Niels Onstad. Henie had a shrewd head for money and marriage, and her third, to Onstad, resulted in the Center. They put together a fine collection of early 20th-century art, with important works by Leger, Munch, Picasso, Bonnard, and Matisse. Henie died in 1969, but she still skates her way through many a late-night movie. The three-time Olympic gold-medal winner was the first to realize the potential of the ice show, and her technical assistant, Frank Zamboni, has been immortalized in skating rinks around the world by the ice-finishing machine he developed just for her, the Zamboni. Buses 151, 152, and 251 from Oslo S Station stop near the entrance to the Henie-Onstad Center grounds. ⊠ *1311 Høvikodden,* ☎ *67/54–30–50.* 🎦 *NKr50.* 🕐 *Mon. 9–5, Tues.– Fri. 9–9, weekends 11–9.*

One of Oslo's fashionable suburbs, Bærum is about 20 minutes from the city. The area is mostly residential, but along the banks of the Lomma **2** River you'll find charming **Bærums Verk.** In the 1960s, the owners of the Bærums Verk iron foundry fixed up their old industrial town and made it into a historical site. Created in the 17th century after iron ore was discovered in the region, the ironworks of Bærum quickly became the country's primary iron source. Anna Krefting, a woman who ran the works during the 18th century, believed that workers who spent their days and nights in the foundry should live there as well and be protected by it. The ironworks of Bærum thus became a village in its own right.

As you explore the beautifully restored village, you'll first notice the cramped wooden cottages lining **Verksgata** where the workers once lived. Notice that the doors are in the back of the buildings; this was in case a fire from the works spread through the main street. Crafts makers now lease space in the former living quarters. Here you can purchase wares from a doll maker, a glassblower, a carpenter, a chocolatier, and an embroiderer.

Cross the Lomma River to the entrance of the **Ovnmuseet** (Stove Museum), which displays centuries-old cast-iron stoves in the basement of the iron foundry's enormous smelter. Bærums Verk stoves were exported for centuries and still serve as antique fireplaces in many Oslo homes and service establishments. From Oslo, follow E16 in the direction of Hønefoss. Veer north on Route 168, following signs to Bærums Verk Senteret until you reach the tourist information office. ⊠ *Verksgt. 8B, Boks 39, 1353 Bærum,* ☎ *67/13–00–18 (information office).* 🕐 *Verksgata weekdays 10–6, Sat. 10–3; some shops open Sun. Stove Museum weekends noon–3. Other times on request.*

NEED A
BREAK?   Stop in at **Pannekake Huset** (The Pancake House, ⊠ Verksgt. 9, ☎ 67/ 15–07–02) for sweet or salty Dutch-style crepes and a cherry beer or hot chocolate. It's open Tuesday–Sunday noon to 8.

Dining

$$$ ✕ **Værtshuset Bærums Verk.** Norway's oldest standing restaurant, ★ this spot is a must on any itinerary that includes the neighboring iron works. The inn opened in 1640 and was a frequented stop on the "King's" road from Oslo to Bergen. Restored in 1987, it is now one of Norway's finest restaurants. Low ceilings, pastel-painted wooden floors, shiny pewter tableware, and the tick-tock of a grandfather

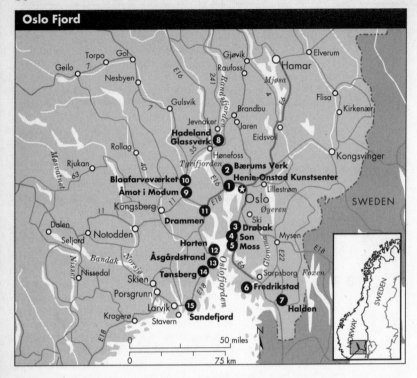

Oslo Fjord

clock in the dining room all create the impression that you are walking into 19th-century Scandinavia. Each room has a charm of its own, from the quiet, oblong Doctor's Room to the rustic kitchen with a blazing fire. Perhaps the most innovative menu of the year, which lasts only three days in March, is one modeled after the famous meal served in the film *Babette's Feast*, complete with a faux turtle soup (it is illegal to hunt turtles in Norway), blinis, and quail. ⊠ *Vertshusvn. 10, Brums Verk,* ☎ *67/80–02–0. AE, DC, MC, V. No lunch.*

East of the Oslo Fjord

The eastern side of the Oslo Fjord is summer-vacation country for many Norwegians, who retreat to cabins on the water during July. The towns have developed facilities to cater to them and brag that they inhabit the "sunny" side of the fjord.

Many towns along the fjord offer history and culture as well as a place to bathe. Viking ruins and inscriptions, fortified towns, and bohemian 19th-century artists' colonies provide just a glimpse into the region's rich past.

Some of the towns mentioned can easily be visited as day trips from Oslo. Roads can be winding, though, so you might want to devote several days to exploring the area. Note that ferries shuttle cars and people back and forth between the archipelago islands and either side of the fjord, so it is possible to combine this tour with the West of the Oslo Fjord (☞ *below*) and make a complete circle without backtracking.

Drøbak

❸ *35 km (21 mi) south of Oslo.*

Mention the summer resort town of Drøbak to many Norwegians, and strangely enough, they'll start talking about Father Christmas. Although there is some question as to where the *Julenisse* (literally, "Christmas elf") came from, Norwegians claim—at least his adopted home—is here in Drøbak.

Norwegian legend says that Julenisse is one of many elves who live in the woods and have magical powers. This Julenisse, who has established his own post office, **Julenissens Posthuset** in Drøbak, responds to nearly 30,000 letters a year from children all over the world, the majority of which come from Japan. ✉ *Julenissen, 1440 Drøbak.*

The inviting **Tregaardens Julehus** (Christmas House) dominates the town's central square. Just around the corner from the post office, this 1876 house was once a mission for seafarers unable to reach Oslo because the fjord was frozen over. Now it sells Christmas wares and gifts such as wooden dolls and mice made of cloth—all handmade by Eva Johansen, the store's creator and owner. Spin-offs of this ever-so-authentic Christmas shop include Drøbak's gift of a fir tree to the cities of Berlin and Osaka. ✉ *1440 Drøbak,* ☎ *64/93–41–78.*

NEED A
BREAK?

Back on the main square, stop in **Det Gamle Bageri Ost & Vinstue** (The Old Bakery Wine and Cheese Room, ☎ 64/93–21–05) for some home-brewed smoky-tasting *Rauchbier,* a German specialty. Originally a bakery, this tiny pub serves wine with cheese and fruit plates on heavy wood-slab tables by the central oven.

LODGING

$–$$ 🏨 **Reenskaug Hotel.** The Norwegian author Knut Hamsun frequented this hotel and wrote a book here at the turn of the century. Back then, it was just a wooden house on a dirt road. The 100-year-old hotel's whitewashed exterior complements the quaintness of the town's main road. Inside, the rooms are rather small and nondescript, but they are nonetheless clean. Reasonable summer prices make it worth your while to stay the night in Drøbak. ✉ *Storgt. 32, 1440 Drøbak,* ☎ *64/93–33–60,* 🆁🆇 *64/93–36–66. 29 rooms. Restaurant, bar, nightclub, meeting rooms. AE, MC, V.*

Son

❹ *25 km (15 mi) south of Drøbak.*

You can swim, sail, or sun on the banks of Son (pronounced *soon*), just south of Drøbak. An old fishing and boating village, this resort town has traditionally attracted artists and writers. Artists still flock here, as do city folk in summer. With them comes a rash of activity, which loungers on the immense boulders by the water can hear in the distance.

In the summer season, you can count on **Klubben Soon** (☎ 64/95–70–42) for a good mix of disco, jazz, concerts and stand-up comedy.

Moss

❺ *10 km (6 mi) south of Son.*

Although the area has been inhabited since Viking times, Moss gained borough status in the 18th century and is one of the area's main commercial and shipping centers. This industrial town is also home to the manufacturers of Helly-Hansen sportswear, which is becoming ever-so-popular in the United States—you'll find it in sporting goods stores from Duluth, Minnesota, to New York City.

OFF THE
BEATEN PATH

GALLERI F15 – A 5-km (3-mi) ride outside Moss, on the island of Jeløy, is an art center set in an old farm. Exhibits displayed here range from photography to Scandinavian crafts, or just stroll the beautiful grounds. ⊠ *Alby Gård,* ☎ *69/27–10–33.* 🖼 *NKr20.* ⊙ *June–Sept., Tues.–Sun. 11–7; Oct.–May, Tues.–Sat. 11–5, Sun. 11–7.*

DINING AND LODGING

$$$ ✕🖼 **Refsnes Gods.** Refsnes has one of Norway's best kitchens and a
★   wine cellar with some of the oldest bottles of Madeira in the country. Chef Erwin Stocker utilizes the fjords' resources and adds a French touch to traditional Norwegian seafood. The main building dates from 1770, when it was a family estate, but it did not become a hotel until 1938. In the back is a long, tree-lined promenade extending to the shores of the Oslo Fjord. The blue-and-beige rooms are airy and pretty. ⊠ *Box 236, 1502 Moss,* ☎ *69/27–04–11,* 🖷 *69/27–25–42. 61 rooms. Restaurant, pool, sauna, beach, boating, meeting rooms. AE, DC, MC, V.*

Fredrikstad

❻ *34 km (20 mi) south of Moss.*

Norway's oldest fortified city, Fredrikstad lies peacefully at the mouth of the Glomma, the country's longest river. Its bastions and moat date from the 1600s. The **Gamlebyen** (Old Town) has been preserved and has museums, art galleries, cafés, artisans' workshops, antiques shops, and old bookstores.

The **Fredrikstad Museum** documents the town's history. ☎ *69/30–68–75.* 🖼 *NKr20.* ⊙ *May–Sept., weekdays 11–5, Sun. noon–5.*

Just east of the Fredrikstad town center is **Kongsten Festning** (Kongsten Fort), which mounted 200 cannons and could muster 2,000 men at the peak of its glory in the 16th century. ☎ *69/32–05–32.* 🖾 *Free.* ⊙ *May–Sept., 24 hrs. Call for guided tour.*

Halden

❼ *30 km (18 mi) south of Fredrikstad.*

Halden is practically at the Swedish border, a good enough reason to fortify the town. Norwegians and Swedes had ongoing border disputes, and the most famous skirmish at Fredriksten fortress resulted in the death of King Karl XII in 1718. Few people realize that slavery existed in Scandinavia, but until 1845 there were up to 200 slaves at Fredriksten, mostly workers incarcerated and sentenced to a lifetime of hard labor for trivial offenses.

Fredriksten Festning (⊠ Fredriksten Fort, ☎ 69/17–35–00), built on a French star-shaped plan in the late 17th century, is perched on the city's highest point. Inside the fort itself is **Fredriksten Kro**, a good, old-fashioned pub with outdoor seating. ☎ *69/17–52–32.* 🖾 *NKr25.* ⊙ *Mid-May–mid-Sept., Mon.–Sat. 10–5, Sun. 10–6.*

East of the Oslo Fjord A to Z

ARRIVING AND DEPARTING

By Boat: A ferry links Drøbak, on the east side of the fjord, with Hurum, on the west side just north of Horten. Contact Drøbak Turistinformasjon (☞ *below*) for schedule information.

By Bus: Bus 541 from Oslo's City Hall to Drøbak affords great glimpses of the fjord (and its bathers). The trip takes an hour, and buses depart roughly every half hour during the week, with reduced service weekends. Bus 117 links Halden and Fredrikstad eight times a day during the week, with reduced service Saturdays. Contact **Nor-Way Bussekspress** (☎ 22/17–52–90) for schedules.

By Car: Follow Route E18 southeast from Oslo to Route E6. Follow signs to Drøbak and Son. Continue through Moss, following signs to Halden, farther south on E6. The route then takes you north to Sarpsborg, where you can turn left to Fredrikstad.

By Train: Trains for Halden leave from Oslo S Station and take two hours to make the 136-km (85-mi) trip, with stops in Moss, Fredrikstad, and Sarpsborg.

CONTACTS AND RESOURCES

Visitor Information: Drøbak (Drøbak Turistinformasjon, ☎ 64/93–50–87). **Fredrikstad** (Fredrikstad Turistkontor, ⊠ Turistsentret vøstre Brohode and ⊠ 1632 Gamle Fredrikstad, ☎ 69/32–03–30 or 69/32–10–60). **Halden** (Halden Turist Kontor, ⊠ Storgt. 6, Box 167, 1751 Halden, ☎ 69/17–48–40). **Moss** (Moss Turistkontor, ⊠ Fleischersgt. 17, 1531 Moss, ☎ 69/25–32–95). **Son** (Son Kystkultursenter, ⊠ 1555 Son, ☎ 64/95–89–20).

West of the Oslo Fjord

Towns lining the western side of the fjord are more industrial on the whole than their neighbors on the eastern side. Still, the western towns have traditionally been some of Norway's oldest and wealthiest, their fortunes derived from whaling and lumbering. Although these activities no longer dominate, their influence is seen in the monuments and in the wood architecture.

Jevnaker

Follow E16 toward Hønefoss, then follow Rte. 241 to Jevnaker, which is about 70 km (42 mi) northwest of Oslo; it's about a 2-hr drive.

A day trip to Jevnaker combines a drive along the Tyrifjord, where you can see some of the best fjord views in eastern Norway, with a visit to a glass factory that has been in operation since 1762. At **Hadeland Glassverk** you can watch artisans blowing glass, or, if you get there early enough, you can blow your own. Both practical table crystal and one-of-a-kind art glass are produced here, and you can buy (first quality and seconds) at the gift shop. The museum and gallery have a collection of 15,000 items, with about 800 on display. Bus 171, marked "Hønefoss," leaves from the university on Karl Johans Gate at seven minutes after the hour. Change in Hønefoss for the Jevnaker bus (it has no number). ⊠ *Rte. 241, Postboks 85, 5320 Jevnaker,* ☎ *61/31–05–55.* ⊙ *June–Aug., Mon.–Sat. 9–6, Sun. 11–6; Sept.–May, weekdays 9–4, Sat. 10–3, Sun. noon–5.*

Åmot i Modum

Take Rte. 35 south, along the Tyrifjord. If you are coming from the E18, take Rte. 11 west to Hokksund, and Rte. 35 to Åmot. Then turn onto Rte. 287 to Sigdal. 70 km (45 mi) from Oslo.

The small village of Åmot is famous for its cobalt mines. The blue mineral was used to make dyes for the world's glass and porcelain industries. The **Blaafarveværket** (Cobalt Works) was founded in 1773 to extract cobalt from the Modum mines. Today the complex is a museum and a national park. A permanent collection displays old cobalt-blue glass and porcelain. For children there's a petting farm, and there's a restaurant that serves Norwegian country fare. Up the hill from the art complex is Haugfossen, the highest waterfall in eastern Norway. Outdoor concerts are held on the grounds throughout the summer. The bus to Modum leaves from the university on Karl Johans Gate at 9:45 AM on Tuesday, Thursday, and Saturday. ⊠ *Rte. 507, 3370 Morud,* ☎ *32/78–49–00.* ⊠ *Special exhibitions NKr50; cobalt works free. Guided tours in English.* ◷ *Late May–Sept., daily 10–6.*

Drammen

⓫ *40 km (25 mi) from Oslo; 45 km (27 mi) south of Åmot i Modum.*

Drammen, a timber town and port for 500 years, is an industrial city of 50,000 on the Simoa River at its outlet to a fjord. It was the main harbor for silver exported from the Kongsberg mines. Today cars are imported into Norway through Drammen.

The **Spiralen** (Spiral), Drammen's main attraction, is a corkscrew road tunnel that makes six complete turns before emerging about 600 ft above, on Skansen Ridge. The entrance is behind the hospital by way of a well-marked road. ⊠ *NKr10 parking fee.*

Drammens Museum, a small county museum, is on the grounds of Marienlyst Manor, which dates from 1750. Glass from the Nøstetangen factory, which was in operation between 1741 and 1777, and a collection of rustic painted pieces are on display here. Its newer addition looks like a small temple set in the manor garden. ⊠ *Konnerudgt. 7,* ☎ *32/83–89–48.* ⊠ *NKr30.* ◷ *May–Oct., Tues.–Sat. 11–3, Sun. 11–5; Nov.–Apr., Tues.–Sun. 11–3.*

DINING AND LODGING

$$ ✕ **Spiraltoppen Café.** At the top of Bragernes Hill, this café offers excellent views and generous portions of Norwegian food. Try the meatballs with stewed cabbage or the open-face sandwiches. ⊠ *Bragernesåsen, Drammen,* ☎ *32/83–78–15. Reservations not accepted. AE, DC, MC, V.*

$$ 🏨 **Rica Park.** As with all Rica hotels, the atmosphere is relaxed and the rooms are comfortable. The nightclub at this hotel is popular with the over-30 crowd. ⊠ *Gamle Kirkepl. 3, 3019 Drammen,* ☎ *32/83–82–80,* 🖷 *32/89–32–07. 95 rooms. 2 restaurants, 2 bars, nightclub. AE, DC, MC, V.*

Horten

⓬ *30 km (17 mi) south of Drammen.*

Off the main route south, the coastal village of Horten has some distinctive museums. The town was once an important naval station and still retains the officers' candidates school.

The **Marinemuseet** (Royal Norwegian Navy Museum), built in 1853 as a munitions warehouse, displays relics from the nation's naval history. Outside is the world's first torpedo boat, from 1872, plus some one-person submarines from World War II. ⊠ *Karl Johans Vern,* ☎ *33/04–20–81.* ⊠ *Free.* ◷ *May–Oct., weekdays 10–4, weekends noon–4; Nov.–Apr., weekdays 10–3, Sun. noon–4.*

The **Redningsselskapets Museum** (Museum of the Sea Rescue Association) traces the history of ship-rescue operations. The organization has rescued more than 320,000 people since it was founded more than 100 years ago. ⊠ *Strandpromenaden 8, near Horten Tourist Office,* ☎ *33/04–70–66.* ⊠ *NKr10.* ◷ *May.–Oct., Fri.–Sun. noon–4.*

The **Preus Fotomuseum** houses one of the world's largest photographic collections. Exhibits include a turn-of-the-century photographer's studio and a tiny camera that was strapped to a pigeon for early aerial photography. ⊠ *Langgt. 82,* ☎ *33/04–27–37.* ⊠ *NKr30.* ◷ *May–Aug., daily 10–4; Sept.–Apr., daily 10:30–2.*

Just beyond Horten, between the road and the sea, lies a Viking grave site, **Borrehaugene,** with five earth and two stone mounds and the 12th-century Borre church.

Åsgårdstrand

⑬ *10 km (6 mi) south of Horten.*

The coastal town of Åsgårdstrand was known as an artists' colony for outdoor painting at the turn of the century. Edvard Munch painted *Girls on the Bridge* here and earned a reputation as a ladies' man. Munch spent seven summers at **Munchs lille hus** (little house), now a museum. ⊠ *Munchsgt.,* ☎ *33/03–17–08 (Horten Tourist Office).* 🎫 *NKr10.* ☉ *May, Sept., weekends 1–7; Jun.–Aug., Tues.–Sun. 11–7.*

En Route Travel south from Åsgårdstrand toward Tønsberg and you'll pass **Slagen,** the site where the Oseberg Viking ship, dating from around AD 800, was found. (It's now on display at Vikingskiphuset in Oslo.) Look for the mound where it was buried as you pass Slagen's church.

Tønsberg

⑭ *11 km (6½ mi) south of Åsgårdstrand.*

According to the sagas, Tønsberg is Norway's oldest settlement, founded in 871. The town's fortunes took a turn for the worse after the Reformation, and the city did not recover until shipping and whaling brought it into prominence in the 18th century. Little remains of Tønsberg's early structures, although the ruins at **Slottsfjellet** (Castle Hill), by the train station, include parts of the city wall, the remains of a church from around 1150, and a 13th-century brick citadel, the **Tønsberghus.** Other medieval remains are below the cathedral and near Storgata 17.

The **Vestfold Fylkesmuseum** (County Museum), north of the railroad station, houses a small Viking ship, several whale skeletons, and some inventions. There's an open-air section, too. ⊠ *Farmannsvn. 30,* ☎ *33/31–29–19.* 🎫 *NKr20.* ☉ *Mid-May–mid-Sept., Mon.–Sat. 10–5, Sun. noon–5; mid-Sept.–mid-May, weekdays 10–2.*

Sandefjord

⑮ *125 km (78 mi) south of Oslo; 25 km (15 mi) south of Tønsberg.*

Once the whaling capital of the world and possibly Norway's wealthiest city at the turn of the century, Sandefjord celebrated its 150th birthday in 1995. Now the whales are gone and all that remains of that trade is a monument to it. Thanks to shipping and other industries, however, the city is still rich and draws many illustrious Norwegians to its beaches, such as film actress Liv Ullmann, who has a cottage here.

Kommandør Christensens Hvalfangstmuseum (Commander Christensen's Whaling Museum) traces the development of the industry from small primitive boats to huge floating factories. An especially arresting display chronicles whaling in the Antarctic. ⊠ *Museumsgt. 39,* ☎ *33/46–32–51.* 🎫 *NKr20.* ☉ *May–Sept., daily 11–5; Oct.–Apr., daily 11–3.*

DINING AND LODGING

$$–$$$ ✕ **Ludl's Gourmet Odd Ivar Solvold.** The Austrian chef, Ludl, shows
★ Norwegians that there's more in the sea than cod and salmon. Ludl is a champion of the local cuisine, and specials may include ocean catfish, stuffed sole, a fish roulade, and lobster. Ludl's desserts are equally good, especially the cloudberry marzipan basket. ⊠ *Rådhusgt. 7, Sandefjord,* ☎ *33/46–27–41. AE, DC, MC, V.*

$$–$$$$ ⊞ **Rica Park Hotel.** It *looks* formal for a hotel built right on the water in a resort town, but there's no dress code. The decor is 1960s style, but surprisingly, it doesn't seem passé. Ask for one of the newer rooms. ⊠ *Strandpromenaden 9, 3200 Sandefjord,* ☎ *33/46–55–50,* FAX *33/46–79–00. 174 rooms, 8 suites. 2 restaurants, bar, indoor pool, health club, nightclub, convention center. AE, DC, MC, V.*

$–$$$ ⊞ **Comfort Home Hotel Atlantic.** The Atlantic Home was built in 1914, when Sandefjord was a whaling center. The history of whaling is traced in exhibits in glass cases and in pictures throughout the hotel. There's no restaurant, but the hotel provides *aftens,* a supper consisting of bread and cold cuts, plus hot soup and light beer, as part of the room rate. A coffeemaker and waffle iron are at your disposal at all times. ⊠ *Jernbanealleen 33, 3201 Sandefjord,* ☎ *33/46–80–00,* FAX *33/46–80–20. 72 rooms. Lobby lounge, sauna. AE, DC, MC, V.*

West of the Oslo Fjord A to Z

ARRIVING AND DEPARTING

By Boat: The most luxurious and scenic way to see the region is by boat: there are guest marinas at just about every port.

By Bus: Because train service to towns south of Drammen is infrequent, bus travel is the best alternative to cars. Check with **Nor-Way Bussekspress** (☎ 22/17–52–90) for schedules.

By Car: Route E18 south from Oslo follows the coast to the towns of this region.

By Train: Take a suburban train from Nationaltheatret or trains from Oslo S Station to reach Horten, Tønsberg, and Sandefjord.

CONTACTS AND RESOURCES

Visitor Information: Blaafarveværket (☎ 32/78–49–00). **Drammen** (Drammen Kommunale Turistinformasjonskontor, ⊠ Bragernes Torg 6, 3008 Drammen, ☎ 32/80–62–10). **Hadeland** (☎ 61/31–10–00). **Horten and Åsgårdstrand** (Horten Turist Kontor, ⊠ Tollbugt. 1a, 3187 Horten, ☎ 33/03–17–08). **Sandefjord** (Sandefjord Reiselivsforening, ⊠ Torvet, 3201 Sandfjord, ☎ 33/46–05–90). **Tønsberg** (Tønsberg og Omland Reiselivslag, ⊠ Nedre Langgt. 36 B, 3110 Tønsberg, ☎ 33/31–02–20).

4 Telemark and the Setesdal Valley

The interior region of southern Norway, Telemark and the Setesdal Valley, lies in the shadow of the famed beaches and fjords of the coast, but certainly doesn't lack majestic scenery—forested hills meet deeply etched valleys, and lakes stretch across the serene countryside.

A LAND OF WIDE-OPEN VISTAS and deep forests, the Telemark region is veined with swift-flowing streams and scattered with peaceful lakes—a natural setting so powerful and silent that a few generations ago, trolls were the only reasonable explanation for what lurked in, or for that matter plodded through, the shadows. These legendary creatures, serious Norwegians explain, boast several heads and a couple of noses (used to stir their porridge, of course) and can grow to the size of a village. Fortunately for humans, however, they turn to stone in sunlight.

Telemark was the birthplace of downhill skiing as well as the birthplace of many ancestors to Norwegian-Americans, for the poor farmers of the region were among the first to emigrate to the United States during the 19th century.

The quiet Setesdal Valley stretches north–south next to Telemark and sits atop rich mineral resources. The region is rich with history and is well-known for its colorful traditional costume and the intricate silver jewelry that decorates it.

Kongsberg

⑯ *84 km (52 mi) southwest of Oslo.*

Kongsberg, with 20,000 people today, was Norway's silver town for more than 300 years. It was here that silver was discovered in its purest form. King Christian IV saw the town's natural potential when he noticed that a cow's horn had rubbed moss off a stone to expose silver. Thereupon, the Danish builder-king began construction of the town. Thus, Norway's first industrial town rose to prominence. The mines are now closed, but the Royal Mint is still going strong.

The **Norsk Bergverksmuseum** (Norwegian Mining Museum), in the old smelting works, documents the development of silver mining and exhibits pure silver, gold, emeralds, and rubies from other Norwegian mines. The **Royal Mint Museum,** in the same building, is a treasure trove for coin collectors, with a nearly complete assemblage of Norwegian coins. Children can pan for silver during summer. The **Kongsberg Ski Museum,** also part of the mining complex, houses exhibits of ancient skis and 23 Olympic and World Championship medals won by Kongsberg skiers. ⊠ *Hyttegt. 3,* ☎ *32/73–32–60.* 🎫 *NKr40.* ☉ *Mid-May–late May and mid-Aug.–late Aug., daily 10–4; June–mid-Aug., weekdays 10–6, weekends 10–4; Sept., daily noon–4; Oct.–mid-May, Sun. noon–4. Otherwise, by appointment.*

....

OFF THE **SØLVGRUVENE –** In Saggrenda, about 8 km (5 mi) outside Kongsberg
BEATEN PATH toward Notodden, you can visit silver mines. Guided mine tours include a 2⅓-km (1½-mi) ride on the mine train into Kongensgruve (the King's mine) and a ride on the first personnel elevator. The temperature in the mine is about 6°C (43°F) and the tour takes about one hour and 20 minutes, so dress accordingly. ☎ *32/73–32–60.* 🎫 *NKr50.* ☉ *Tours mid-May–June and mid-Aug.–late Aug., daily at 11, 12:30, 2; July–mid-Aug., daily at 11, 12:30, 2, 3:30; Sept.–mid-May, Sun. at 2.*

....

Kongsberg Kirke (Kongsberg Church), finished in 1761, was built during the heyday of the silver mines, with an impressive gilded Baroque altar, organ, and pulpit all on one wall. It seats 3,000. The royal box and the galleries separated the gentry and mine owners from the workers. Organ concerts are given Wednesdays at 6 in summer. ☎ *32/73–*

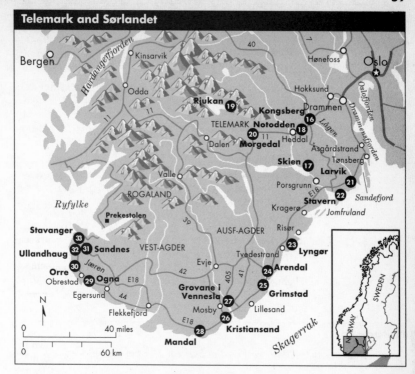

Telemark and Sørlandet

19–02. ▨ NKr20. ☾ Mid-May–Aug., weekdays 10–4, Sat. 10–1; Sept.–mid-May, Tues.–Fri. 10–2. Sun. services at 11 with tours afterward until 1:30. Call to confirm times.

The Arts

Every June jazz fans descend on Kongsberg for its annual **jazz festival.** Contact the tourist office (☞ Telemark and the Setesdal Valley A to Z, *below*) for information.

Dining and Lodging

$$ ✕ **Gamle Kongsberg Kro.** This café next to the waterfall at Nybrofossen offers hearty Norwegian dishes at moderate prices. There's a miniature golf course nearby. ⊠ *Thornesvn. 4,* ☎ *32/73–16–33,* ☏ *32/73–26–03. DC, MC, V.*

$–$$ 🏨 **Quality Grand Hotel.** A statue of Kongsberg's favorite son, Olympic ski jumper Birger Ruud, stands in the park in front of this modern, centrally located hotel. ⊠ *Kristian Augustsgt. 2, 3600,* ☎ *32/73–20–29,* ☏ *32/73–41–29. 97 rooms, 2 suites. 2 restaurants, 2 bars, indoor pool, exercise room, nightclub, meeting rooms. AE, DC, MC, V.*

Skien

17 88 km (55 mi) south of Kongsberg on Rtes. 32 and 36.

Best known as the birthplace of playwright Henrik Ibsen, Skien, with a population of 50,000, is the capital of the Telemark region. Ibsen's hometown celebrates its favorite son every August with the **Ibsen-Kultur-festival** (⊠ Skien Tourist Office, Box 192, 3701 Skien, ☎ 35/58–19–10), which includes concerts as well as drama.

The **Fylkesmuseet** (County Museum), a manor house from 1780, has a collection of Ibsen memorabilia, including his study and bedroom and the "blue salon" from his Oslo flat (other interiors are at the Norsk Folkemuseum in Oslo). Also on display is Telemark-style folk art, including rosemaling and wood carving. ⊠ *Øvregt. 41,* ☎ *35/52–35–94.* ⌨ *NKr20.* ⊙ *Garden mid-May–Aug., daily 10–8; museum mid-May–Aug., daily 10–6; Sept., Sun. 10–6.*

Venstøp looks just as it did when the Ibsen family lived here from 1835 to 1843. The attic was the inspiration for *The Wild Duck*. This house, part of Skien's County Museum, is 5 km (3 mi) northwest of the city. ☎ *35/52–35–94.* ⌨ *NKr20.* ⊙ *Mid-May–Aug., daily 10–6; Sept., Sun. 10–6.*

Dining and Lodging

$$ ✕ **Boden Spiseri.** Boden serves excellent French-influenced Norwegian-style food, such as medallions of reindeer. For dessert, *Gjoegler Boden*—ice cream with rum, raisins, and a touch of ginger—is a delight. ⊠ *Landbrygga 5,* ☎ *35/52–61–70. AE, DC, MC, V. No lunch.*

$–$$ ⌂ **Rainbow Høyers Hotell.** The old-fashioned quality of the exterior, with cornices and pedimented windows, is reflected in the Høyers's lobby, which is an incongruous mixture of old and new. The rooms are modern and light, thanks to the big windows. ⌨ *Kongensgt. 6, 3700,* ☎ *35/52–05–40,* ⌨ *35/52–26–08. 69 rooms, 1 suite. Restaurant, bar, meeting rooms. AE, DC, MC, V.*

Notodden

⑱ *68 km (42 mi) northwest of Skien and 35 km (20 mi) west of Kongsberg.*

Notodden today is not much more than a small industrial town (although it's well-known for its blues fest). It is believed that the area must have been a prosperous one in the Middle Ages, though, because of the size of the town's stavkirke—85 ft high and 65 ft long.

Heddal Stave Church is Norway's largest. The church dates from the middle of the 12th century and has exceptional stylized animal ornamentation, along with grotesque human heads, on the portals. ☎ *35/02–08–40.* ⌨ *NKr15.* ⊙ *Mid-May–June and late Aug.–mid-Sept., Mon.–Sat. 10–5; late June–late Aug., Mon.–Sat. 9–7. Sunday service at 12:30* PM *mid-May–mid-Sept.*

Notodden is famous for its **summer blues festival** in August, which lasts four days and brings in Norwegian and American acts such as the Robert Cray Band. Some acts require reserved tickets, which can be done in advance at any post office in Norway (or call ☎ 75/15–75–16 from outside Norway). For more information contact Notodden tourist information (☞ Telemark and the Setesdal Valley A to Z, *below*).

En Route   Route 37 northwest from Notodden to Rjukan passes the 6,200-ft **Gaustatoppen,** a looming, snow-streaked table of rock popular with hikers.

Rjukan

⑲ *96 km (59 mi) from Notodden.*

The town of Rjukan may not ring a bell, but mention "heavy water," and anyone who lived through World War II or saw the film *The Heroes of Telemark* with Kirk Douglas knows about the sabotage of the heavy water factory there, which thwarted German efforts to develop an atomic bomb. Rjukan's history actually began in the decade between 1907 and 1916, when the population grew from a few hundred to 10,000 because of a different kind of water, hydroelectric power. Norsk Hydro, one of Norway's largest industries, which uses hydroelectric power to manufacture chemicals and fertilizer, was started here.

Heavy water (used in nuclear reactors as a moderator) was produced as a by-product in the manufacture of fertilizer at Vemork, 6 km (4 mi) west of Rjukan along Route 37, where a museum, **Industriarbeidermuseet Vemork,** has been built. Exhibits document both the development of hydroelectric power and the World War II events. Every year on the first Saturday in July, the work of the saboteurs is commemorated, but their 8-km (5-mi) path, starting at Rjukan Fjellstue (mountain lodge) and finishing at the museum, is marked and can be followed at any time. ☎ *35/09–51–53.* ✉ *NKr50.* ☉ *May–mid-Aug., daily 10–6; mid-Aug.–Sept., weekdays 10–4, weekends 11–6; Oct. and March–Apr., Sat. 11–4.*

Rjukan is the site of northern Europe's first cable car, **Krossobanen,** built in 1928 by Hydro to transport people to the top of the mountain. ✉ *NKr20.* ☉ *Mid-Apr.–mid-Sept. Times vary; call Rjukan tourist information for details,* ☎ *35/09–15–11.*

Lodging

$$ ⌂ **Euro Park Hotell.** This small hotel with a traditional family atmosphere is in the center of town. The rooms are decorated in light colors. The restaurant, with the curious name Ammonia, offers a wide selection. ✉ *Sam Eydes Gt. 67, 3660,* ☎ *35/09–02–88,* ℻ *35/09–05–25. 39 rooms. Restaurant, bar, pub, nightclub. AE, DC, MC, V.*

$$ ⌂ **Gaustablikk Høyfjellshotell.** Built at the foot of Gaustatoppen near Rjukan, this modern timber hotel is a popular ski resort, with nine downhill slopes and 80 km (50 mi) of cross-country trails. In summer, these marked trails are perfect for walks and hikes. ✉ *3660,* ☎ *35/09–14–22,* ℻ *35/09–19–75. 83 rooms, 14 suites. Restaurant, bar, indoor pool, sauna, exercise room. AE, DC, MC, V.*

Morgedal

⑳ *77 km (46 mi) southwest of Rjukan via Åmot.*

In the heart of Telemark is Morgedal, the birthplace of modern skiing, thanks to a persistent Sondre Nordheim, who in the 19th century perfected his skis and bindings and practiced jumping from his roof. His innovations included bindings that close behind the heel and skis that narrow in the middle to facilitate turning. In 1868, after revamping his skis and bindings, he took off for a 185-km (115-mi) trek to Oslo just to prove it could be done. A hundred years ago, skiers used one long pole, held diagonally, much like high-wire artists. Eventually the use of two short poles became widespread, although purists feel that the one-pole version is the "authentic" way to ski. Nordheim's traditional Telemark skiing is now the rage in Norway, though the revival was begun in the United States.

☾ The **Norsk Skieventyr** (Norwegian Skiing Adventure) in Morgedal guides you through the history of the winter sport with life-size exhibits of typical ski cottages and authentic skis and costumes. Displays include the inside of Norway's original and last ski-wax factory where specialists melted a variety of secret ingredients, including cheese, to make uphill and downhill slides smoother. The sport of yore meets its match on the last leg of the exhibit where a multiscreen-panoramic video shows modern-day footage of the don't-try-this-at-home sort. Teenagers in techno-gear and professional ski-trekkers in Telemark-style sweaters zoom around the snow to traditional fiddle music. ✉ *On Rte. 11 between Brunkeberg and Høydalsmo,* ☎ *35/05–42–50.* ✉ *NKr50.* ☉

May–mid-June and mid-Aug.–mid-Sept., daily 11–5; mid-June–mid-Aug., daily 9–7; late Sept.–Apr., weekends 11–5.

Dalen

The Dalen area is the place to hike, bike, and be outdoors. From Skien you can take boat tours on the Telemark waterways, a combination of canals and natural lakes between Skien and either Dalen or Notodden (☞ Notodden, *above*). The trip to Dalen takes you through Ulefoss, where you can leave the boat and visit the neoclassical **Ulefoss Manor** (✉ Hovedgård, ☎ 35/94–56–10), which dates from 1807. It's open weekdays June through September from 2 PM to 4 PM and Sunday from noon to 3. The historic **Viking Dalen Hotel** (☞ *below*) is worth a peek, whether or not you stay there. A number of royal families have stayed there, and locals are said to think ghosts haunt its creaky wooden walls. *For trips to Dalen, call Telemarkreiser, ☎ 35/53–03–00; for Notodden, contact Telemarksbåtene, ✉ 3812 Akkerhaugen, ☎ 35/95–82–11, ☎ 35/95–82–96.*

Dining and Lodging

$$$ ✕☎ **Viking Dalen Hotel.** At the end of the Telemark Canals stands this opulent, Victorian "Swiss-style" hotel, complete with dragonhead carvings, stained-glass windows, and a balcony overlooking the stunning entrance hall. Rooms are relatively small and furnished with plain Norwegian antiques. All meals are provided on request. ✉ *3880 Dalen, ☎ 35/07–70–00, ☎ 35/07–70–11. 38 rooms. Breakfast room, lobby lounges, meeting rooms. AE, V. Closed Christmas–Easter.*

$–$$ ☎ **Telemarkstunet Natadal Uppigård.** This cluster of 18th-century farmhouses with grass roofs provides an authentic alternative to a hotel stay. Set on a steep mountainside about an hour's drive from Dalen, the cabins could be on display in Oslo's Folkemuseum. Activities here are plentiful, including horseback riding, pond swimming, and strawberry picking—all the Norwegian favorites. A stay in these rustic accommodations is comparable to camping: breakfast, linens, and housekeeping cost extra. The cabins come with kitchenettes but not always individual bathrooms. ✉ *3841 Flatdal, ☎ 35/05–23–00, ☎ 35/05–20–30. 3 cabins with room for 21 people; 4 individual rooms in main house. No credit cards.*

Valle

The Setesdal road, Rte. 39, follows the Otra River downstream and then runs alongside the Byglandsfjord; Valle is 56 km (35 mi) southeast of Dalen.

Near Valle sits **Sylvartun,** a clump of grass-roofed cottages that house a local silversmith's workshop, a jewelry shop, and an art gallery. It's also a cultural center that hosts concerts, displays local crafts, and holds summertime "Setesdal Evenings" at which professional musicians and folk dancers perform while a traditional Norwegian dinner is served. ✉ *Rte. 39, Nomeland (near Valle), ☎ 37/93–63–06. ☉ Silversmith's shop: May–Oct., Mon.–Sat. 10–6, Sun. 11–6. Folk dances: summer only. Call for opening hours and program schedules.*

OFF THE   **SETESDAL MINERAL PARK –** About 97 km (57 mi) from Valle, just south of
BEATEN PATH   Evje on Route 39, is an interesting park where rock formations from Norway and elsewhere are displayed inside a dark mountain. ✉ *4660 Evje, ☎ 37/19–85–33. ☎ NKr60. ☉ Late June–late Aug., daily 10–6.*

Telemark and the Setesdal Valley A to Z

Arriving and Departing

BY BUS

The many bus lines that serve the region are coordinated through **Nor-Way Bussekspress** in Oslo (⊠ Bussterminalen, Galleri Oslo, ☎ 22/17–52–90, FAX 22/17–59–22).

BY CAR

On Route E18 from Oslo, the drive southwest to Kongsberg takes a little more than an hour. If you arrive by way of the Kristiansand ferry, the drive up Route 37 to Evje will take about an hour as well.

BY TRAIN

The train from Oslo S Station to Kongsberg takes 1 hour and 25 minutes; bus connections to Telemark are available.

Getting Around

BY BUS

Buses in the region rarely run more than twice a day, so get a comprehensive schedule from the tourist office or Nor-Way Bussekspress (☞ *above*) and plan ahead.

BY CAR

Roads in the southern part of the interior region are open and flat, but others are still curvy and mountainous. Route 11 passes through Heddal and Morgedal, and connects with 37, which goes north to Rjukan and south toward Dalen. Route 11 also connects with 37, the main Setesdal road, which goes through Evje and Valle all the way to Kristiansand.

BY TRAIN

The only train service in the southern part of the region is the Oslo–Stavanger line (via Kristiansand).

Contacts and Resources

VISITOR INFORMATION

Kongsberg (⊠ Storgt. 35, ☎ 32/73–50–00). **Notodden** (⊠ Storgt. 39, ☎ 35/01–20–22). **Rjukan** (⊠ Torget 2, ☎ 35/09–15–11). **Setesdal** (☎ 4660 Evje, tel. 37/93–14–00). **Skien** (⊠ Reiselivets Hus, N. Hjellegt. 18, ☎ 35/95–00–61).

5 Sørlandet: Along the Coast

In summer, Oslo's residents migrate to the southern coast to soak up some sunshine. Southern Norway is an outdoor paradise, with a mild summer climate and terrain varying from coastal flatland to inland mountains and forests.

SCANDINAVIA BY TRAIN

The best way to experience the sights Scandinavia has to offer is by train.

With a *Scanrail Pass* choose unlimited rail travel throughout Denmark, Finland, Norway and Sweden for as many days as you need. Individual country rail passes are also available.

And with a *Scanrail 'n Drive,* you can take advantage of the benefits of both rail *and* car to get even more out of your Scandinavian vacation.

For information or reservations call your travel agent or Rail Europe:

1-800-4-EURAIL(US)

1-800-361-RAIL(CAN)

Your one source for European travel!

Pick up the phone.

Pick up the miles.

MCI Calling Card

415 555 1234 2244
J.D. SMITH

WorldPhone

Use your MCI Card® to make an international call from virtually anywhere in the world and earn frequent flyer miles on one of seven major airlines.

Enroll in an MCI Airline Partner Program today. In the U.S., call **1-800-FLY-FREE.** Overseas, call MCI collect at **1-916-567-5151.**

1. To use your MCI Card, just dial the WorldPhone access number of the country you're calling from.
   (For a complete listing of codes, visit www.mci.com.)
2. Dial or give the operator your MCI Card number.
3. Dial or give the number you're calling.

# Austria (CC) ♦	022-903-012		# Netherlands (CC) ♦	0800-022-91-22
# Belarus (CC)			# Norway (CC) ♦	800-19912
From Brest, Vitebsk, Grodno, Minsk	8-800-103		# Poland (CC) ÷	00-800-111-21-22
From Gomel and Mogilev regions	8-10-800-103		# Portugal (CC) ÷	05-017-1234
# Belgium (CC) ♦	0800-100-12		Romania (CC) ÷	01-800-1800
# Bulgaria	00800-0001		# Russia (CC) ÷ ♦	
# Croatia (CC) ★	99-385-0112		To call using ROSTELCOM ■	747-3322
# Czech Republic (CC) ♦	00-42-000112		For a Russian-speaking operator	747-3320
# Denmark (CC) ♦	8001-0022		To call using SOVINTEL ■	960-2222
# Finland (CC) ♦	08001-102-80		# San Marino (CC) ♦	172-1022
# France (CC) ♦	0-800-99-0019		# Slovak Republic (CC)	00-421-00112
# Germany (CC)	0130-0012		# Slovenia	080-8808
# Greece (CC) ♦	00-800-1211		# Spain (CC)	900-99-0014
# Hungary (CC) ♦	00▼800-01411		# Sweden (CC) ♦	020-795-922
# Iceland (CC) ♦	800-9002		# Switzerland (CC) ♦	0800-89-0222
# Ireland (CC)	1-800-55-1001		# Turkey (CC) ♦	00-8001-1177
# Italy (CC) ♦	172-1022		# Ukraine (CC) ÷	8▼10-013
# Kazakhstan (CC)	8-800-131-4321		# United Kingdom (CC)	
# Liechtenstein (CC) ♦	0800-89-0222		To call using BT ■	0800-89-0222
# Luxembourg	0800-0112		To call using MERCURY ■	0500-89-0222
# Monaco (CC) ♦	800-90-019		# Vatican City (CC)	172-1022

Is this a great time, or what? :-)

SØRLANDET, OR SOUTHERN NORWAY, is a land of wide beaches toasted by the greatest number of sunny days in Norway, waters warmed by the Gulf Stream, and long, fertile tracts of flatland. Not a people to pass up a minute of sunshine, the Norwegians have sprinkled the south with their hytter (cabins) and made it their number one domestic holiday spot. Nonetheless, even at the height of summer, you can sail to a quiet skerry or take a solitary walk through the forest.

There's plenty of fish in the rivers and lakes, as well as along the coast. The region is particularly well suited to canoeing, kayaking, rafting, and hiking. Beavers, deer, foxes, and forest birds inhabit the area, so bring binoculars if you'd like to see them more closely.

The coast bordering the Skagerak, the arm of the North Sea separating Norway and Denmark, is lined with small communities stretching from Oslo as far as Lindesnes, which is at the southernmost tip. Sørlandet towns are often called "pearls on a string," and in the dusk of a summer evening, reflections of the white-painted houses on the water have a silvery translucence.

The two chief cities of Norway's south, Kristiansand on the east coast and Stavanger on the west coast, differ sharply. Kristiansand is a resort town, scenic and relaxed, whereas Stavanger, once a fishing center, is now the hub of the oil industry and Norway's most cosmopolitan city. Stavanger has many more good restaurants than other cities of comparable size, thanks to the influx of both foreigners and money. More than 100 restaurants, bars, and cafés offer everything from Thai, Chinese, and Indian to Italian, French, and, of course, Norwegian cooking. Try the restored warehouse area in the harbor for some of the best restaurants.

Between Kristiansand and Stavanger is the coastal plain of Jæren, dotted with prehistoric burial sites and the setting for the works of some of the country's foremost painters.

Numbers in the margin correspond to points of interest on the Telemark and Sorlandet map in chapter 4.

Larvik

㉑ *128 km (79 mi) from Oslo, 19 km (12 mi) south of Sandefjord.*

Larvik is the last of the big whaling towns. It's still a port, but now the traffic is made up of passengers to Fredrikshavn, Denmark.

Kong Haakons Kilde (King Haakon's Spring), also called Farris Kilde (Farris Spring), is Norway's only natural source of mineral water. A spa was built here in 1880, but people now drink the water rather than bathe in it. The spring is near the ferry quays. ⊠ *Fjellvn, 3256,* ☎ *33/18–20–00.* 🎫 *Free.* ☉ *Late June–mid-Aug., weekdays.*

The noble Gyldenløve family once owned the large estate, **Herregården,** which dates back to 1677. Inside, the furnishings are masterful examples of trompe l'oeil: Scandinavian nobility had to make do with furniture painted to look like marble rather than the real thing. ⊠ *Herregaardssletta 1, 3257,* ☎ *33/13–04–04.* 🎫 *NKr25.* ☉ *Late May–late Aug., daily noon–5; early Sept.–late May, Sun. noon–5.*

The **Maritime Museum** is in Larvik's former customs house and chronicles the town's seafaring history. There's heavy coverage of Thor Heyerdahl's voyages, with models of *Kon-Tiki* and *Ra II.* 🎫 ☉ *Charges and opening times vary; check with the tourist office.*

OFF THE
BEATEN PATH   **PORSGRUNN PORSELÆNFABRIK ASA** – About 27 km (17 mi) west of
Larvik in Porsgrunn is a porcelain factory where you can take a tour and
purchase factory seconds. ⊠ *Porselensgt. 12,* ☎ *35/55–00–40.* ⊡
NKr10. ⊙ *Late May–Aug., tours weekdays at 10, 11, and 1.*

Dining and Lodging

$$ ✕⊡ **Grand.** The rooms are spotless and the service attentive in this large
hotel overlooking the fjord. The restaurant is a good spot to sample
the local fish soup and smoked-meat platters—especially at lunch. ⊠
Storgt. 38–40, 3256, ☎ *33/18–78–00,* ⅨⅩ *33/18–70–45. 97 rooms.
Restaurant, bar, pub, dance club, nightclub. AE, DC, MC, V.*

Stavern

㉒ *8 km (5 mi) south of Larvik.*

A popular sailing center today, Stavern was Norway's main naval sta-
tion between 1750 and 1850, then called Fredriksvern, named for
King Fredrik V.

A fine example of Scandinavian Rococo architecture, **Stavern Church**
was built in 1756. Its pews were designed so their backs could be folded
down to make beds in case the church had to be used as a field hos-
pital in time of war. ⊠ *On the water east of town,* ☎ *33/19–99–75.*
⊙ *Guided tours by appointment.*

En Route   From Stavern to Lyngør, you'll pass through Kragerø, a picturesque
town with its own small archipelago. Theodor Kittelsen (1857–1914),
famous for his drawings of trolls and illustrations of Norwegian fairy
tales, lived in Kragerø, and his birthplace is now a museum. The next
pearl on the string after Kragerø is Risør, which is just off E18 on the
coast. On the first weekend in August the town holds a festival that
fills the harbor with beautiful antique boats.

Lyngør

㉓ *18 km (11 mi) south of Risør. To get to Lyngør, follow E18 to the sign
for Sørlandsporten (Gateway to the South). Turn off just after the sign
and drive 26 km (16 mi) to Lyngørfjorden Marina (☎ 37/16–68–00),
where you can take a five-minute watertaxi ride for NKr80.*

Hardly changed since the days of sailing ships, Lyngør is idyllic and
carless, lined with rows of white-painted houses bearing window boxes
filled with pink and red flowers. This island community, on four tiny
rocky islands off the coast, is considered by some to be Europe's best-
preserved village. In winter the population is 110, but every summer
thousands descend on the village. You'll find white houses all along
the south coast, a tradition that began more than 100 years ago, when
Dutch sailors traded white paint for wood. Until that time, only red
paint was available in Norway.

NEED A
BREAK?   In a historic late-19th-century white house with blue trim, **Den Blå
Lanterne** (☎ 37/16–64–80) is Lyngør's only restaurant. Although it's
pricey, you can eat as much of the famous fish soup as you like at this
well-regarded restaurant—and there's often live music. It's open May
through September.

Arendal

㉔ *33 km (20½ mi) from Lyngør on E18.*

Picturesque Arendal has more of the tidy white houses that are common to the area. In Tyholmen, the old town, you'll see many of these, as well as some brightly colored well-preserved wooden houses. This is a good town for strolling around. For a more formal tour, ask about the summer walking tours at the tourist office.

OFF THE BEATEN PATH

MERDØGAARD MUSEUM – On the island of Merdøy, a 30-minute boat ride from Arendal's Langbrygga (long wharf), is an early 18th-century sea captain's home, now a museum. ☎ 37/08–52–43. ☞ NKr10. ◷ Late June–mid-Aug., daily 11–5. Guided tours on the hr until 4.

Dining and Lodging

$$ ✕ **Madam Reiersen.** This authentic restaurant on the waterfront serves good food in an informal atmosphere. ⊠ *Nedre Tyholmsvn. 3, 4800,* ☎ 37/02–19–00. AE, DC, MC, V.

$$ ▥ **Clarion Tyholmen Hotel.** This maritime hotel, built in 1988, is in Tyholmen, with the sea at close quarters and a magnificent view of the fjord. The open-air restaurant is great in summer. ⊠ *Teaterpl. 2, 4800* ☎ 37/02–68–00, ℻ 37/02–68–01. 60 rooms. 2 restaurants, bar, sauna. AE, DC, MC, V.

Grimstad

㉕ *15 km (9.2 mi) south of Arendal.*

Grimstad's glory was in the days of sailing ships—about the same time the 15-year-old Henrik Ibsen worked as an apprentice at the local apothecary shop. Grimstad Apotek is now a part of **Ibsenhuset** (the Ibsen House) and has been preserved with its 1837 interior intact. Ibsen wrote his first play, *Catlina,* here. ⊠ *Henrik Ibsensgt. 14, 4890,* ☎ 37/04–46–53. ☞ NKr25. ◷ Mid-May–mid-Sept., Mon.–Sat. 11–5, Sun. 1–5.

Kristiansand

㉖ *55 km (34.1 mi) south of Grimstad on E18.*

Kristiansand, with 68,000 inhabitants, is one of Sørlandet's most prosperous cities and the domestic summer-vacation capital of Norway. According to legend, in 1641 King Christian IV marked the four corners of Kristiansand with his walking stick, and within that framework the grid of wide streets was drawn. The center of town, called the **Kvadrat,** still retains the grid, even after numerous fires.

Kristiansand's **Fisketorvet** (fish market) is near the south corner of the town's grid, right on the sea. **Christiansholm Festning** (fortress) is on a promontory opposite Festningsgata. Completed in 1672, the circular building with 15-ft-thick walls has played more a decorative than a defensive role; it was used once, in 1807, to defend the city against British invasion. Now it contains art exhibits.

The Gothic Revival **cathedral** from 1885 is the third-largest church in Norway. It often hosts summertime concerts in addition to an annual weeklong International Church Music Festival in mid-May (☎ 38/02–13–11 for information) that includes organ, chamber, and gospel music. ⊠ *Kirkegt., 4610,* ☎ 38/02–11–88. ☞ Free. ◷ June–Aug., daily 9–2.

A wealthy merchant-shipowner built **Gimle Gård** (Gimle Manor) around 1800 in the Empire style. It displays furnishings from that period, paintings, silver, and hand-blocked wallpaper. To get there from the city center, head north across the Otra River on Bus 22 or drive to Route E18 and cross the bridge over the Otra to Parkveien. Turn left onto Ryttergangen and drive to Gimleveien, where you'll turn right. ⊠ *Gimlevn. 23, 4630,* ☎ *38/09–02–28.* 🎫 *NKr20.* ۞ *July–Aug., Tues.– Sat. noon–4, Sun. noon–6.*

The runestone in the cemetery of **Oddernes Kirke** (Oddernes Church) tells that Øyvind, godson of Saint Olav, built this church in 1040 on property he inherited from his father. One of the oldest churches in Norway, it is dedicated to Saint Olav. ⊠ *Oddernesvn, 6430,* ☎ *38/ 09–01–87 or 38/09–03–60.* 🎫 *Free.* ۞ *May–Aug., Sun.–Fri. 9–2.*

At **Kristiansand Kanonmuseum** (Cannon Museum) you can see the cannon that the German occupying force rigged during World War II. With a 38-centimeter caliber, the cannon was said to be capable of shooting a projectile halfway to Denmark. ⊠ *Møvik,* ☎ *38/08-50-90.* 🎫 *NKr40.* ۞ *May–mid-June and Sept., Thurs.–Sun. 11–6; late-June– Aug., daily 11–6.*

You'll see dwellings and workshops on a reconstructed city street at **Vest-Agder Fylkesmuseum** (County Museum). Here you can visit two *tun*—farm buildings traditionally set in clusters around a common area, which suited the extended families. The museum is 4 km (3 mi) east of Kristiansand on Route E18. ⊠ *Kongsgård, 4631,* ☎ *38/09–02–28.* 🎫 *NKr20.* ۞ *Mid-June–mid-Aug., Mon.–Sat. 10–6; late May–mid-June and mid-Aug.–mid-Sept., Sun. noon–6; mid-Sept.–mid-May, Sun. noon– 5; or by appointment.*

A favorite with hikers and strolling nannies, **Ravnedalen** (Raven Valley) is a lush park that's filled with flowers in springtime. Wear comfortable shoes and you can hike the narrow, winding paths up the hills and climb 200 steps up to a 304-ft lookout. ⊠ *Northwest of town.*

Ⓒ One of Norway's most popular attractions, **Kristiansand Dyrepark** is actually five separate parks, including a water park (bring bathing suits and towels), a forested park, an entertainment park, a fairy-tale park, and a zoo, which contains an enclosure for Scandinavian wolves and Europe's (possibly the world's) largest breeding ground for Bactrian camels. The fairy-tale park, **Kardemomme By** (Cardamom Town), is named for a book by Norwegian illustrator and writer Thorbjørn Egner. His story comes alive here in a precisely replicated village, with actors playing townsfolk, shopkeepers, pirates, and a delightful trio of robbers. Families who are hooked can even stay overnight in one of the village's cozy apartments or nearby cottages (reserve at least a year in advance). The park is 11 km (6 mi) east of town. ⊠ *Kristiansand Dyrepark, 4609 Kardemomme By,* ☎ *38/04–97–00.* 🎫 *NKr170 includes admission to all parks and rides.* ۞ *Mid-May–mid-June, weekdays 9–4, weekends 10–6; late June–mid-Aug., daily 10–6; late Aug.– mid-Sept., weekdays 10–4, weekends 10–6; late Sept.–early May, weekdays 10–3, weekends 10–4.*

Dining and Lodging

$$–$$$ ✕ **Sjøhuset.** Built in 1892 as a salt warehouse, this white-trimmed red building has since become a restaurant. The specialty is seafood, appropriately, and the monkfish with Newburg sauce on green fettuccine is colorful and delicious. ⊠ *Østre Strandgt. 12, 4610,* ☎ *38/02–62– 60. AE, DC, MC, V.*

$$ ✕ **Restaurant Bakgården.** At this small and intimate restaurant the menu varies from day to day, but the seafood platter and lamb tenderloin are standard. The staff is especially attentive. ⊠ *Tollbodgt. 5, 4611,* ☎ *38/02–79–55. AE, DC, MC, V. No lunch.*

$ ✕ **Mållaget Kafeteria.** At this cafeteria everything is homemade (except for the gelatin dessert). That includes such dishes as meatballs, brisket of beef with onion sauce, and trout in sour-cream sauce. It's the best deal in town, but it closes right around 6 PM, the time most people think about eating dinner. ⊠ *Gyldenløves Gt. 11, 4611,* ☎ *38/02–22–93. No credit cards.*

$$–$$$ 🏨 **Clarion Ernst Park Hotel.** The rooms are decorated with chintz bedspreads and drapes and practical furniture. The corner rooms have a tower nook at one end. On Saturday the atrium restaurant is the local spot for a civilized tea and lovely cakes. ⊠ *Rådhusgt. 2, 4611,* ☎ *38/02–14–00,* FAX *38/02–03–07. 112 rooms, 4 suites. Restaurant, 3 bars, nightclub, meeting rooms. AE, DC, MC, V.*

$$ 🏨 **Rainbow Hotel Norge.** This quiet, family hotel in the heart of town has an entrance more modern than that of the Ernst Park, but upstairs the difference is negligible. Here the rooms are furnished in bright colors and dark woods. Get up for breakfast to taste the homemade breads and rolls. ⊠ *Dronningens Gt. 5, 4610,* ☎ *38/02–00–00,* FAX *38/02–35–30. 114 rooms. Restaurant, library, meeting rooms. AE, DC, MC, V.*

Outdoor Activities and Sports

BIKING

Kristiansand has 70 km (43 mi) of bike trails around the city. The tourist office (☞ Visitor Information *in* Sørlandet A to Z, *below*) can recommend routes and rentals.

FISHING

Just north of Kristiansand there is excellent trout, perch, and eel fishing at Lillesand's **Vestre Grimevann** lake. You can get a permit at any sports store or at the tourist office (☞ Visitor Information *in* Sørlandet A to Z, *below*).

HIKING

In addition to the gardens and steep hills of **Ravnedalen** (☞ *above*), the **Baneheia Forest,** just a 15-minute walk north from the city center, is full of evergreens, small lakes, and paths that are ideal for a lazy walk or a challenging run.

WATER SPORTS

Kuholmen Marina (⊠ Roligheden Camping, ☎ 38/09–67–22) rents boats, water skis, and water scooters. **Anker Dykkersenter** (⊠ Randesundsgt. 2, Kuholmen, ☎ 38/09–79–09) rents scuba equipment. **Kristiansand Diving Club** (⊠ Myrbakken 3, ☎ 38/01–03–32 between 6 PM and 9 PM) has information on local diving.

Combining history and sailing, the magnificent full-rig, square-sail school ship ***Sørlandet*** (⊠ Gravene 2, 4610 Kristiansand, ☎ 38/02–98–90), built in 1927, takes on passengers for two weeks, usually stopping for several days in a northern European port. The price is about NKr7,000.

Grovane i Vennesla

㉗ *20 km (13 mi) north of Kristiansand. Follow Rte. 39 from Kristiansand to Mosby, veer right onto 405, and continue to Grovane.*

At Grovane i Vennesla you will find the **Setesdalsbanen** (Setesdal Railway), a 4¾-km-long (3-mi-long) stretch of narrow-gauge track on which a steam locomotive from 1894 and carriages from the early 1900s run. ⊠ *Vennesla Stasjon, 4700,* ☎ *38/15–55–08.* 🎫 *NKr50.* ☺ *Mid-June–late June and Aug., Sun. at 11:30; July, Tue.–Fri. at 6 and weekends at 11:30 and 2.*

Mandal

② *42 km (28 mi) southwest from Kristiansand and 82 km (51 mi) from Evje.*

Mandal is Norway's most southerly town, famous for its historic core of well-preserved wooden houses and its beautiful long beach, Sjøsanden.

Mandal Kirke, built in 1821, is Norway's largest Empire-style wooden church. ☎ 38/26–35–77. ☉ *Tues.–Fri. 11–2.*

Lindesnes Fyr, Norway's oldest lighthouse, was built on the southernmost point of the country. The old coal-fired light dates from 1822. ☎ 38/25–88–51. ☉ *Mid-May–mid-Sept., 8 AM–10 PM; rest of yr, open during daylight hours.*

En Route   The road from Mandal climbs and weaves its way through steep, wooded valleys and then descends toward the sea. Here you'll find the small town of Flekkefjord, which is known for its **Hollenderbyen** (Dutch Town), a historic district with small, white-painted houses lining narrow, winding streets. From Flekkefjord you can take Route E18, which heads inland here, to Stavanger. It is more rewarding, however, to go on the coast road—Route 44. Follow the coast road 40 km (25 mi) past the fishing port of Egersund to Ogna.

Ogna

② *93 km (57 mi) from Flekkefjord on Rte. 42.*

Ogna is known for the stretch of sandy beach that inspired so many Norwegian artists, among them Kitty Kjelland.

Hå Gamle Prestegaard (Old Parsonage), built in the 1780s, is now a cultural center for the area. ▣ NKr20. ☉ *May–mid-Sept., weekdays 11–7, Sat. noon–5, Sun. noon–7; late Sept.–Apr., Sat. noon–5, Sun. noon–7.*

Whichever road you choose to continue on out of Ogna, they both head northward along the rich agricultural coastal plain of the **Jæren district.** Flat and stony, it is the largest expanse of level terrain in this mountainous country. The mild climate and the absence of good harbors mean that the population here turned to agriculture, and the miles of stone walls are a testament to their labor.

Ancient monuments in Jæren are still visible, notably the **Hå gravesite** below the Hå parsonage near the Obrestad light. It consists of about 60 mounds, including two star-shaped and one boat-shaped, dating from around AD 500, all marked with stones. Take coastal Route 44.

Outdoor Activities and Sports

BIRD-WATCHING

The **Jærstrendene** in Jæren, from Randabergvika in the north to Ogna in the south, is a protected national park—and a good area for spotting puffins, cormorants, and black guillemots, as well as such waders as dunlins, little stints, and ringed plovers. Some areas of the park are closed to visitors, and it is forbidden to pick flowers or, for that matter, to disturb anything.

FISHING

Three of the 10 best fishing rivers in Norway, the **Ognaelva, Håelva,** and **Figgjo,** are in Jæren, just south of Stavanger. Fishing licenses, sold in grocery stores and gas stations, are required at all of them.

Orre

③ *North on Rte. 507 26 km (16 mi) from Ogna.*

Orre is the site of a medieval stone church. It also has one of the few preserved Viking graveyards, dating from the Bronze Age and Iron Age. Near Orre pond, slightly inland, is a bird-watching station.

Dining

$$ ✕ **Time Station.** This eatery (in fact the only one in Bryne) is next to the town's train station. Bryne is just up the road from Orre off Highway 507 and about a 40-minute train ride from Stavanger. Though the meat dishes are tasty, the house specialty is the seafood platter, with salmon, monkfish, ocean catfish, mussels, and ocean crayfish in a beurre blanc sauce. For dessert, try the *krumkake,* a cookie baked on an iron, wafer thin, shaped into a cone, and filled with blackberry cream. ✉ *Storgt. 346, 4340 Bryne,* ☎ *51/48–22–56. Reservations essential. AE, DC, MC, V. Closed Sun. No lunch weekdays.*

Sandnes

③ *25 km (16 mi) south of Stavanger, 52 km (32 mi) north of Orre.*

☺ In Sandnes is **Havana Badeland,** Norway's largest indoor aquapark for kids and adults, complete with a 300-ft water slide, whirlpool baths, saunas, a Turkish steambath, and massage parlors. ✉ *Hanaveien 17, 4300 Sandnes,* ☎ *51/62–92–00.* 🎟 *NKr95.* ☉ *Mid-June–mid-Aug., daily 10–8; late Aug.–early June, Tues., Thurs. 1–8, Wed., Fri., Sat. 10–9.*

Ullandhaug

③ *15 km (9 mi) west of Sandnes.*

Take your imagination further back in time at Ullandhaug, a reconstruction of an Iron Age farm. Three houses have been built around a central garden, and guides wearing period clothing demonstrate the daily activities of 1,500 years ago. ✉ *Grannesvn.,* ☎ *51/55–76–56.* 🎟 *NKr20.* ☉ *Mid-June–Aug., daily noon–5; early May–mid-June and early Sept., Sun. noon–4.*

You can see the place where what we know as Norway was founded by traveling 1½ km (1 mi) east on Grannesveien Ullandhaug to the **Harfsfjord.** In 872, in the Battle of Harfsfjord, Harald Hårfagre (Harald the Fair-Haired), the warrior king from the eastern country of Vestfold, finally succeeded in quelling the resistance of local chieftains in Rogaland and was promptly declared king of all Norway. A memorial in the shape of three giant swords plunged halfway into the earth marks the spot.

OFF THE BEATEN PATH
UTSTEIN KLOSTER – Originally the palace of Norway's first king, Harald Hårfagre, and later the residence of King Magnus VI, Utstein was used as a monastery from 1265 to 1537, when it reverted to the royal family. One of the best-preserved medieval monuments in Norway, the monastery opened to the public in 1965 and is today used to host classical and jazz concerts on Sunday afternoons during the summer.

After the concert, try the *Får i kål* (mutton, potatoes, and cabbage boiled in a peppery juice) at **Utstein Kloster Vertshus,** approximately 2 km (1 mi) from the monastery along the water's edge. To get to Utstein: buses depart from Stavanger at 12:15, returning from the monastery at 4:05, weekdays. It's about a half-hour drive from Stavanger. By car, travel north on coastal highway 1, through the world's second-longest undersea car tunnel. There is a toll of NKr75, plus NKr25 per pas-

senger for the tunnel passage. ⊠ *4156 Mosterøy,* ☎ *51/72–01–00.* 🖼
NKr20. ☉ *May–mid-Sept., Tues.–Sat. 1–4, Sun. noon–5.*

Stavanger

③③ *5 km (3 mi) east of Ullandhaug, 198 km (123 mi) from Kristiansand, 6 hrs from Bergen by car and ferry.*

Stavanger has always prospered from the riches of the sea. During the 19th century, huge harvests of brisling and herring established it as the sardine capital of the world. A resident is still called a Siddis, from S(ta-vanger) plus *iddis,* which means "sardine label," and the city's symbol, fittingly enough, is the key of a sardine can.

During the past two and a half decades, a different product from the sea has been Stavanger's lifeblood—oil. Since its discovery in the late 1960s, North Sea oil has transformed both the economy and the lifestyle of the city. In the early days of drilling, expertise was imported from abroad, chiefly from the United States. Although Norwegians have now taken over most of the projects, foreigners constitute almost a tenth of the inhabitants, making Stavanger the country's most international city. Though the population hovers around 142,000, the city has all the agreeable bustle of one many times its size. However, the city's charm still remains—in the heart of **Old Stavanger** you can wind down narrow cobblestone streets past small, white houses and craft shops with many-paned windows and terra-cotta roof tiles.

Stavanger Domkirke (cathedral), a large, well-preserved medieval church, is in the city center next to Breiavatnet, a small pond. Construction was begun in 1125 by Bishop Reinald of Winchester, who was probably assisted by English craftsmen. Largely destroyed by fire in 1272, the church was rebuilt to include a Gothic chancel. The result: its once elegant lines are now festooned with macabre death symbols and airborne putti. Next to the cathedral is **Kongsgård,** formerly a residence of bishops and kings but now a school and not open to visitors. 🖼 *Free.* ☉ *Mid-May–mid-Sept., Mon.–Sat. 9–6; mid-Sept.–mid-May, Mon.–Sat. 9–2, Sun. 1–6.*

Breidablikk manor house has been perfectly preserved since the '60s and feels as if the owner has only momentarily slipped away. An outstanding example of what the Norwegians call "Swiss-style" architecture, this house was built by a Norwegian shipping magnate. In spite of its foreign label, the house is uniquely Norwegian, inspired by national romanticism. ⊠ *Eiganesvn. 40A, 4009,* ☎ *51/52–60–35.* 🖼 *NKr30. Also includes admission to Ledaal, Norsk Hermetikkmuseum, and Sjøfartsmuseet.* ☉ *Mid-June–mid-Aug., daily 11–4; mid-Aug.–mid-June, Sun. 11–4.*

Ledaal, the royal family's Stavanger residence, is a stately house built by the Kielland family in 1799. The second-floor library is dedicated to the writer Alexander Kielland, a social critic and satirist. ⊠ *Eiganesvn. 45, 4009,* ☎ *51/52–06–18.* 🖼 *NKr30. Also includes admission to Breidablikk, Norsk Hermetikkmuseum, and Sjøfartsmuseet.* ☉ *Mid-June–mid-Aug., daily 11–4; mid-Aug.–mid-June, Sun. 11–4.*

☾ This fascinating, albeit obscure, museum, the **Norsk Hermetikkmuseum** (Canning Museum), is housed in a former canning factory. Exhibits document the processing of brisling and sardines—the city's most important industry for nearly 100 years, thanks greatly to savvy turn-of-the-century packaging (naturally, the inventor of the sardine-can key was from Stavanger). ⊠ *Øvre Strandgt. 88A, 4005,* ☎ *51/53–49–89.* 🖼 *NKr30. Also includes admission to Ledaal, Breidablikk, and Sjø-*

fartsmuseet. ☉ *Mid-June–mid-Aug., daily 11–4; early June and late Aug., Tues.–Fri. 11–3, Sun. 11–4; Sept.–May, Sun. 11–4.*

Along Strandkaien, warehouses face the wharf; the shops, offices, and apartments face the street on the other side. Housed in the only two shipping merchants' houses that remain completely intact is the **Sjø-fartsmuseet** (Maritime Museum). Inside, the house is just as it was a century ago, complete with office furniture, files, and posters, while the apartments show the standard of living for the mercantile class at that time. Although signs are only in Norwegian, an English-language guidebook and guided tours outside normal opening hours are available. ⊠ *Nedre Strandgt. 17–19, 4005,* ☎ *51/52–59–11.* ⊠ *NKr30. Also includes admission to Ledaal, Breidablikk, and Norsk Her-metikkmuseum.* ☉ *Mid-June–mid-Aug., daily 11–4; early June and late Aug., Sun. 11–4.*

You can easily spot the spiky **Valbergtårnet** (⊠ Valberget 4, ☎ 51/89–55–01) from any spot on the quay. Built on the highest point of the old city, this tower was a firewatch. Today it is a crafts center, which may not interest you, but it's still worth a visit for the view.

If you are of Norwegian stock you can trace your roots at **Det Norske Utvandresenteret** (Norwegian Emigration Center). Bring along any information you have, especially where your ancestors came from in Norway and when they left the country. The center is on the fourth floor of the brick *Ligningskontoret* (Tax Office) building a few minutes' walk from the harbor. You can make arrangements via fax to have the center do research for you, but the wait for this service is long. If you're in the area in early summer, call for information on the "emigration festival" that the center organizes each June. ⊠ *Bergjelandsgt. 30, 4012 Stavanger,* ☎ *51/50–12–74,* ℻ *51/50–12–90.* ⊠ *Free, but each written request costs NKr180.* ☉ *Weekdays 9–3, Sat. 9–1.*

Rogaland Kunstmuseum houses the country's largest collection of works by Lars Hertervig, a Romantic painter who is considered one of the country's greatest artists. Other exhibits include Norwegian art from the early 19th century to the present. The museum is near Mosvannet (Moss Lake), which is just off highway E18 at the northern end of downtown. ⊠ *Tjensvoll 6, 4021 Mosvannsparken,* ☎ *51/53–09–00.* ⊠ *NKr30.* ☉ *Tues.–Fri. 10–2, Sat. 11–2, Sun. 11–5.*

⟳ **Kongeparken Amusement Park** has a 281-ft-long figure of Gulliver and a lifelike dinosaur exhibit as its main attractions, and plenty of rides. ⊠ *4330 Ålgård,* ☎ *51/61–71–11.* ⊠ *NKr110.* ☉ *Mid-May–mid-June, weekends 10–6; mid-June–mid-Aug., daily 10–7; mid-Aug.–Sept., weekends 10–7.*

OFF THE BEATEN PATH

PREKESTOLEN – Pulpit Rock, a huge cube with a vertical drop of 2,000 ft, is not a good destination if you suffer from vertigo but is great for a heart-stopping view. The clifflike rock sits on the banks of the finger-shaped Lysefjord. You can join a tour to get there (☞ Guided Tours, *in* Sørlandet A to Z, *below*), or you can do it on your own from June 16 to August 25 by taking the ferry from Fiskepiren across Hildefjorden to Tau. (It takes about 40 minutes from Stavanger.) In summer, a bus runs regularly from the ferry to the parking lot at the Pulpit Rock Lodge. It takes 1½ to 2 hours to walk from the lodge to the rock—the well-marked trail crosses some uneven terrain, so good walking shoes or boots are vital. Food and lodging are near the trail.

LYSEFJORDSENTERET – Lysefjord Center, whose shape mimics the mountains, takes visitors through a multimedia simulation of how a trickling brook created this sliver of a fjord. A ferry to the bottom side of Pulpit

Rock will drop off passengers midway (for more information, call Clipper Fjord Sightseeing, ☎ 51/89–52–70). Note that at press time the center's future opening times were uncertain, but the center will always gladly open for visitors with an appointment, so be sure to call ahead. ✉ Oanes 4110 Forsand, ☎ 51/70–31–23. ✎ NKr50. ☉ May, daily 11–6; June–Aug., daily 10–8; Sept.–Apr., Sun. 11–6.

Dining and Lodging

$$$$ ✕ **Jans Mat & Vinhus.** The cellar setting is rustic, with old stone walls
★   and robust sideboards providing a nice counterpoint to the refined menu. Saddle of Rogaland county lamb is boned and rolled around a thyme-flavored stuffing, and the fillet is topped with a crunchy mustard crust. For dessert, try the nougat parfait dusted with cocoa. ✉ Breitorget 4, 4006, ☎ 51/89–47–73. Reservations essential. Jacket and tie. AE, DC, MC, V. No lunch. Closed Sun.

$$$ ✕ **Sjøhuset Skagen.** Just a few doors down from N.B. Sørensen's (☞ below), this spot is similar in decor, but with a greater variety of food. Try the crêpes stuffed with roe of chapelin, onion, and sour cream, and the marinated salmon, Norwegian style, with potatoes in a dill-and-cream sauce. The Brie served with cloudberries marinated in whiskey is excellent. ✉ Skagen 16, 4006, ☎ 51/89–51–80. AE, DC, MC, V.

$$$ ✕ **Straen Fiskerestaurant.** Right on the quay with two old-fashioned dining rooms, Straen is considered by many the city's best fish restaurant. The three-course meal of the day is always the best value. A rock club, a rock café, and a pub are on the premises. ✉ Nedre Strandgt. 15, 4005, ☎ 51/84–37–00 or 51/52–61–00. AE, DC, MC, V. No lunch. Closed Sun.

$$ ✕ **City Bistro.** Choose from reindeer medallions with rowanberry jelly, deer fillet with lingonberries and pears, or halibut poached in cream with saffron, garnished with shrimp, crayfish, and mussels at this bistro, where you'll dine at massive oak tables in a turn-of-the-century house. ✉ Madlavn. 18–20, 4008, ☎ 51/53–95–70. Reservations essential. AE, DC, MC, V. No lunch.

$$ ✕ **Harry Pepper.** This trendy Mexican restaurant has a popular bar. The color schemes are fun, bright, and gaudy, as are the displays of tacky souvenirs. ✉ Øvre Holmegt. 15, 4006, ☎ 51/89–39–93. AE, DC, V.

$–$$ ✕ **N.B. Sørensen's Dampskibsexpedition.** In a restored warehouse dec-
★   orated with nautical ropes, rustic barrels, and gaslights, this bar and restaurant is right on the quay. The food is nouvelle Norwegian. Try the marinated shrimp appetizer and the baked monkfish. The dish of the day, as well as the red house wine, which is always waiting for customers in an N.B. Sørensen's bottle on each table, is one of the better deals in Stavanger. ✉ Skagen 26, 4006, ☎ 51/89–12–70. AE, DC, MC, V.

$ ✕ **Café Sting.** Right at the foot of the Valbergtårnet, it's a restaurant–gallery–concert hall–meeting place day and night. All food is made in-house and is better than most other inexpensive fare in Norway. There's a skillet dish with crisp fried potatoes and bacon, flavored with leek, and topped with melted cheese and sour cream; and a meat loaf with mashed potatoes and sprinkled with cheese. The chocolate and almond cakes are served with delicious hot chocolate. ✉ Valberget. 3, 4006, ☎ 51/89–38–78. AE, DC, MC, V.

$$$–$$$$ 🛏 **Radisson Atlantic Hotel.** The largest hotel in Stavanger, the Atlantic overlooks Breiavatnet pond in the heart of downtown. The feel is that of an international luxury hotel with several restaurants and the most popular nightclubs in town, but with little local flair. Rooms, which come in four different standards, are immaculate with heavy quilts, thick carpets, and cushy stuffed chairs. 🛏 Olav V's Gt. 3, 4005 Stavanger, ☎

51/52–75–20, FAX 51/53–48–69. 351 rooms, 5 suites. Restaurant, bar, café, pub, dance club, nightclub, meeting rooms. AE, DC, MC, V.

$$–$$$ 🖼 **Skagen Brygge.** Housed in three rehabilitated old sea houses, almost all rooms are different here, from modern to old-fashioned maritime, with exposed beams and brick and wood walls; many have harbor views. The hotel has an arrangement with 14 restaurants in the area—they make the reservations and the tab ends up on your hotel bill. 🖼 *Skagenkaien 30, 4006,* 🕾 *51/89–41–00, FAX 51/89–58–83. 106 rooms. Bar, sauna, Turkish bath, health club, convention center. AE, DC, MC, V.*

$–$$$ 🖼 **Victoria Hotel.** Stavanger's oldest hotel was built at the turn of the century and still retains a clubby, Victorian style, with elegant carved beds and leather sofas. Rooms on the front overlook the harbor. Ask about a discount at the Trimoteket health club, just behind the hotel. 🖼 *Skansegt. 1, 4006 Stavanger,* 🕾 *51/89–60–00, FAX 51/89–54–10. 107 rooms, 3 suites. Restaurant, bar, breakfast room, meeting room. AE, DC, MC, V.*

$–$$ 🖼 **Grand Hotel.** This place on the edge of the town center doesn't aim to be fancy; rooms are comfortable and bright, done in light pastels and white. In summer the rates drop significantly. 🖼 *Klubbgt. 3, Boks 80, 4012,* 🕾 *51/53–30–20, FAX 51/56–19–42. 92 rooms. Bar, breakfast room. AE, DC, MC, V.*

Nightlife and the Arts

NIGHTLIFE

In summer people are out at all hours, and sidewalk restaurants stay open until the sun comes up. Start a sunny evening at **Hansen Hjørnet**'s outdoor restaurant and bar (⊠ Skagenkn. 18, 🕾 51/89–52–80). Walk along **Skagenkaien** and **Strandkaien** for a choice of pubs and nightclubs. Among media junkies the place for a beer and a bit of CNN is the **Newsman** (⊠ Skagen 14, 🕾 51/53–57–09). **Taket Nattklubb** (⊠ Nedre Strandgt. 15, 🕾 51/84–37–00) is for the mid-20s and above crowd, whereas **Berlin** (⊠ Lars Hertervigs Gt. 5, 🕾 51/52–40–40) brings in youngish martini drinkers.

THE ARTS

Stavanger Konserthus (⊠ Concert Hall, Bjergsted, 🕾 51/56–17–16) features local artists and hosts free summertime foyer concerts. Built on an island in the archipelago in the Middle Ages, today **Utstein Kloster** (☞ *above*) is used for its superior acoustics and hosts classical and jazz concerts from June to August.

Outdoor Activities and Sports

BIKING

If you want to cycle around town, you can rent a bike at **Sykkelhuset** (⊠ Løkkevn. 33, 🕾 51/53–99–10). From Stavanger you can take your bike onto the ferry that departs for Finnøy. Spend the day or longer: weeklong cottage rentals are available from **Finnøy Fjordsenter** (⊠ 4160, Judaberg, 🕾 51/71–26–46, FAX 51/54–17–62). For more information about cottages in the archipelago and maps, contact the Stavanger Tourist Board (☞ Visitor Information *in* Sørlandet A to Z, *below*). The Ministry of the Environment can also provide information; call its **Bike Project** (⊠ Sandnes Turistinformasjon, Langgt. 8, 4300 Sandnes, 🕾 51/62–52–40).

FISHING

North of Stavanger is the longest salmon river in western Norway, the **Suldalslågen,** made popular 100 years ago by a Scottish aristocrat who built a fishing lodge there. **Lindum** still has cabins and camping facilities, as well as a dining room. Contact the **Lakseslottet Lindum** (⊠ N–4240 Suldalsosen, 🕾 52/79–91–61). The main salmon season is July through September. On the island of **Kvitsøy,** in the archipelago just west of Stavanger, you can rent an apartment, complete with fish-smoking and -freezing facilities, and arrange to use a small sail- or motorboat. Contact **Kvitsøy Maritime Senter** (⊠ Box 35, 4090 Kvitsøy, ☎ 51/73–51–88).

GOLF

The **Stavanger Golfklubb** (⊠ Longebakken 45, 4042 Hafrsfjord, ☎ 51/55–54–31) offers a lush, 18-hole, international-championship course and equipment rental.

HIKING

Stavanger Turistforening (⊠ Postboks 239, 4001 Stavanger, ☎ 51/52–75–66) can plan a hike through the area, particularly in the rolling **Setesdalsheiene** and the thousands of islands and skerries of the **Ryfylke Archipelago.** The tourist board oversees 33 cabins for members (you can join on the spot) for overnighting along the way. Also in the Ryfylke area is a hike up **Kjerag,** a sheet of granite mountain that soars 3,555 ft, at the Lysefjord, near Forsand—ideal for thrill seekers.

SKIING

Skiing in **Sirdal,** 2½ hours from Stavanger, is good from January to April. Special ski buses leave Stavanger on the weekends at 8:30 AM during the season. Especially recommended is **Sinnes** for its non–hair-raising cross-country terrain. Downhill skiing is available at **Alsheia** on the same bus route. Contact **SOT Reiser** (⊠ Treskeveien 5, 4040 Hafrsfjord, Stavanger, ☎ 51/59–90–66) for transportation information.

WATER SPORTS

Diving is excellent all along the coast—although Norwegian law requires all foreigners to dive with a Norwegian as a way of ensuring that wrecks are left undisturbed. Contact **Dive In** (⊠ Madlaveien 5, Stavanger, ☎ 51/52–99–00), which rents equipment.

Shopping

Figgjo Ceramics (⊠ Rte. E18, 4333 Figgjo, ☎ 51/68–35–00; 51/68–35–70 after 3:30) is outside town; the factory's beginnings in World War II are documented in an adjoining museum. A seconds shop has discounts of about 50%. **Skjæveland Strikkevarefabrikk** (⊠ 4330 Ålgård, ☎ 51/61–85–06) has a huge selection of sweaters at discount prices.

Sørlandet A to Z

Arriving and Departing

BY BOAT

Color Line (⊠ Strandkaien, Stavanger, ☎ 51/52–45–45) has four ships weekly on the Stavanger–Newcastle route. High-speed boats to Bergen are operated by **Flaggruten** (☎ 51/89–50–90). There is also a car ferry from Hirtshals, in northern Denmark, that takes about four hours to make the crossing. Another connects Larvik to Frederikshavn, on Denmark's west coast. In Denmark contact **DSB** (☎ 33/14–17–01); in Norway contact **Color Line** (☎ 51/52–45–45, 38/07–88–88 in Kristiansand) or **DFDS Seaways** (☎ 22/41–90–90).

BY BUS

Aust-Agder Trafikkselskap (☎ 37/02–65–00), based in Arendal, has one departure daily in each direction for the 5½- to six-hour journey between Oslo and Kristiansand.

Sørlandsruta (☎ 38/02–43–80), based in Mandal, has two departures in each direction for the 4½-hour trip from Kristiansand (Strandgt. 33) to Stavanger.

For information about both long-distance and local bus services in **Stavanger,** call ☎ 51/56–71–71; the bus terminal is outside the train station. In **Kristiansand,** call ☎ 38/02–43–80.

BY CAR

From Oslo, it is 329 km (203 mi) to Kristiansand and 574 km (352 mi) to Stavanger. Route E18 parallels the coastline but stays slightly inland on the eastern side of the country and farther inland in the western part. Although seldom wider than two lanes, it is easy driving because it is so flat.

BY PLANE

Kristiansand: Kjevik Airport, 16 km (10 mi) outside town, is served by **Braathens SAFE** (☎ 38/00–80–00), with nonstop flights from Oslo, Bergen, and Stavanger, and **SAS** (☎ 81/00–33–00), with nonstop flights to Copenhagen. **MUK Air** serves Aalborg, Denmark; **Agder Fly** serves Göteborg, Sweden, and Billund, Denmark. Tickets on the last two can be booked with Braathens or SAS.

The **airport bus** departs from the Braathens SAFE office (✉ Vestre Strandgate, ☎ 94/67–22–42) approximately one hour before every departure and proceeds, via downtown hotels, directly to Kjevik. Tickets cost NKr40.

Stavanger: Sola Airport is 14 km (9 mi) from downtown. **Braathens SAFE** (☎ 51/51–10–00) has nonstop flights from Oslo, Kristiansand, Bergen, Trondheim, and Newcastle. **SAS** (☎ 81/00–33–00) has nonstop flights from Bergen, Oslo, Copenhagen, Aberdeen, Göteborg, London, and Newcastle. **KLM** (☎ 51/64–81–20) and **British Airways** (☎ 80/03–00–77) have nonstop flights to Stavanger from Billund and London, respectively. **Air UK** (☎ 51/65–26–30) flies nonstop from London.

The **Flybussen** (airport bus) leaves the airport every 15 minutes. It stops at hotels and outside the railroad station in Stavanger. Tickets cost NKr35.

BY TRAIN

The **Sørlandsbanen** leaves Oslo S Station four times daily for the approximately five-hour journey to Kristiansand and three times daily for the 8½- to nine-hour journey to Stavanger. Two more trains travel the 3½-hour Kristiansand–Stavanger route. Kristiansand's train station is at Vestre Strandgata (☎ 38/07–75–30). For information on trains from Stavanger, call ☎ 51/56–96–00.

Getting Around

BY BUS

Bus connections in Sørlandet are infrequent; the tourist office can provide a comprehensive schedule. Tickets on Stavanger's excellent bus network cost NKr14.

BY CAR

Sørlandet is flat, so it's easy driving throughout. The area around the Kulturhus in the Stavanger city center is closed to car traffic, and one-way traffic is the norm in the rest of the downtown area. Parking is available in numerous marked lots and is free with the **Stavanger Card** (☞ *below*).

BY TAXI

All **Kristiansand** taxis are connected with a central dispatching office (☎ 38/03–27–00), as are **Stavanger** taxis (☎ 51/88–41–00). Journeys within Stavanger are charged by the taxi meter, otherwise by the kilometer. The initial charge is NKr24 (NKr36 at night), with NKr13 per kilometer during the day and NKr15 at night.

Stavanger: The **Stavanger Card,** sold at hotels, post offices, and Stavanger Tourist Information, gives discounts of up to 50% on sightseeing tours, regional and long-distance, buses, car rentals, and other services and attractions. Parking, local buses, and museum admissions are free with the Stavanger Card, which costs NKr110, NKr190, or NKr240 for one, two, or three days, respectively. For more information call the Stavanger tourist office (☎ 51/85–92–00).

Contacts and Resources

DOCTORS AND DENTISTS

Doctors: In Kristiansand, **Kvadraturen Legesenter** (⊠ Vestre Strandgt. 32, 4611, ☎ 38/02–66–11) is open 8–4. **Dentists:** In Kristiansand, **Skoletannklinikken** (⊠ Festningsgt. 40, ☎ 38/02–19–71) is open 7–3.

EMERGENCIES

Police: ☎ 112. **Fire:** ☎ 111. **Ambulance:** ☎ 113. **Car Rescue:** in Kristiansand, ☎ 38/12–47–00; in Stavanger, ☎ 51/58–29–00.

Hospital Emergency Rooms: In Kristiansand, **Røde Kors** (Red Cross) **Legevakt** (Egsvei, ☎ 38/02–52–20) is open weekdays 4 PM–8 AM and weekends 24 hours. In Stavanger, call **Rogaland Sentralsykehus** (☎ 51/51–80–00).

GUIDED TOURS

Kristiansand: Tours of Kristiansand run summer only. The **City Train** (⊠ Rådhusgt. 11, 4611, ☎ 38/03–05–24) is a 15-minute tour of the center. The M/S *Maarten* (⊠ Pier 6 by Fiskebrygga, ☎ 38/12–13–14) offers two-hour tours of the eastern archipelago and a three-hour tour of the western archipelago early June–late August.

Stavanger: A two-hour bus tour leaves from the marina at **Vågen** daily at 1 between June and August. **Rødne Clipperkontoret** (⊠ Skagenkaien 18, 4006, ☎ 51/89–52–70) offers three different tours. **Rogaland Trafikkselskap** (☎ 51/56–71–71 or 51/52–26–00) does the same, in either high-speed boats or ferries.

LATE-NIGHT PHARMACIES

Elefantapoteket (⊠ Gyldenløvesgt. 13, 4611, Kristiansand, ☎ 38/02–20–12) is open weekdays 8:30–8, Saturday 8:30–6, Sunday 3–6. **Løveapoteket** (⊠ Olav V's Gt. 11, 4005, Stavanger, ☎ 51/52–06–07) is open daily 8 AM–11 PM.

VISITOR INFORMATION

Arendal (SørlandsInfo, ⊠ Arendal Næringsråd, Friholmsgt. 1, 4800, ☎ 37/02–21–93). **Kristiansand** (⊠ Dronningensgt. 2, Box 592, 4601, ☎ 38/12–13–14, FAX 38/02–52–55). **Larvik** (⊠ Storgt. 48, 3250, ☎ 33/13–01–00). **Mandal** (Mandal og Lindesnes Turistkontor, ⊠ Bryggegt., 4500, ☎ 38/27–83–00). **Stavanger** (Stavanger Kulturhus, ⊠ Sølvberget, ☎ 51/85–92-00).

6 Bergen

Bergen is the gateway to Norway's fjord country, and though it's Norway's second largest city, it's managed to maintain an intimate, small-town feeling.

PEOPLE FROM BERGEN like to say they do not come from Norway but from Bergen. Enfolded at the crook of seven mountains and fish-boned by seven fjords, Bergen does seem far from the rest of Norway.

Hanseatic merchants from northern Germany settled in Bergen during the 14th century and made it one of their four major overseas trading centers. The surviving Hanseatic buildings on Bryggen (the quay) are neatly topped with triangular cookie-cutter roofs and scrupulously painted red, blue, yellow, and green. A monument in themselves (they are on the UNESCO World Heritage List), they now house boutiques, restaurants, and museums. In the evening, when the harborside is illuminated, these modest buildings, together with the stocky Rosenkrantz Tower and the yachts lining the pier, are reflected in the water—and provide one of the loveliest cityscapes in northern Europe.

During the Hanseatic period, this active port was Norway's capital and largest city. Boats from northern Norway brought dried fish to Bergen to be shipped abroad by the Dutch, English, Scottish, and German merchants who had settled here. By the time the Hansa lost power, the city had an ample supply of wealthy local merchants and shipowners to replace them. For years Bergen was the capital of shipping, and until well into the 19th century, it remained the country's major city.

Culturally Bergen has also had its luminaries, including dramatist Ludvig Holberg, Scandinavia's answer to Molière—whom the Danes claim as their own. Bergensers know better. Norway's musical geniuses Ole Bull and Edvard Grieg also came from the city of the seven hills. Once you've visited Troldhaugen, Grieg's "Hill of Trolls," you'll understand his inspiration. In fact, the city of Bergen has been picked as the European Union's "European Center of Culture" for the year 2000.

About 219,000 people live in the greater metropolitan area now, compared with nearly 500,000 in Oslo. Even though the balance of power has shifted to the capital, Bergen remains a strong commercial force, thanks to shipping and oil, and is a cultural center, with an international music and arts festival every spring. Although it's true that an umbrella and slicker are necessary in this town, the raindrops—actually 219 days per year of them—never obstruct the lovely views.

EXPLORING BERGEN

The heartbeat of Bergen is at Torgalmenningen, the main pedestrian street that runs from the city's central square to the Fisketorget, which sits on the harbor and faces *Bryggen* (the wharf). From here, the rest of the city spreads up the sides of the seven mountains that surround Bergen, with some sights concentrated near the university or a small lake called Lille Lungegårdsvann. Fløyen, the mountain to the east of the harbor, is the most accessible for day-trippers. Before you begin your walking tour, you can take the funicular up to the top of it for a particularly fabulous overview of the city. Bergen is a very walkable city—especially when the sun's shining. If the weather's nice, you may want to take a couple of hours and just wander the streets, exploring the narrow cobblestone alleyways, charming wood houses, and quaint cafés.

Historic Bergen: Bryggen to Fløyen

A Good Walk

Start your tour in the center of town at Torget, also called **Fisketorget** ㉞ or the Fish Market, where fisherman and farmers deal their goods.

Next, walk over to **Bryggen** ③⑤, the wharf on the northeast side of Bergen's harbor. The gabled wood warehouses lining the docks mark the site of the city's original settlement. Take time to walk the narrow passageways between buildings; shops and galleries are hidden among the wooden facades. Follow the pier to the **Hanseatisk Museum** ③⑥ at Finnegården and have a look inside. Afterward, continue your walk down the wharf, past the historic buildings to the end of the Holmen promontory and to **Bergenhus Festning** ③⑦ (Bergenhus Fort), which dates from the 13th century; the nearby **Rosenkrantztårnet** is a 16th-century tower residence. After you've spent some time out here, retrace your steps back to the Radisson SAS Hotel. Beside the hotel is **Bryggens Museum** ③⑧, which houses some magnificent archaeological finds. Just behind the museum is the 12th-century church called **Mariakirken** ③⑨. Around the back of the church up the small hill is Øvregaten, a street that's the back boundary of Bryggen. Walk down Øvregaten four blocks to **Fløybanen** ④⓪, the funicular that runs up and down Fløyen, one of the city's most popular hiking mountains. Don't miss a trip to the top, whether you hike or take the funicular—the view is like no other. At the base of the funicular is Lille Øvregaten. On this street, and in the area of crooked streets and hodgepodge architecture nearby, you'll find most of Bergen's antiques shops. On your left, at the intersection with Kong Oscars Gate is **Bergen Domkirke** ④① (Bergen Cathedral). Last, head back to Torgalmenningen in the center of town for a late afternoon snack at one of the square's cafés.

TIMING

This tour will take a good portion of a day. Be sure to get to the Fisketorget early in the morning, as many days it may close as early as 1 or 2. Also, try to plan your trip up Fløyen for a sunny day. Although it may be tough, as Bergen is renowned for rain, you may want to wait a day or two to see if the skies clear up.

Sights to See

OFF THE
BEATEN PATH

AKVARIET – Penguins—several kinds, one of which has a platinum feather "hairdo," strangely appropriate in this land of blonds—seem to be the main attraction at the aquarium. There are also several seals and 50 tanks with a wide variety of fish. Try to catch the movie on Bergen, which is presented on a 360° "supervideograph" screen; it's directed by one of Norway's most beloved animators, Ivo Caprino. The aquarium is on Nordnes Peninsula, a 15-minute walk from the fish market, or take Bus 4. ✉ *Nordnesparken,* ☎ *55/23–85–53.* ⊡ *NKr50.* ⊙ *May–Sept, daily 9–8; Oct.–Apr., daily 10–6. Feeding times: 11, 2, and 6 in summer; noon and 4 in winter.*

④① **Bergen Domkirke** (Bergen Cathedral). This building is constructed in a profusion of styles. The oldest parts, the choir and lower portion of the tower, date from the 13th century. ✉ *Kong Oscars gt. and Domkirkegt.,* ☎ *55/31–04–70.* ⊙ *Weekdays 11–2 in summer only.*

③⑦ **Bergenhus Festning** (Bergenhus Fortress). The buildings here date from the mid-13th century. **Håkonshallen,** a royal ceremonial hall erected during the reign of Håkon Håkonsson between 1247 and 1261, was badly damaged by the explosion of a German ammunition ship in 1944 but was restored by 1961. The nearby **Rosenkrantztårnet** (Rosenkrantz Tower), also damaged in the same explosion, has been extensively restored as well. The Danish governor of Bergenhus, Erik Rosenkrantz, built this tower in the 1560s as an official residence and fortification. It is furnished in a formal, austere style. ✉ *Bergenhus,* ☎ *55/31–60–67.* ⊡ *NKr15.* ⊙ *Mid-May–mid-Sept., daily 10–4; mid-Sept.–mid-May,*

Bergen

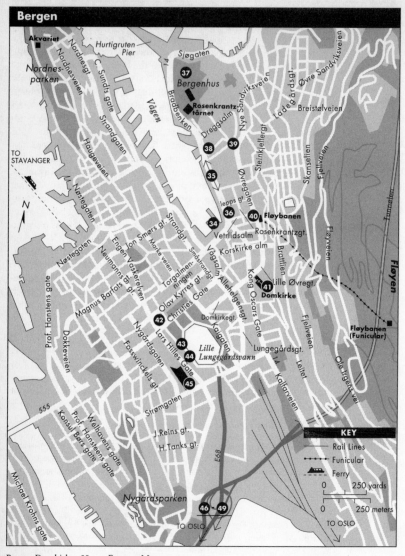

Akvariet

Nordnes-
parken

Hurtigruten
Pier

Sjøgaten

Nordnesveien

Nordnesgt

C. Sundts gate

Strandgaten

Haugeveien

Vågen

Bradbenken

37

Bergenhus

Rosenkrantz
tårnet

Dregasalm

Nye Sandviksveien

Ladegårdsgt.

Øvre Sandviksveien

Breistølveien

TO
STAVANGER

Nøstegaten

N

38

39

35

Steinkjellergt

Skanselien

Fjellveien

Tunnelen

Nøstegaten

Neumanns gt.

Engen

Vaskerelven

Jon Smørs gt.

Marke veien

Strandgt.

Torgalmen-
ningen

Sandstrandgt.

Vågsalm

Allehelgensg.

Øvregaten

Iepps gt.

34

36

Vetrlidsalm

40

Fløybanen

Rosenkrantzgt.

Korskirke alm

Brattlien

Fløyveien

Fløyen

Magnus Barfots gt.

Olav Kyrres gt.

Christies Gate

Kaigaten

Domkirkegt.

Kong Oscars Gate

Lille Øvregt.

41

Domkirke

Fjellveien

Fløybanen
(Funicular)

Prof. Hanstens gate

Dokkeveien

Nygårdsgaten

Lars Hilles Gate

42

43

44

Lille
Lungegårdsvann

Lungegårdsgt.

Leitet

Kalfarveien

Ole Irgens vei

Fosswinckels gt.

45

Strømgaten

555

Welhavens gate

Prof. Hansteens gate

Konsul Børs gate

J. Reins gt.

H. Tanks gt.

F68

KEY

Rail Lines

Funicular

Ferry

0   250 yards

0   250 meters

Michael Krohns gate

Nygårdsparken

46   49

TO OSLO

TO OSLO

daily noon–3, also Thurs. 3–6. Guided tours every hr. Closed during Bergen International Music Festival.

㉟ Bryggen (The Docks, Wharf, or Quays). A trip to Bergen is not complete until you visit Bryggen. One of the most charming walkways in Europe (especially on a sunny day—this town is known for rain, just ask any Bergenser), this row of 14th-century painted wooden buildings facing the harbor was built by Hansa merchants. The buildings, which are on the UNESCO World Heritage List, are mostly reconstructions, with the oldest dating from 1702. Several fires, the latest in 1955, destroyed the original structures.

㊳ Bryggens Museum. Artifacts found during excavations on Bryggen, including 12th-century buildings constructed on site from the original foundations, are on display here. The collection provides a good picture of daily life before and during the heyday of the Hansa, down to a two-seater outhouse. ⊠ *Bryggen, 5020,* ☎ *55/31–67–10.* ⊑ *NKr20.* ☺ *May–Aug., daily 10–5; Sept.–Apr., weekdays 11–3, Sat. noon–3, Sun. noon–4.*

㉞ Fisketorget (Fish Market). At the turn of the century, views of this active and pungent square, with fishermen in Wellington boots and mackintoshes and women in long aprons, were popular postcard subjects. Times haven't changed; the marketplace remains just as picturesque—bring your camera. ☺ *Mon.–Wed. and Fri. 7–4, Thurs. 7–7, Sat. 7–3.*

NEED A
BREAK?

For an inexpensive snack, try one of the open-face salmon sandwiches sold at the Fish Market. In summer, an array of beautiful, juicy berries is usually available at the adjacent fruit stands. The Norwegian *jordbær* (strawberries) are sure to be some of the best you'll ever have—smaller, but much more flavorful than most American varieties.

㊵ Fløybanen (Fløyen Funicular). The most astonishing view of Bergen is from the top of **Fløyen,** the most popular of the city's seven mountains. A funicular (a cable car that runs on tracks on the ground) takes you to a lookout point 1,050 ft above the sea. Several marked trails lead from Fløyen into the surrounding wooded area, or you can walk back to town on Fjellveien, which is a common Sunday activity for many locals. ⊑ *NKr30; one-way tickets are half-price.* ☺ *Rides every half hour 7:30 AM–11 PM, Sat. from 8 AM, Sun. from 9 AM. It runs until midnight May–Sept.*

㊱ Hanseatisk Museum (Hanseatic Museum). One of the best-preserved buildings in Bergen, it was the office and home of an affluent German merchant. The apprentices lived upstairs, in boxed-in beds with windows cut into the wall so the tiny cells could be made up from the hall. Although claustrophobic, they retained body heat, practical in these unheated buildings. The 16th-century interior here will give you a feel for the life of a Hanseatic merchant. ⊠ *Bryggen,* ☎ *55/31–41–89.* ⊑ *NKr35; off-season NKr20.* ☺ *June–Aug., daily 9–5; Sept.–May, daily 11–2. Ticket is also valid for entrance to Schøtstuene, Hanseatic Assembly Rooms.*

㊴ Mariakirken (St. Mary's Church). It began as a Romanesque church in the 12th-century but gained a Gothic choir, richly decorated portals, and a splendid Baroque pulpit, much of it added by the Hanseatic merchants who owned it during the 15th and 16th centuries. Organ recitals are held Tuesday and Thursday mid-June through late August. ⊠ *Dreggen, 5020,* ☎ *55/31–59–60.* ⊑ *NKr10 in summer.* ☺ *Mid-May–early Sept., weekdays 11–4; early Sept.–mid-May, Tues.–Fri. noon–1:30.*

Rasmus Meyers Allé and Grieghallen

A Good Walk

From Torgalmenningen, walk to Nordahl Bruns Gate and turn left for the **Vestlandske Kunstindustrimuseum** ㊷, the West Norway Museum of Applied Art. After viewing some of the museum's elaborately crafted works, exit the museum and head for Christies Gate. Follow it along the park and turn left on Rasmus Meyers Allé, which runs along the small lake, Lille Lungegårdsvann, to reach **Stenersens Samling** ㊸, an art museum that has some very impressive holdings, with works by Kandinsky and Klee. Just beyond Stenersens is **Rasmus Meyers Samlinger** ㊹, another museum with equally exciting works, including a large Munch collection. Behind these museums on Lars Hills Gate is **Grieghallen** ㊺, Bergen's famous music hall. Although the building's architecture is interesting from street level, try to get a peek of it from the top of Fløyen, where the shape may remind you of a grand piano.

TIMING

All of the museums on this tour are quite small and very near to each other, so you probably won't need more than half a day to complete this tour.

Sights to See

㊺ **Grieghallen.** Home of the Bergen Philharmonic Orchestra and stage for the annual International Music Festival, this music hall is a conspicuous slab of glass and concrete, but the acoustics are marvelous. Built in 1978, the hall was named for the city's famous son, composer Edvard Grieg (1843–1907). ✉ *Lars Hills Gt. 3A,* ☎ *55/21–61–50.*

㊹ **Rasmus Meyers Samlinger.** Meyer, a businessman who lived from 1858 to 1916, assembled a superb art collection, with many names that are famous today but were unknown when he acquired them. Here you'll see the best Munch paintings outside Oslo, as well as major works by Scandinavian impressionists. The gallery hosts summertime Grieg concerts. ✉ *Rasmus Meyers Allé 7,* ☎ *55/56–80–00.* ✉ *NKr35.* ☉ *Mid-May–mid-Sept., Tues., Wed., Fri. 10–3, Thurs. noon–7, Sat. 11–4, Sun. noon–5; late Sept.–early May, Tues.–Sun. noon–3.*

㊸ **Stenersens Samling.** This is an extremely impressive collection of modern art for a town the size of Bergen. Modern artists represented at this museum include Max Ernst, Paul Klee, Vassily Kandinsky, Pablo Picasso, and Joan Miró, as well as—guess who—Edvard Munch. There is also a large focus here on Norwegian art since the mid-18th century. ✉ *Rasmus Meyers Allé 3,* ☎ *55/56–80–00.* ✉ *NKr35.* ☉ *Mid-May– mid-Sept., Tues., Wed., Fri. 10–3, Thurs. noon–7, Sat. 11–4, Sun. noon–5; mid-Sept.–mid-May, Tues.–Sun. noon–3.*

㊷ **Vestlandske Kunstindustrimuseum** (West Norway Museum of Applied Art). Seventeenth- and 18th-century Bergen silversmiths were renowned throughout Scandinavia for their heavy, elaborate Baroque designs. Tankards embossed with flower motifs or inlaid with coins form a rich display. ✉ *Permanenten, Nordahl Bruns Gt. 9,* ☎ *55/32–51–08.* ✉ *NKr20.* ☉ *Mid-May–mid-Sept., Tues.–Sun. 11–4; mid-Sept.–mid-May, Tues.–Sat. noon–3, Thurs. noon–6, Sun. noon–4 PM.*

Troldhaugen, Fantoft, Lysøen, and Ulriken

A Good Drive

If you get your fill of Bergen's city life, you can head out to the countryside to four of the area's interesting, but low-key attractions. Follow Route 1 (Nesttun/Voss) out of town about 5 km (3 mi) to **Troldhaugen** ㊻, the villa where Edvard Grieg spent 22 years of his life.

After you've spent some time wandering the grounds of Troldhaugen, head for **Lysøen** ㊼, the Victorian dream castle of Norwegian violinist Ole Bull. Getting here is a 30-minute trek by car and ferry, but it's well worth the effort. From Troldhaugen, get back on Route 1 or Route 586 to Fana, over Fanafjell to Sørestraumen. Follow signs to Buena Kai. From here, take the ferry over to Lysøen. After visiting Lysøen, on your way back to Bergen, you can see the **Fantoft Stavkirke** ㊽, which unfortunately was badly damaged in a fire in 1992 but has been completely rebuilt. Lastly, end your day with a hike up **Ulriken Mountain** ㊾, the tallest of Bergen's seven mountains. If you're too worn out from your day of sightseeing, but still want take in the view from the top, you can always take the Ulriken cable car.

TIMING

Driving time (or bus time) will consume much of your day on this tour. However, the landscape is beautiful, so visiting these sights is a pleasant way to explore Bergen's environs with some direction. You can enjoy the day at a leisurely pace, but note closing times below. Try to take your tour on a Monday or Friday so you can end your day with a "Music on the Mountain" concert at Ulriken.

Sights to See

★ ㊽ **Fantoft Stavkirke** (Fantoft Stave Church). Originally built in the early 12th century in Sognefjord, this ancient wooden stave church was later moved to its present site. Stave churches are unique to Norway, representing a sort of first step, spiritually and architecturally, into Christianity, without complete relinquishment of pagan beliefs. They also parallel Viking ships, as they are built of strips of wood laid edge to edge rather than in log-cabin style. (The church was badly damaged by an arsonous fire in 1992 but has been completely rebuilt.) From *sentral bystasjonen* (the main bus station next to the railway station), take any bus leaving from Platform 19, 20, or 21. ⊠ *Paradis,* ☎ *55/ 28–07–10.* ⊑ *NKr 30.* ☉ *Mid-May–mid-Sept., daily 10:30–1:30 and 2–5:30; for other times, please call.*

㊼ **Lysøen.** Ole Bull, not as well known as some of Norway's other cultural luminaries, was a virtuoso violinist and patron of visionary dimension. In 1850, after failing to establish a "New Norwegian Theater" in America, he founded the National Theater in Norway. He then chose the young, unknown playwright Henrik Ibsen to write full-time for the theater and later encouraged and promoted another neophyte—15-year-old Edvard Grieg.

Built in 1873, this villa, complete with an onion dome, gingerbread gables, curved staircase, and cutwork trim just about everywhere, has to be seen to be believed. Inside, the music room is a frenzy of filigree carving, fretwork, braided and twisted columns, and gables with intricate openwork in the supports, all done in knotty pine. Bull's descendants donated the house to the national preservation trust in 1973. The entrance fee includes a guided tour of the villa.

The ferry, *Ole Bull,* leaves from Buena Kai on the hour Monday–Saturday noon–3 and Sunday 11–4; the last ferry leaves Lysøen Monday–Saturday at 4, Sunday at 5; return fare is NKr30. By bus, take the "Lysefjordruta" bus from Gate 20 at the main bus station to Buena Kai. From here take the *Ole Bull* ferry. Return bus fare is NKr68. ☎ *56/ 30–90–77.* ⊑ *NKr25.* ☉ *Mid-May–late Aug., Mon.–Sat. noon–4, Sun. 11–5; Sept., Sun. noon–4.*

㊻ **Troldhaugen** (Troll Hill). Composer Edvard Grieg began his musical career under the tutelage of his mother, then went on to study music in Leipzig and Denmark, where he met his future wife, Nina, a Danish soprano. Even in his early compositions, his own unusual chord progressions fused with elements of Norwegian folk music. Norway and its landscape were always an inspiration to Grieg, and nowhere is this more in evidence than at his villa by Nordåsvannet, where he and his wife, Nina, lived for 22 years beginning in about 1885. An enchanting white clapboard house with restrained green gingerbread trim, it served as a salon and gathering place for many Scandinavian artists and it's brimming with paintings, prints, and other memorabilia. On Grieg's desk you'll see a small red troll—which, it is said, he religiously bade good night before he went to sleep. The house also contains his Steinway piano, which is still used for special concerts. Behind the grounds, at the edge of the fjord, you'll find a sheer rock face that was blasted open to provide a burial place for the couple. **Troldsalen** (Troll Hall), with seating for 200 people, is used for concerts. Catch a bus from Platform 19, 20, or 21 at the bus station, and get off at Hopsbroen, turn right, walk 200 yards, turn left on Troldhaugsveien, and follow the signs for 20 minutes. ☎ 55/91–17–91. ✑ NKr40. ☉ Mid-Apr.–Sept., daily 9–6; Oct.–Nov. and Apr., weekdays, 10–2, Sat. noon–4, Sun. 10–4; Feb.–Mar., weekdays 10–2, Sun. 10–4.

49 **Ulriken Mountain.** Admire summer sunsets from the highest of the seven Bergen mountains—Ulriken—while enjoying free "Music on the Mountain" concerts Mondays and Fridays at 7, May through September. The Ulriken cable car will transport you up the mountain. You can catch the cable car near Haukeland hospital. It's best reached near the Montana Youth Hostel (Buses 2 or 4). ⊠ Ulriken 1, 5009 Bergen, ☎ 55/29–31–60. ✑ NKr50. ☉ The cable car operates 9–9 in summer, 9–sunset in winter.

DINING

Among the most characteristic of Bergen dishes is a fresh, perfectly poached whole salmon, served with new potatoes and parsley-butter sauce. To try another typical Bergen repast, without the typical bill, stroll among the stalls at Fisketorvet, where you can munch bagfuls of pink shrimp, heart-shaped fish cakes, and round buns topped with salmon. Top it off with another local specialty, a skillingsbolle, a big cinnamon roll, sometimes with a custard center but most authentic without.

$$$$ ✕ **Kafé Kristall.** This small, intimate restaurant is one of the most
★ fashionable in town. The chef here combines his own eclectic contemporary style with traditional Norwegian ingredients. ⊠ Kong Oscars Gt. 16, ☎ 55/32–10–84. AE, DC, MC, V. Closed Sun. No lunch.

$$$$ ✕ **Lucullus.** Although the decor seems a bit out of kilter—modern art matched with lace doilies and boardroom chairs—the food in this restaurant is always good. This is a good place to splurge on the four-course meal that's offered. ⊠ Hotel Neptun, Walckendorfsgt. 8, ☎ 55/90–10–00. Jacket and tie. AE, DC, MC, V. Closed Sun. No lunch.

$$$–$$$$ ✕ **Finnegaardstuene.** This classic Norwegian restaurant near Bryggen
★ has four small rooms that make for a snug, intimate atmosphere. Some of the timber interior dates from the 18th century. The seven-course menu emphasizes seafood, although the venison and reindeer are excellent. Traditional Norwegian desserts such as cloudberries and cream are irresistible. ⊠ Rosenkrantzgt. 6, ☎ 55/31–36–20. AE, DC, MC, V. Closed Sun.

$$$ ✕ **To Kokker.** The name means "two cooks," and that's what there are.
★ Ranked among Bergen's best restaurants by many, this spot is on Bryggen, in a 300-year-old building complete with crooked floors and slanted moldings. Try the roasted reindeer or the marinated salmon.

Desserts use local fruit. ✉ *Enhjørningsgården,* ☎ *55/32–28–16. Reservations essential. AE, DC, MC, V. Closed Sun. No lunch.*

$$ ✕ **Bryggeloftet & Stuene.** It's always full, upstairs and down. The menu's the same in both places, but only the first floor is authentically old. Poached halibut served with boiled potatoes and cucumber salad, a traditional favorite, is the specialty, but there's also sautéed ocean catfish with mushrooms and shrimp, and grilled lamb fillet. ✉ *Bryggen 11,* ☎ *55/31–06–30. AE, DC, MC, V.*

$$ ✕ **Munkestuen.** With its five tables and red-and-white-check table-
★ cloths, this mom-and-pop place looks more Italian than Norwegian, but locals regard it as a hometown legend—make reservations as soon as you get into town, if not before (they can be booked up to four weeks in advance). Try the monkfish with hollandaise sauce or the fillet of roe deer with morels. ✉ *Klostergt. 12,* ☎ *55/90–21–49. Reservations essential. AE, DC, MC, V. Closed weekends and 3 wks in July. No lunch.*

$ ✕ **Baker Brun.** This Bergen institution, now in several locations, is great
★ for a quick bite. Try skillingsbolle or *skolebrød,* a sweet roll with custard and coconut icing—both are scrumptious. For something less sweet, this bakery serves fresh-baked wheat rolls with Norwegian *hvit ost* (white cheese) and cucumber. ✉ *Zachariasbryggen,* ☎ *55/31–51–08;* ✉ *Søstergården, Bryggen,* ☎ *55/31–65–12. No credit cards.*

$ ✕ **Børs Café.** What began as a beer hall in 1894 is now more of a pub, with hearty homemade food at reasonable prices. The corned beef with potato dumplings is served only on Thursday and Friday; meat cakes with stewed peas, fried flounder, and the usual open-face sandwiches are always on the menu. ✉ *Strandkaien 12,* ☎ *55/32–47–19. No credit cards.*

$ ✕ **Kjøbmandsstuen** and **Augustus.** You can't beat these two cafeterias under the same management for lunch or for cake and coffee in the afternoon. Vegetarians will be impressed by the number of salads and quiches, in addition to pâté and open-faced sandwiches. ✉ *Kjømandsstuen: C. Sundtsgt. 24,* ☎ *55/30–40–00.* ✉ *Augustus: Galleriet,* ☎ *55/32–35–25. AE, DC, MC, V.*

$ ✕ **Pasta Sentralen.** If you're looking for good cheap eats, this place will give you bang for your buck. You can't beat the 45-kroner daily special, which includes a generous main course, bread, and soda. More than 40 types of delicious homemade pasta are served here, as are pizzas and other Italian dishes. ✉ *Vestre Strømkaien 6 (near Lars Hilles Gate),* ☎ *55/96–00–37. No credit cards.*

LODGING

From June 20 through August 10, special summer double-room rates are available in 21 Bergen hotels; rooms can be reserved only 48 hours in advance. In the winter, weekend specials are often a fraction of the weekday rates, which are geared toward business travelers. The tourist office (☎ 55/32–14–80) will assist in finding accommodations in hotels, guest houses, or private houses.

$$–$$$ 🏨 **Clarion Admiral Hotel.** This dockside warehouse from 1906, right on
★ the water across Vågen from Bryggen, was converted into a hotel in 1987. The building is geometric Art Nouveau, and although the small rooms are ordinary, the larger rooms overlooking the harbor have some of the best nighttime views in town. The harborside restaurant, Emily, has a small but good buffet table. ✉ *C. Sundts Gt. 9, 5004,* ☎ *55/23–64–00,* FAX *55/23–64–64. 152 rooms, 3 suites. Restaurant, bar. AE, DC, MC, V.*

$$–$$$ 🏨 **Radisson SAS Hotel Norge.** Other hotels come and go, but the Norge stays. It's an established luxury hotel in the center of town, right by the park. The architecture is standard modern, with large rooms that blend contemporary Scandinavian comfort with traditional warmth. The warm, thick *dyner* (featherbed-like comforters) are so comfy, it's hard to get out of bed in the mornings. ⊠ *Ole Bulls Pl. 4, 5012,* ☎ *55/21–01–00,* 𝖥𝖠𝖷 *55/21–02–99. 347 rooms, 14 suites. 2 restaurants, 2 bars, indoor pool, health club, nightclub, meeting rooms. AE, DC, MC, V.*

$$–$$$ 🖭 **Radisson SAS Royal Hotel.** This popular Bergen hotel opened in 1982 behind the famous buildings at Bryggen on the site of old warehouses. Ravaged by nine fires since 1170, the warehouses have been rebuilt each time in the same style, which SAS has incorporated into the architecture of the hotel. The rooms are small but pleasant. ⊠ *Bryggen, 5003,* ☎ *55/54–30–00,* 𝖥𝖠𝖷 *55/32–48–08. 273 rooms, 7 suites. 2 restaurants, bar, pub, indoor pool, sauna, health club, dance club, convention center. AE, DC, MC, V.*

$–$$ 🖭 **Augustin Hotel.** This small but comfortable hotel in the center of town has been restored to its original late–Art Nouveau character. ⊠ *C. Sundts Gt. 22–24, 5004,* ☎ *55/23–00–25,* 𝖥𝖠𝖷 *55/30–40–10. 83 rooms. Meeting rooms. AE, DC, MC, V.*

$–$$ 🖭 **Romantik Hotel Park Pension.** Near the university, this small family-run hotel is in a well-kept Victorian building. Both the public rooms and the guest rooms are furnished with antiques. It's a 10-minute walk from downtown. Don't oversleep and miss the simple and delicious Norwegian breakfast—fresh bread, jams, cheeses, and cereal—included in the price. ⊠ *Harald Hårfagres Gt. 35, 5000,* ☎ *55/32–09–60,* 𝖥𝖠𝖷 *55/31–03–34. 21 rooms. Breakfast room. AE, DC, MC, V.*

$–$$ 🖭 **Tulip Inn Bryggen Orion.** Facing the harbor in the center of town, the Orion is within walking distance of many of Bergen's most famous sights, including Bryggen and Rosenkrantztårnet. The rooms are decorated in warm, sunny colors. The open fireplace at the bar is cozy in the winter. ⊠ *Bradbenken 3,* ☎ *55/31–80–80,* 𝖥𝖠𝖷 *55/32–94–14. 229 rooms. Restaurant, bar, nightclub. AE, DC, MC, V.*

$ 🖭 **Fantoft Sommerhotell.** This student dorm, 6 km (3½ mi) from downtown, becomes a hotel from May 20 to August 20. Family rooms are available. Accommodation is simple but adequate. Take Bus 18, 19, or 20 to Fantoft. ⊠ *5036 Fantoft,* ☎ *55/27–60–00,* 𝖥𝖠𝖷 *55/27–60–30. 72 rooms. Restaurant. AE, DC, MC, V.*

NIGHTLIFE AND THE ARTS

Nightlife

Bars and Clubs

Most nightlife centers on the harbor area. **Zachariasbryggen** is a restaurant and entertainment complex right on the water. **Engelen** (the Angel) at the SAS Royal Hotel attracts a mixed weekend crowd when it blasts hip-hop, funk, and rock. The **Hotel Norge** piano bar and disco are more low-key, with an older crowd. **Dickens** (⊠ 8–10 Ole Bulls Pl., ☎ 55/90–07–60), across from the Hotel Norge, is a relaxed meeting place for an afternoon or evening drink. Right next to Dickens is **Losjehagen** (☎ 55/90–08–20), an outdoor patio especially popular in summer. **Wesselstuen,** also on Ole Bull Plads (☎ 55/90–08–20) is a cozy place where you'll find students and the local intelligentsia. **Café Opera** (⊠ 24 Engen, ☎ 55/23–03–15) is a sumptuous place to go for a drink or a coffee. It's great for people-watching and whiling away the time. **Banco Rotto** (⊠ Vågsalmenningen 16, ☎ 55/32–75–20), in a 19th-century bank building, is one of Bergen's most popular watering holes, for young and old alike. The café here—one of the fanciest in town—serves delicious desserts. The three-story **Rick's Café & Salonger** (⊠ Veiten 3, ☎ 55/23–03–11) has a disco, an Irish pub, and Bergen's longest bar; the decor is straight out of the film *Casablanca*.

Bergen has an active gay community with clubs and planned events. Call **Landsforeningen for Lesbisk og Homofil Frigjøring** (National Association for Lesbian and Gay Liberation, ⊠ Nygårdsgt. 2A, ☎ 55/31–21–39) Wednesday 7–9 to ask about events in the city. **Café Finken** (⊠ Nygårdsgt. 2A, ☎ 55/31–21–39) is open daily until 1 AM.

Live Music

Bergensers love jazz, and the **Bergen Jazz Festival** (⊠ Georgernes Verft 3, 5011 Bergen, ☎ 55/32–09–76) is held here during the third week of August. **Bergen Jazz Forum** (same address) is *the* place, both in winter and summer, when there are nightly jazz concerts. For rock, **Hulen** (the Cave) (⊠ Olav Ryesvei 47, ☎ 55/32–32–87) has live music on weekends.

The Arts

Bergen is known for its **Festspillene** (International Music Festival), held each year during the last week of May and the beginning of June. It features famous names in classical music, jazz, ballet, the arts, and theater. Tickets are available from the Festival Office at **Grieghallen** (⊠ Lars Hilles Gt. 3, 5015, ☎ 55/21–61–00).

During the summer, twice a week, the **Bjørgvin folk dance group** performs a one-hour program of traditional dances and music from rural Norway at Bryggens Museum. Tickets are sold at the tourist office and at the door. ⊠ *Bryggen,* ☎ *55/31–67–10.* ⊠ *NKr70. Performances June–Aug., Tues. and Thurs. at 8:30.*

A more extensive program, **Fana Folklore** is an evening of folklore, with traditional wedding food, dances, and folk music, plus a concert, at the 800-year-old Fana Church. The event has been going on for more than 40 years. ⊠ *A/S Kunst (Art Association) Torgalmenning 9,* ☎ *55/91–52–40;* ⊠ *Fana Folklore, 5047 Fana,* ☎ *55/91–52–40.* ⊠ *NKr200 (includes dinner).* ☉ *June–Aug., Mon., Tues., Thurs., and Fri. at 7 PM (for groups 6:45 PM). Return trip back to the city center by 10:30 PM.*

Concerts are held at **Troldhaugen,** home of composer Edvard Grieg (☞ Exploring, *above*), all summer. Tickets are sold at the tourist office or at the door. Performances are given late June–August, Wednesday and Sunday at 7:30, Saturday at 2, and September–October, Sunday at 2.

OUTDOOR ACTIVITIES AND SPORTS

Below is a sampling of activities for the Bergen area, but outdoors lovers should be aware that the city is within easy reach of the Hardangervidda, the country's great plateau, which offers limitless outdoor possibilities (☞ Hardangervidda *in* Chapter 7).

Fishing

The **Bergen Angling Association** (⊠ Fosswinckelsgt. 37, ☎ 55/32–11–64) provides information on permits; it's closed in July. Among the many charters in the area, the *Fiskestrilen* (☎ 56/33–75–00 or 56/33–87–40) offers evening fishing tours from Glesvaer on the island of Sotra, about an hour's drive from Bergen, where you can catch coal fish, cod, mackerel, or haddock. On the sail home, they'll cook part of the catch.

Hiking

Take the funicular up **Fløyen** (☞ Exploring, *above*), and minutes later you'll be in the midst of a forest. For a simple map of the mountain, ask at the tourist office for the cartoon "Gledeskartet" map, which outlines 1½- to 5-km (1- to 3-mi) hikes. **Ulriken Mountain** (☞ Exploring, *above*) is popular with walkers. Maps of the many walking tours around Bergen are available from bookstores and from **Bergens Turlag** (touring club, ✉ Tverrgata 2–4, 5017 Bergen, ☎ 55/32–22–30), which arranges hikes and maintains cabins for hikers.

In the archipelago west of Bergen, there are many hiking options, ranging from the simple path between Morland and Fjell to the more rugged mountain climb at Haganes. For details, contact the **Sund Tourist Office** (✉ 5382 Skogsvåg, ☎ 56/33–75–00).

Yachting

The **Bergen Yachting Club** (☎ 55/22–65–45) has its harbor at Hjellestad, about a half-hour bus ride from the city bus station. If you want to do more than ogle the boats, however, the 100-year-old Hardanger yacht *Mathilde* (✉ Stiftinga Hardangerjakt, 5600 Kaldestad, ☎ 56/55–22–77), with the world's largest authentic yacht rigging, does both one- and several-day trips, as well as coastal safaris.

SHOPPING

Shopping Centers

Sundt City (✉ Torgalmenningen 14, ☎ 55/31–80–20) is the closest you'll get to a traditional department store in Norway, with everything from fashion to interior furnishings. However, you'll find better value for your kroner if you shop around for souvenirs and sweaters. **Kløver-huset** (✉ Strandkaien 10, ☎ 55/21–37–90), between Strandgaten and the fish market, has 40 shops under one roof. You'll find outlets for the ever-so-popular Dale knitwear, souvenirs, leathers, and fur. **Galleriet,** on Torgalmenningen, is the best of the downtown shopping malls. Here you will find **Christiana Glasmagasin** and more exclusive small shops along with all the chains, like **Hennes & Mauritz** and **Lindex. Bystasjonen,** a small shopping center by the bus terminal, is conveniently located for last-minute items.

Specialty Stores

Antiques

There are many antiques shops on **Øvregaten,** especially around Fløy-banen. **Cecilie Antikk** (✉ Kong Oscarsgt. 32, ☎ 55/96–17–53) deals primarily in antique Norwegian glass, ceramics, and old and rare books.

Glass, Ceramics, Pewter

Viking Design (✉ Torgalmenning 1, ☎ 55/31–05–20) specializes in pewter—you'll find that some pieces can be picked up quite reasonably. **Tilbords, Bergens Glasmagasin** (✉ Olav Kyrresgt. 9, ☎ 55/31–69–67) claims to have the town's largest selection of glass and china, both Scandinavian and European designs. **Prydkunst-Hjertholm** (✉ Olav Kyrresgt. 7, ☎ 55/31–70–27) is the ideal shop for gifts; most everything is of Scandinavian design. You'll find pottery and glassware of the highest quality—much of it from local artisans.

Handicrafts

Husfliden (✉ Vågsalmenning 3, ☎ 55/31–78–70) caters to all your handicrafts needs, including a department for Norwegian national costumes. This is one of the best places to pick up handmade Norwegian goods, especially handwoven textiles and hand-carved wood items. **Berle** (✉ Bryggen 5, ☎ 55/31–73–00) has a huge selection of traditional knitwear and other souvenir items—don't miss the troll cave. Downstairs is an interior design shop with Scandinavian furniture. There's also an automatic foreign-money exchange machine.

Jewelry
Theodor Olsens Eftf (⊠ Ole Bulls Pl. 7, ☎ 55/55–14–80) stocks silver jewelry of distinctive Norwegian and Scandinavian design.

BERGEN A TO Z

Arriving and Departing

By Boat
Boats have always been Bergen's lifeline to the world. **Color Line** (⊠ Skuteviksboder 1–2, 5023, ☎ 55/54–86–60) ferries serve Newcastle. Others connect with the Shetland and Faroe islands, Denmark, Scotland, and Iceland. All dock at Skoltegrunnskaien.

Express boats between Bergen and Stavanger run three times daily on weekdays, twice daily on weekends, for the four-hour trip. All arrive and depart from Strandkai Terminalen (☎ 55/23–87–80).

The *Hurtigruten* (⊠ Coastal Express, Veiten 2B, 5012, ☎ 55/23–07–90) departs daily from Frielenes Quay, Dock H, for the 11-day round-trip to Kirkenes in the far north.

By Bus
The summer-only bus from Oslo to Bergen, **Geiteryggekspressen** (literally, "Goat-Back Express," referring to the tunnel through Geiteryggen Mountain, which looks like a goat's back, between Hol and Aurland) leaves the Nor-Way bus terminal (⊠ Galleri Oslo, ☎ 22/17–52–90) at 8 AM and arrives in Bergen 12½ hours later. Buses also connect Bergen with Trondheim and Ålesund. Western Norway is served by several bus companies, which use the station at Strømgaten 8 (☎ 177).

By Car
Bergen is 485 km (300 mi) from Oslo. Route 7 is good almost as far as Eidfjord at the eastern edge of the Hardangerfjord, but then it deteriorates considerably. The ferry along the way, crossing the Hardanger Fjord from Brimnes to Bruravik, runs continually 5 AM to midnight and takes 10 minutes. At Granvin, 12 km (7 mi) farther north, Route 7 joins Route E68, which is an alternative route from Oslo, crossing the Sognefjorden from Refsnes to Gudvangen. From Granvin to Bergen, Route E68 hugs the fjord part of the way, making for spectacular scenery.

Driving from Stavanger to Bergen involves from two to four ferries and a long journey packed with stunning scenery. The Stavanger tourist information office can help plan the trip and reserve ferry space.

By Plane
Flesland Airport is 20 km (12 mi) south of Bergen. **SAS** (☎ 81/00–33–00) and **Braathens SAFE** (☎ 55/23–55–23) are the main domestic carriers. **British Airways** (serviced by Braathens SAFE) and **Lufthansa** (☎ 55/99–82–30) also serve Flesland.

Between the Airport and Downtown: Flesland is a 30-minute bus ride from the center of Bergen at off-peak hours. The **Flybussen** (Airport Bus) departs three times per hour (less frequently on weekends) from the SAS Royal Hotel via Braathens SAFE's office at the Hotel Norge and from the bus station. Tickets cost NKr35.

Driving from Flesland to Bergen is simple, and the road is well marked. Bergen has an electronic toll ring surrounding it, so any vehicle entering the city weekdays between 6 AM and 10 PM has to pay NKr5. There is no toll in the other direction.

A taxi stand is outside the Arrivals exit. The trip into the city costs about NKr200.

By Train
Bergensbanen has five departures daily, plus an additional one on Sunday, in both directions on the Oslo–Bergen route; it is widely acknowledged as one of the most beautiful train rides in the world. Trains leave from Oslo S Station for the 7½- to 8½-hour journey. For information about trains out of Bergen, call ☎ 55/96–60–50.

Getting Around

The best way to see the small center of Bergen is on foot. Most sights are within walking distance of the marketplace.

By Bus
Tourist tickets for 48 hours of unlimited travel within the town boundaries cost NKr70, payable on the yellow city buses. All buses serving the Bergen region depart from the central bus station at Strømgaten 8 (☎ 177). Buses between the main post office (Småstrandgt. and Olav Kyrres Gt.) and the railway station are free.

By Car
Downtown Bergen is enclosed by an inner ring road. The area within is divided into three zones, which are separated by ONE WAY and DO NOT ENTER signs. To get from one zone to another, return to the ring road and drive to an entry point into the desired zone. It's best to leave your car at a parking garage (the Birkebeiner Senter is on Rosenkrantz Gate, and there is a parking lot near the train station) and walk. You pay a NKr5 toll every time you drive into the city—but driving out is free.

By Taxi
Taxi ranks are located in strategic places downtown. All taxis are connected to the central dispatching office (☎ 55/99–70–00) and can be booked in advance (☎ 55/99–70–10).

Sightseeing Passes
The 24-hour **Bergen Card,** which costs NKr120 (NKr190 for 48 hours), gives free admission to most museums and attractions, and rebates of 25% to 50% off sightseeing, rental cars, and transportation to and from Bergen. It is available at the tourist office and in most hotels.

Contacts and Resources

Dentists
The dental emergency center at Lars Hilles Gate 30 (☎ 55/32–11–20) is open daily 10–11 AM and 7–9 PM.

Emergencies
Emergency Rooms: The outpatient center at Lars Hilles Gate 30 (☎ 55/32–11–20), near Grieghallen, is open 24 hours.

Guided Tours
Bergen is the guided-tour capital of Norway because it is the starting point for most fjord tours. Tickets for all tours are available from the tourist office.

Fjord Tours: Bergen is the much-acclaimed "Gateway to the Fjords," with dozens of fjord-tour possibilities. The following is only meant as a sampling; check with the tourist office (☞ *below*) for additional recommendations. The ambitious all-day **"Norway-in-a-Nutshell"** bus-train-boat tour (you can book through the tourist office) goes through Voss, Flåm, Myrdal, and Gudvangen—truly a breathtaking trip—and is the best way to see a lot in a short amount of time.

Traveling by boat is an advantage because the contrasts between the fjords and mountains are greatest at water level, and the boats are comfortable and stable (the water is practically still), so seasickness is rare. Stops are frequent, and all sights are explained. **Fjord Sightseeing** (☎ 55/31–43–20) offers a four-hour local fjord tour. **Fylkesbaatane** (County Boats) **i Sogn og Fjordane** (☎ 55/32–40–15) has several combination tours. Tickets are sold at the tourist office (☞ *below*) and at the quay.

Orientation Tours: Bergen Guided Tours (☎ 55/59–32–00 or 55/96–55–00) offers three city tours departing from Hotel Norge, including one to Edvard Grieg's home and the Fantoft Stave Church. The excellent **Bryggen Guiding** (1½ hours, June–Aug., ☎ 55/31–67–10) offers a historic tour of the buildings at Bryggen, as well as entrance to Bryggens Museum, the Hanseatic Museum, and Schøtstuene after the tour, conducted by knowledgeable guides. **Bergens-Expressen** (☎ 55/18–10–19), a "train on tires," leaves from Torgalmenningen for a one-hour ride around the center of town, summer only.

Late-Night Pharmacies
Apoteket Nordstjernen (☎ 55/31–68–84), by the bus station, is open daily from 7:30 AM to midnight, Sundays from 8:30 AM.

Money and Expenses
Exchanging Money: Outside normal banking hours, the Tourist Information Office on Bryggen can change money. Post offices exchange money and are open Monday through Wednesday and Friday 8 to 5, Thursday 8 to 6, and Saturday 9 to 2.

Opening and Closing Times
Most shops are open Monday–Wednesday and Friday 9–5. On Thursday, as well as Friday for some shops, the hours are 9–7. On Saturday shops are open 9–3. The shopping centers are open weekdays 9–8 and Saturdays 9–6.

Visitor Information
The **Tourist Information Office** (☎ 55/32–14–80) at Bryggen has brochures and maps and can arrange for accommodations and sightseeing. There is also a currency exchange.

7 Central Norway: The Hallingdal Valley to Hardangerfjord

In summer, the rugged peaks and flat plateaus of central Norway provide a spectacular backdrop for hikers and bikers: crystal clear streams ramble down mountainsides, flocks of sheep graze in the pastures, and snowcapped summits glisten in the distance. Come winter this area—especially Geilo, Gol, and Hemsedal—teems with skiers, both cross-country and downhill.

NORWAY'S INTERIOR BETWEEN Oslo and Bergen is a land of superlatives—the tallest peaks, the biggest national park, and the highest mountain plateau in Europe. There are several varied national parks in this region, and the southern part of Norway's interior, around Hardangervidda, has one of the most popular. It's prime vacation land for wilderness-sports lovers, with fishing, canoeing, rafting, hiking, and horseback riding over the plateau in the summer, and skiing, particularly on the slopes of Geilo, in winter.

Hallingdal Valley

120 km (74½ mi) from Oslo; 92 km (57 mi) from Drammen to Nesbyen.

Route 7 from Drammen winds through the historic Hallingdal Valley, which is lined with small farming communities and ski resorts. Hallingdal is known for its many well-preserved wooden log buildings. **Nesbyen,** a small town in the heart of the valley, has a folk museum as well as many campsites and a youth hostel.

En Route About 21 km (13 mi) from Nesbyen you'll come across the small community of **Gol.** This town is popular with campers in summer and skiers in winter who throng the mountains to the north and east of Gol during ski season.

Hemsedal

50 *35 km (21½ mi) from Gol.*

Spring, summer, winter, or fall, the valley of Hemsedal, and its surrounding area, is a great destination. Clear streams, blue lakes, and striking mountains provide plenty of outdoor activities; hikers and skiers (both alpine and cross-country) will find hundreds of miles of trails. In fact, here in Hemsedal, Norwegian World Cup skiers often practice in the top local ski center (☞ Skiing, *below*).

Outdoor Activities and Sports
SKIING

Hemsedal Skisenter (☎ 32/05–53–00) has 34 km (21 mi) of alpine slopes, 175 km (108 mi of cross-country trails), and 17 ski lifts. The **Vinterlandkortet ski pass** is accepted at all 71 ski slopes in Geilo, Hemsedal, Gol, and Ål and is available at ski centers and tourist offices.

Torpo

51 *52 km (32 mi) from Hemsedal.*

Driving from Gol to Geilo, you'll pass through the tiny town of Torpo, known for its church, presumably the oldest building in Hallingdal. **Torpo stave church** is believed to have been built in the late 12th century. Its colorful painted ceiling is decorated with scenes from the life of Saint Margaret. It's open June through August, daily 9:30–5:30.

Geilo

52 *35 km (21 mi) west of Torpo; 251 km (155½ mi) from Oslo; 256 km (159 mi) from Bergen.*

Geilo, population 3,500, is dead-center between Bergen and Oslo. The country's most popular winter resort, it often draws more than a million visitors a year from throughout northern Europe and Scandi-

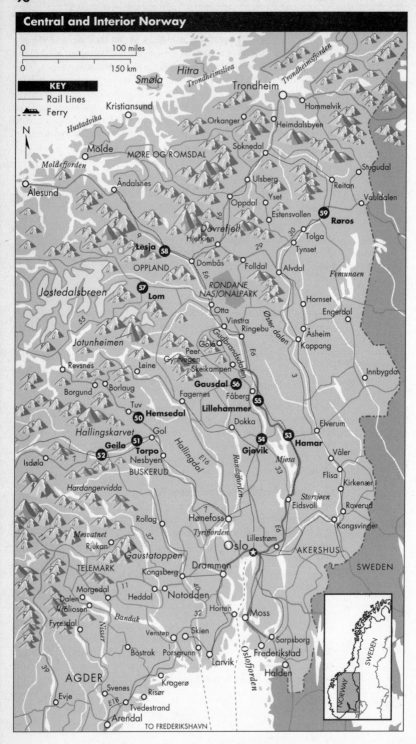

Central and Interior Norway

0 ——— 100 miles
0 ——— 150 km

KEY
——— Rail Lines
⛴ Ferry

N

Smøla
Hitra
Trondheimslia
Trondheimsfjorden
Trondheim
Hommelvik
Kristiansund
Orkanger
Heimdalsbyen
Hustadvika
Soknedal
Stugudal
MØRE OG ROMSDAL
Molde
Ulsberg
Reitan
Moldefjorden
Åndalsnes
Oppdal
Yset
Vauldalen
Ålesund
Estensvollen
59 Røros
Dovrefjell
Tolga
Hjerkinn
30
58 Lesja
Dombås
Folldal
Alvdal
Tynset
OPPLAND
29
Femunaen
57 Lom
RONDANE
NASJONALPARK
Jostedalsbreen
55
Otta
Hornset
Engerdal
Vinstra
Ringebu
Åsheim
Jotunheimen
Gola
Koppang
Revsnes
Peer
Gyntvegen
Skeikampen
Leine
Innbygda
Borlaug
Gausdal 56
Fagernes
Fåberg
Borgund
Tuv
55
Lillehammer
Elverum
50 Hemsedal
Dokka
Våler
Hallingskarvet
Gol
54
53 Hamar
51 Geilo
Torpo
Gjøvik
Flisa
52
Nesbyen
Mjøsa
Kirkenær
Isdøla
BUSKERUD
33
Hardangervidda
Randsfjorden
Storsjøen
Roverud
Rollag
Eidsvoll
Møsvatnet
Hønefoss
Kongsvinger
Rjukan
7
Gaustatoppen
Tyrifjorden
Lillestrøm
AKERSHUS
TELEMARK
Kongsberg
Oslo
SWEDEN
Morgedal
11
Heddal
Notodden
Dalen
32
Kviliosen
Bandak
Horten
Moss
Fyresdal
Nisser
Venstøp
Skien
Sarpsborg
Bøstrak
Porsgrunn
Frederikstad
Larvik
AGDER
39
Kragerø
Oslofjorden
Halden
Evje
Svenes
Risør
E18
Tvedestrand
Arendal
TO FREDERIKSHAVN

SVERIGE
SWEDEN
NORGE

In case you want to see the world.

At American Express, we're here to make your journey a smooth one. So we have over 1,700 travel service locations in over 120 countries ready to help. What else would you expect from the world's largest travel agency?

do more

Travel

In case you want to be welcomed there.

We're here to see that you're always welcomed at establishments everywhere. That's why millions of people carry the American Express® Card – for peace of mind, confidence, and security, around the world or just around the corner.

do more

Cards

In case you're running low.

We're here to help with more than 118,000 Express Cash locations around the world. In order to enroll, just call American Express before you start your vacation.

do more

Express Cash

And just in case.

We're here with American Express® Travelers Cheques and Cheques *for Two*.® They're the safest way to carry money on your vacation and the surest way to get a refund, practically anywhere, anytime.

Another way we help you...

do more ®

**Travelers
Cheques**

navia to its alpine slopes and cross-country trails; many people ski directly from their hotels and cabins. Recently Geilo has become a popular summer destination, with fishing, boating, hiking, and riding—although, admittedly, it still looks like a winter resort minus the snow. Plan ahead if you want to visit at Easter, when Norwegians flock there for a final ski weekend.

On the first Saturday in August, the **Holsdagen** festival presents folk music and a traditional wedding ceremony in the **Hol Stave Church** and **Hol Folkemuseum** (⊠ Hol Kommune, Kulturkontoret, 3576 Hol, ☎ 32/08–81–40).

Dining and Lodging

$$$ ✕☆ **Dr. Holms Hotell.** Truly a place to see and be seen (which means
★ it can be quite a scene), Holms Hotell is among Norway's top resort hotels. Chef Jim Weiss has made the gourmet restaurant (not to be confused with the dining room) worth a special trip. Don't miss the game sausages, which are full of flavor, and the butterscotch pudding with crunchy topping—it's sensational. An après-ski stop at the bar-lounge is a must. ⊠ *3580 Geilo*, ☎ *32/09–06–22*, FAX *32/09–16–20. 124 rooms. Restaurant, 3 bars, 2 indoor pools, hot tub, sauna, exercise room, meeting rooms. AE, DC, MC, V.*

Outdoor Activities and Sports

RAFTING AND CANOEING

In Geilo they've combined rafting and canoeing with skiing, outfitting rubber rafts with a wood rudder and taking off down the slopes for a bracing, if peculiar, swoosh. Contact the tourist board for details. **Flaate Opplevelser** (☎ 61/23–50–00) and **Norwegian Wildlife and Rafting** (☎ 61/23–87–27) also have trips in the Sjoa and Dagali areas.

SKIING

Just to the north, between Bergen and Oslo, is **Geilo Skiheiser** (☎ 32/09–03–33) with 24 km (15 mi) of alpine slopes, 130 km (81 mi) of cross-country trails, 18 lifts, and also a ski-board tunnel. Among the area's other four ski centers, **Vestlia** (☎ 32/09–01–88), west of the Ustedalsfjord, is a good choice for families, as children can play under the guidance of the Troll Klub while their parents ski; **Halstensgård** (☎ 32/09–10–20) and **Slaatta** (☎ 32/09–17–10) have a range of alpine and cross-country trails; and **Havsdalsenteret** (☎ 32/09–17–77) attracts a young crowd to its long alpine slopes. One ski pass gives access to all lifts in all five centers for NKr185. The **Vinterlandkortet ski pass** is accepted at all 71 ski slopes in Geilo, Hemsedal, Uvdal, and Ål and is available at ski centers and tourist offices.

Shopping

Brusletto & Co. (☎ 32/09–02–00), in central Geilo, is a purveyor of high-quality hunting knives with silver-inlaid handles made from burnished metal, walnut, and rosewood. Norwegian men wear these knives, used for hunting and hiking, on their belts—something akin to jewelry.

Hardangervidda

90 km (56 mi) from Geilo to Eidfjord; Rte. 7 is the main road that crosses Hardangervidda.

Geilo is the gateway to Hardangervidda, Europe's largest mountain plateau and Norway's biggest national park—10,000 square km (3,861 square mi) of unique scenery, with the largest herd of wild reindeer in Europe, lakes and streams teeming with trout and char, and home to many birds and animals on the endangered list. It also has rich and varied flora, about 450 different species. Flat in the east and at its center, the plateau is more mountainous in the west. Touring the plateau, either on horseback or on foot, you can find a trail for any level of proficiency, and along the trails, the Norwegian Touring Association (DNT) has built cabins.

About an hour's drive north of Geilo is Hardangervidda's highest peak, **Hardangerjøkulen** (Hardanger Glacier), at 6,200 ft above sea level. Near Hardangerjøkulen you can take a guided hike to the archaeological digs of 8,000-year-old Stone Age settlements. Contact the Geilo Tourist Office (☎ 32/09–13–00).

At the base of the plateau is the innermost arm of the **Hardangerfjord.** Although it's not as dramatic as some of the other fjords, it is pastoral, with royal-blue water and lush apple orchards.

En Route   The western settlement of Finse (on the Bergen railroad), about 34 km (21 mi) from Geilo is one of the most frigid places in southern Norway, with snow on the ground as late as August. Here polar explorers Nansen and Scott tested their equipment and the snow scenes in the *Star Wars* movies were filmed. It, too, is a good starting point for tours of Hardangervidda.

If you'd like to try summer skiing, contact the **Finse Skisenter** (3590 Finse, ☎ 56/52–67–44).

Central Norway A to Z

Arriving and Departing
BY TRAIN
This region is served by the Oslo–Bergen line, which is as much an attraction as a means of transportation.

Contacts and Resources
VISITOR INFORMATION
The main tourist offices of the region are in **Geilo** (☎ 32/09–13–00); **Gol** (☎ 32/07–51–15); and **Nesbyen** (☎ 32/07–01–70).

8 Interior Norway: Lillehammer to Røros

Colorful farmhouses dot Norway's interior countryside, where rivers run wild through rolling valleys and mountains reach up to the sky. You'll see medieval stave churches, preserved mining towns, open-air museums, and the world's oldest paddleboat in this land with a rich heritage. Lillehammer hosted the 1994 Winter Olympics.

NORTHWARD IN NORWAY'S INNER MIDSECTION, the land turns to rolling hills and leafy forests, and the principal town, Lillehammer, attracts skiers from around the world to its slopes and trails; in 1994 it hosted the Winter Olympics. As you travel north, you'll enter Gubrandsdalen (*dal* means valley), one of the longest and most beautiful valleys in the country. Gudbrandsdalen extends from Lake Mjøsa, north of Oslo, diagonally across the country to Åndalsnes. At the base of the lake is Eidsvoll, where Norway's constitution was signed on May 17, 1814. Most visitors come to the region for the beautiful scenery and outdoor activities; tourism has increased substantially in this area since the 1994 Winter Olympics.

At the northern end of the region is the copper-mining town of Røros—which is on UNESCO's World Heritage List—a bucolic little town that's changed little for the past 100 years. The tourist board aptly calls the triangle between Oppland and Hedmark counties, south to Lillehammer, Troll Park. In a reminiscent tribute to the much celebrated 1994 games, this area is also billed as the "Olympic" part of Norway. The otherworldly quality of oblique northern light against wildflower-covered hills has inspired centuries of folk tales as well as artists from Wagner to Ibsen, who was awarded a government grant to scour the land for these very stories. Even today, locals claim he applied for the grant just to have the opportunity to hike the hills.

Numbers in the margin correspond to points of interest on the Central and Interior Norway map in chapter 7.

Hamar

53 *134 km (83 mi) from Oslo; 66 km (41 mi) from Eidsvoll.*

During the Middle Ages, Hamar was the seat of a bishopric. Four Romanesque arches, which are part of the cathedral wall, remain the symbol of the city today. Ruins of the town's 13th-century monastery now form the backbone of a glassed-in exhibition of regional artifacts that date back to the Iron Age but also include more recent findings. Also on the grounds of the **Hedmarksmuseet and Domkirkeodden** (Hedemark Museum and Cathedral) sit 50 or so idyllic grass-roofed houses from the region, and a local favorite, the proliferating herb garden. ⊠ *2301 Hamar,* ☎ *62/53–11–66.* ⊡ *NKr30.* ☉ *Late-May–mid-June and mid-Aug.–Sept., daily 10–4; mid-June–mid-Aug., daily 10–6.*

Hamar got a new lease on life in 1994 when the **Hamar Olympiahall** played host to the speed-skating and figure-skating events of the Lillehammer Winter Olympics. Now used for local exhibitions and conferences, the hall takes the shape of an upside-down Viking ship. Looking out on the town's nature reserve, the hall was built according to the highest environmental and construction standards. Its special laminated wood is so dense that no fire could burn it down. Contact Hamar Olympiahall (⊠ Åkersvika, 2300 Hamar, ☎ 62/51–02–25) for details on tours and sports facilities.

One of Europe's first railway museums, the **Jernbanemuseet** documents how Norway's railways developed, with life-sized locomotives on narrow-gauge tracks outside and train memorabilia inside. Tertittoget, NSB's last steam locomotive, gives rides from mid-May to mid-August. ⊠ *Strandvn. 132,* ☎ *62/51–31–60.* ⊡ *NKr30.* ☉ *June and Aug., daily 10–4; July, daily 10–6.*

The world's oldest paddleboat, the 140-year-old D/S *Skibladner*, also called the "White Swan of the Mjøsa," departs from Hamar, connecting the towns along the lake. The steamer stops daily at Hamar and creeps up to Lillehammer three days a week. The other days it stops at Eidsvoll. Many Norwegian emigrants to North America took the paddler's route from Lillehammer to Eidsvoll to connect with an Oslo-bound train. Be sure to ask for a schedule from the tourist information or the *Skibladner* office. A traditional dinner, consisting of poached salmon and potatoes, with strawberries and cream for dessert, is available for an extra fee. ✉ *Parkgt. 2., 2300 Hamar,* ☎ *62/52–70–85.* ☉ *Mid-June– mid-Aug. The Skibladner is available for charter late May–late Sept.*

NEED A
BREAK?

Sea Side Mat & Vin Hus (☎ 62/52–62–10) sits on the dock near where the *Skibladner* calls; the brass fixtures and lakeside view will surely put you in a maritime mood. The simple fare includes sandwiches, salads, and omelets.

Gjøvik

54 *45 km (30 mi) from Hamar.*

The *Skibladner* stops several times a week at this quiet, hillside town, which claims to be home to the world's largest underground auditorium. So if you get a chance, check out the **Gjøvik Olympiske Fjellhall** (Olympic Mountain Hall), buried 400 ft below the midtown mountain. ☎ *61/13–82–00.*

OFF THE
BEATEN PATH

GILE GÅRD – Farmhouses dot the rolling green countryside along this side of the Mjøsa. Some of them serve as lodgings, and others are just picturesque stops along the way. The Gile family has owned the Gile Farm since the 18th century, although the land has been used as farmland for some 5,000 years. In summer, a variety of uncommon flowers sprout atop the many Viking burial mounds that lie untouched around the house. Call in advance for a schedule of events at the farmhouse. ✉ *2850 Lena (off Rte. 33),* ☎ *61/16–03–73.* ☉ *Tues. Call for more information.*

Lillehammer

55 *40 km (25 mi) from Gjøvik, 60 km (37 mi) from Hamar.*

The winter-sports center of Lillehammer has 23,000 inhabitants. In preparation for the 1994 Winter Olympics, this small town built a ski-jumping arena, an ice-hockey hall, a cross-country skiing stadium, and a bobsled and luge track, in addition to other venues and accommodations. However, farsighted planning kept expansion surprisingly minimal, ensuring that the town was not left in a state of Olympic obsolescence. After the games, which proved hugely successful, many of the structures built to house the foreign media were turned over to the regional college, and one-third of the athletes' quarters were transported to Tromsø to be used as housing.

Kulturhuset Banken, a magnificent, century-old bank building, is the main locale for cultural events. It is decorated with both contemporary and turn-of-the-century art. Don't miss the murals on the ceiling of the ceremonial hall. ✉ *Kirkegt. 41,* ☎ *61/26–68–10.* ☉ *Tours for groups by appointment only.*

The **Olympiaparken** (Olympic Park) includes the Lysgårdsbakkene ski-jumping arena, where the Winter Olympics' opening and closing ceremonies were held. From the tower you can see the entire town. Also in the park are **Håkons Hall,** used for ice hockey, and the **Birkebeineren Stadion** (ski stadium), which holds cross-country and biathlon events. ✉ *Elvegaten 19,* ☎ *61/26–07–00.* ✑ *Free, but admission fee charged at individual facilities.*

Norges Olympiske Museum (Olympic Museum), new in June 1998, focuses on the major Olympic sports achievements of Norwegian and other European sports teams. The architects of Maihaugen's "We Won the Land" (☞ *below*) have also created the exhibits here; you'll see many similarities—mannequins, antique sports equipment, video footage, and sound and light effects. ☒ *Håkons Hall, Olympic Park.* ☎ *61/25–21–00.* ☜ *NKr50.* ☉ *June–Sept., daily 10–6; Oct.–May, Tues.–Sun. 11–4.*

The winter-sports facilities provide amusement all year-round in Lillehammer. You can try the **Downhill and Bobsled simulator** between Håkons Hall and Kristins Hall in the Olympic Park. It's a five-minute ride that replicates the sensations of being on a bobsled. ☜ *NKr25.* ☉ *Jan.–late June, daily 11–4; late June–mid-Aug., daily 10–7; late Aug., daily 11–4.*

Those older than the age of 12 can try the **Bobsled on Wheels**—it's the real thing with wheels instead of blades—at the Lillehammer Bobsled and Luge Stadion. Speeds of 100 km (60 mi) per hour are reached, so you'll get a distinct impression of what the sport is all about. ☎ *94/ 37–43–19.* ☜ *Arena NKr 15.* ☉ *Daily 8–8.* ☜ *Wheeled bobsled NKr125.* ☉ *Late May–early June and mid-Aug.–mid-Sept., daily noon– 5; June–mid-Aug., daily 11–7.*

A highlight of Lillehammer's ski year is the **Birkebeineren cross-country ski race,** which commemorates the trek of two warriors whose legs were wrapped in birchbark (hence *birkebeiner*—birch legs), which was customary for people who couldn't afford wool or leather leggings. They raced across the mountains from Lillehammer to Østerdalen in 1205, carrying the 18-month-old prince Håkon Håkonsson away from his enemies. The race attracts 8,000 entrants annually. Cartoon figures of Viking children representing Håkon on skis and his aunt Kristin (on ice skates) were the official mascots for the Olympic games.

★ ☾ Lillehammer claims fame as a cultural center as well. Sigrid Undset, who won the Nobel Prize in literature in 1928, lived in the town for 30 years. It is also the site of **Maihaugen,** Norway's oldest (and, according to some, Scandinavia's largest) open-air museum, founded in 1887. The massive collection was begun by Anders Sandvik, an itinerant dentist who accepted folksy odds and ends—and eventually entire buildings—from the people of Gudbransdalen in exchange for repairing their teeth. Eventually Sandvik turned the collection over to the city of Lillehammer, which provided land for the museum.

Maihaugen's permanent indoors exhibit, **"We Won the Land,"** will leave you slack-jawed. Completed in 1993, this inventive meander chronicles Norway's history, starting in 10,000 BC when life was somewhere inside a mere drop of melting ice. After walking past life-sized, blue-hued dolls representing periods from the Black Death and 400 years of Danish rule, you will arrive in the 20th century to unsettling visions of the postwar West: a mannequin-junkie sits crumpled in a city stairwell and a lonely old lady tosses feed to the pigeons. Sound effects, period music (including the Rolling Stones), and realistic smells bring each room eerily to life. ☒ *Maihaugvn 1,* ☎ *61/28–89–00.* ☜ *NKr60. Ticket includes guided tour.* ☉ *June–Aug., daily 9–7; May and Sept., daily 10–5; Oct.–Apr., Tues.–Sun. 11–4.*

One of the most important art collections in Norway is housed at the **Lillehammer Kunstmuseum** (Lillehammer Art Museum). In addition to Munch pieces, the gallery has one of the largest collections of works from the national romantic period. ☒ *Stortorgt. 2,* ☎ *61/26–94–44.* ☜ *NKr30.* ☉ *June–Aug., Mon.–Thurs. 11–4, Fri.–Sun., 11–8; Sept.– May, Tues.–Sun. 11–4; call for hrs of guided tours.*

OFF THE
BEATEN PATH

HUNDERFOSSEN PARK – This amusement park takes pride in displaying the world's biggest troll, who sits atop a fairy-tale cave where carved-boulder trolls hold up the ceilings, and scenes from troll tales are depicted. There's a petting zoo for small children, plenty of rides, plus an energy center, with Epcot-like exhibits about oil and gas, and a five-screen theater. The park is 13 km (8 mi) north of Lillehammer. ⊠ *2638 Fåberg,* ☎ *61/27–72–22.* 🖾 *NKr135.* ⊙ *Early June–mid-Aug., daily 10–8.*

Dining and Lodging

When the world came to Lillehammer in 1994, not everyone could stay in downtown hotels. A delightful alternative is a farm stay, which many VIPs took advantage of during the Olympics. Many farms lie in the vicinity around Lillehammer, with a good number on the other side of Lake Mjøsa. For more information and a photo-packed brochure, call **Country Holidays in Troll Park** (⊠ Olympia Utvikling, ☎ 61/28–99–70).

$$–$$$ ✕ **Lundegården Brasserie & Bar.** A piece of the Continent in the middle of Storgata, this restaurant is a haven where guests can enjoy a light snack in the bar area or a full meal. The menu offers such dishes as baked salmon with pepper-cream sauce and seasonal vegetables. The rattan furnishings in the bar and the starched white tablecloths in the dining room make for a pleasant interior. ⊠ *Storgt. 108A,* ☎ *61/26–90–22. Reservations essential. AE, DC, MC, V. No lunch.*

$$–$$$ ✕ **Nikkers Spiseri.** The staff is service-minded at this classic Norwegian restaurant, which serves cakes, sandwiches, and hot dishes. Lunch specials and à la carte evening meals are offered. ⊠ *Elvegt. 18,* ☎ *61/27–05–56. AE, DC, MC, V.*

$$–$$$ 🏨 **Comfort Home Hotel Hammer.** This 1990s hotel is named after the original Hammer farm, which first opened its doors to guests in 1665. The rooms are decorated in shades of green with oak furniture, both modern and rustic. Waffles, coffee, light beer, and an evening meal are included in the price. ⊠ *Storgt. 108, 2600,* ☎ *61/26–35–00,* 🖾 *61/26–37–30. 71 rooms. Lobby lounge, sauna, meeting rooms. AE, DC, MC, V.*

$$–$$$ 🏨 **Mølla Hotell.** A converted mill houses one of Lillehammer's newer hotels. The intimate reception area on the ground floor gives the feeling of a private home. The top-floor bar—called Toppen—has a good view of Mjøsa, the town, and the ski-jump arena. Downstairs is a cheaper eatery called Egon. ⊠ *Elvegt. 12,* ☎ *61/26–92–94,* 🖾 *61/26–92–95. 58 rooms. Bar, sauna, exercise room. AE, DC, MC, V.*

$$–$$$ 🏨 **Rica Victoria Hotel.** This classic, centrally located hotel has small, relaxing rooms, some of which look out on the main street and the outdoor café it owns, Terassen. **Victoria Stuene,** the hotel's restaurant, is among Norway's best. ⊠ *Storgt. 84b, 2600,* ☎ *61/25–00–49,* 🖾 *61/25–24–74. 121 rooms. Lobby lounge, 2 restaurants, outdoor café, nightclub, meeting rooms, conference center. AE, DC, MC, V.*

$$ 🏨 **Gjestehuset Ersgaard.** Dating from the 1500s, originally called Eiriksgård (Eirik's Farm), today this white manor house has all modern facilities but retains its homey atmosphere. The surroundings are beautiful, including views of Lillehammer and Lake Mjøsa, which can be enjoyed from the large terrace. ⊠ *Nordsetervn. 201 (at the Olympic Park),* ☎ *61/25–06–84,* 🖾 *61/25–06–84. 30 rooms, 20 with bath. AE, DC, MC, V.*

$-$$ ⊞ **Birkebeineren Hotel, Motell & Apartments.** Rooms are functional
in these central accommodations. ⊠ *Olympiaparken,* ☎ *61/26–47–
00,* FAX *61/26–47–50. 52 hotel rooms, 35 motel rooms, 40 apartments.
Dining room, sauna. AE, DC, MC, V.*

$-$$ ⊞ **Breiseth Hotell.** This friendly hotel is right beside the railroad sta-
tion and within walking distance of shops and businesses. The Døla-
heimen Kafe serves hearty Norwegian meals. ⊠ *Jernbanegt. 1–5,* ☎
61/26–95–00, FAX *61/26–95–05. 89 rooms. Bar, brasserie, sauna. AE,
DC, MC, V.*

Outdoor Activities and Sports

FISHING

Within the Troll Park, the **Gudbrandsdalåen** is touted as one of the
best-stocked rivers in the country, and the size of Mjøsa trout (locals
claim 25 pounds) is legendary. For seasons, permits (you'll need both
a national and a local license), and tips, call local tourist boards (☞
Visitor Information *in* Interior Norway A to Z, *below*).

RAFTING AND CANOEING

The **Sjoa River,** close to Lillehammer, offers some of the most challenging
rapids in the country. Contact **Heidal Rafting** (☎ 61/23–60–37).

SKIING

Lillehammer, the 1994 Winter Olympics town, is a major skiing center (20 km of alpine, 400 km of cross-country trails; 7 ski lifts). However, downtown Lillehammer is a good half-hour drive from most ski
areas. If you want to ski right out the door of your hotel, call the tourist
office to book a hotel by the slopes. Within the Lillehammer area, there
are five ski centers: **Hafjell** (☎ 61/27–70–78), 10 km (6 mi) north, is
an Olympic venue with moderately steep slopes; **Kvitfjell** (☎ 61/28–
21–05), 50 km (31 mi) north, another Olympic site, has some of the
most difficult slopes in the world; **Skei** and **Peer Gynt** (☞ Skiing *in* Gausdal, *below*), 30 km (19 mi) north and 80 km (50 mi) northwest, respectively; and **Galdhøpiggen Sommerskisenter** (☞ Skiing *in* Lom,
below), 135 km (84 mi) northwest of Lillehammer. One ski-lift ticket,
called a **Troll Pass** (🎟 NKr175), is good for admission to all the lifts
at all five sites.

Gausdal

🗺 *18 km (11 mi) northwest of Lillehammer.*

The composer of Norway's national anthem and the 1903 Nobel Prize
winner in literature, Bjørnstjerne Bjørnson lived at **Aulestad,** in Gausdal, from 1875 until he died in 1910. After his wife, Karoline, died in
1934, their house was opened as a museum. ⊠ *2620 Follebu,* ☎ *61/
22–03–26.* 🎟 *NKr30.* ☉ *Late May–Sept., daily 10–3:30.*

At Gausdal, just north of Lillehammer, you can turn onto the scenic,
well-marked **Peer Gynt Vegen** (Peer Gynt Road), named for the real-
life person behind Ibsen's character. A feisty fellow, given to tall tales,
he is said to have spun yarns about his communing with trolls and riding reindeer backward. As you travel along the rolling hills sprinkled
with old farmhouses and rich with views of the mountains of Rondane,
Dovrefjell, and Jotunheimen, the road is only slightly narrower and
just 3 km (2 mi) longer than the main route. It passes two major resorts, **Skeikampen/Gausdal** and **Golå/Wadahl,** before rejoining E6 at
Vinstra. Between Vinstra and Harpefoss, at the Sødorp Church, you
can visit Peer Gynt's stone grave and what is said to be his old farm.
Although you can walk the grounds, the 15th-century farm is privately
owned.

En Route The E6 highway passes through **Vinstra,** the village of Peer Gynt, where, around mid-August every year, the Peer Gynt Festival celebrates the character and his lore. The road continues along the great valley of the River Lågen, birthplace of *Gudbrandsdalsost,* a sweet brown goat cheese. From this road you'll see lovely, rolling views of red farmhouses and lush green fields stretching from the valley to the mountainsides.

Dining and Lodging

$$$ ✕🖬 **Golå Høyfjellshotell og Hytter.** Tucked away in Peer Gynt terri-
★ tory north of Vinstra, this peaceful hotel is furnished in Norwegian country style. The restaurant has a simple menu of fresh local fish and game, which is elegantly prepared. ✉ 2646 Golå, ☎ 61/29–81–09, FAX 61/29–85–40. 42 rooms. Restaurant, pool, downhill skiing, children's programs, meeting rooms. AE, DC, MC, V.

Outdoor Activities and Sports

HIKING
You can pick up maps and the information-packed **"Peer Gynt"** pamphlet at the tourism office in Vinstra; then hike anywhere along the 50-km (31-mi) circular route, passing Peer's farm, cottages, and monument. Overnighting in cabins or hotels is particularly popular on the Peer Gynt Trail, where you can walk to each of the **Peer Gynt hotels.** (✉ Box 115, N–2647 Hundorp, ☎ 61/29–66–66, FAX 61/29–66–88).

SKIING
Skei (☎ 61/22–85–55), near Gausdal, has both cross-country and alpine trails. **Peer Gynt** (☎ 61/29–85–28) has respectable downhill but is stronger as a cross-country venue. One ski-lift ticket, called a **Troll Pass** (🎟 NKr175), is good for admission to lifts at five sites in the area (☞ Skiing *in* Lillehammer, *above*).

Lom

🔵 *At Otta, Rte. 15 turns off for the 62-km (38-mi) drive to Lom.*

Lom, in the middle of Jotunheimen national park, is a picturesque, rustic town, with log-cabin architecture, a stave church from 1170, and plenty of decorative rosemaling.

Lom Stavkirke (Lom Stave Church), a mixture of old and new construction, is on the main road. The interior, including the pulpit, a large collection of paintings, pews, windows, and the gallery, is Baroque. ☎ 61/21–12–86. 🎟 NKr20. ☉ June–Aug., daily 9–9.

Dining and Lodging

$–$$ ✕🖬 **Fossheim Turisthotell.** Arne Brimi's cooking has made this hotel
★ famous. He's a self-taught champion of the local cuisine and now a household name in Norway; his dishes are based on nature's kitchen, with liberal use of game, wild mushrooms, and berries. Anything with reindeer is a treat in his hands, and his thin, crisp wafers with cloudberry parfait make a lovely dessert. ✉ 2686, ☎ 61/21–10–05, FAX 61/21–15–10. 54 rooms. Restaurant, bar. AE, DC, MC, V.

$$ 🖬 **Vågå Hotel.** About halfway between Otta and Lom on Route 15, this homey, no-frills hotel lies in the lovely mountain village that hosts a number of hang-gliding competitions every summer. It's a good place to park for the night if you're skiing, hiking, or rafting the next day. ✉ 2680 Vågåmo, ☎ 61/23–70–71, FAX 61/23–75–25. 60 rooms. Restaurant, bar, indoor pool, meeting rooms. AE, D, MC, V.

$ ☒ **Elveseter Hotell.** There are many reasons to overnight at this unusually original hotel, including a swimming pool in a barn dating from 1579. About 24 km (15 mi) from Lom in Bøverdalen, this family-owned hotel feels like a museum: every room has a history, and doors and some walls have been painted by local artists. The public rooms are filled with museum-quality paintings and antiques. ☒ *2687 Bøverdalen,* ☎ *61/21–20–00,* FAX *61/25–48–74. 100 rooms. 2 restaurants, bar, indoor pool, meeting rooms. AE, MC, V. Closed mid-Sept.–May.*

Outdoor Activities and Sports

DOGSLEDDING

In Jotunheimen, Magnar Aasheim and Kari Steinaug (☒ Sjoa Rafting, ☎ 61/23–98–50) have one of the biggest kennels in Norway, with more than 30 dogs. You can travel as a sled-bound observer or control your own team of four to six dogs, most of which are ridiculously friendly Siberian and Alaskan huskies.

HIKING

In summer you can hike single-file (for safety purposes, in case of calving or cracks) on the ice and explore ice caves on the **Galdhøpiggen** glacier. Call Lom Fjellføring (☎ 61/21–21–42) or the tourist board (☞ Visitor Information *in* Interior Norway A to Z, *below*). For hikers with sturdy legs, there's a path along a mountain ridge overlooking Gjende lake that makes for a good daylong hike (it's a favorite with Norwegians). A boat will drop you at the path's starting point and you'll end up atop **Bessegen** in Jotunheimen. For information, call Vågåmo Tourist Office (☞ *below*).

NATIONAL PARKS

In this region you'll find **Ormtjernkampen,** a virgin spruce forest, and **Jotunheimen,** a rougher area spiked with glaciers, as well as Norway's highest peak, the **Galdhøpiggen.**

SKIING

To the east of the Gudbrandsdalen is the **Troll-løype** (Troll Trail), 250 km (150 mi) of country trails that vein across a vast plateau that's bumped with mountains, including the Dovrefjells to the north. For information, contact the Otta Tourist Office (☒ 2670 Otta, ☎ 61/23–02–44). **Beitostølen** (9 km [5 mi] of downhill slopes, 150 km [93 mi] of cross-country trails; 7 ski lifts), on the southern slopes of the Jotunheim range, has everything from torchlit night skiing to hang gliding. **Galdhøpiggen Sommerskisenter** (☒ 2686 Bøverdalen, ☎ 61/21–21–42 or 61/21–17–50) sits on a glacier, which makes it great for summer skiing.

Lesja

🔢 *159 km (99 mi) from Lom.*

As you follow Route E6 towards Lesja, the broad, fertile valleys and snowcapped mountains of the Upper Gudbrandsdal provide staggering scenery for the drive. The area around Lesja is trout-fishing country; Lesjaskogvatnet, the lake, has a mouth at either end, so the current changes in the middle. The landscape becomes more dramatic with every mile as jagged rocks loom up from the river, leaving the tiny settlement of **Marstein** without sun for five months of the year.

OFF THE
BEATEN PATH   **JORUNDGÅRD MIDDELALDER SENTER –** Anyone who read Sigrid Undset's 1928 Nobel Prize–winning trilogy, *Kristin Lavransdatter,* will remember that the tale's heroine grew up on a medieval farm of the same name. In 1996, the film actress Liv Ullmann directed a film based on the book a few feet away from where the story was said to have taken place. The authentic medieval farm she built now serves as Jorundgård Medieval Center, a historical and cultural museum. ☒ *Sel,* ☎ *61/23–37–00 or*

61/23–02–44. ☎ *NKr40, guided tours every ½ hr.* ☉ *June–mid-Sept., daily 10–6.*

Outdoor Activities and Sports

GUIDED TOURS

From 1932 to 1953, musk ox were transported from Greenland to the Dovrefjell, where about 60 still roam—bring binoculars to see them. For information on safari-like tours, call the Dombås Tourist Office (☎ 61/24–14–44).

NATIONAL PARKS

The scrubby, flat, and wide **Rondane** to the southeast of Lesja, and **Dovre-fjell,** peaked to the north, have some of the country's steepest mountains and are home to wild musk ox, reindeer, and birds.

Røros

❺❾ *317 km (197 mi) from Lesja; 157 km (97 mi) from Trondheim.*

At the northern end of the Østerdal, the long valley to the east of Gudbrandsdalen, lies Røros. For more than 300 years practically everyone who lived in this one-company town was connected with the copper mines. Notice there are two main axes: one leading to the church, the other to the company. Since many of the early settlers were German engineers, Røros resembles more closely a crowded German *dorf* (hamlet or village) than it does a more spread-out Norwegian farm village. The last mine in the region closed in 1986, but the town has survived thanks to other industries, including tourism, especially after it was placed on UNESCO's World Heritage List.

Røros's main attraction is the **Old Town,** with its 250-year-old workers' cottages, slag dumps, and managers' houses, one of which is now City Hall. Descendants of the man who discovered the first copper ore in Røros still live in the oldest of the nearly 100 protected buildings. The tourist office has 75-minute guided tours of this part of town, starting at the information office and ending at the church. ☎ *NKr40.* ☉ *Tours early June and late Aug.–mid-Sept., Mon.–Sat. at 11; late June–mid-Aug., Mon.–Sat. at 10, noon, 1, 2, and 3, Sun. at 3; mid-Sept.–May, Sat. at 11.*

The **Røroskirke** (Røros Church), which rises above all the other buildings in the town, is an eight-sided stone structure from 1784 (the mines' symbol is on the tower). It can seat 1,600, quite surprising in a town with a population of only 3,500 today. The pulpit looms above the center of the altar, and seats encircle the top perimeter. Two hundred years ago wealthy locals paid for the privilege of sitting there. ☎ *72/41–00–00.* ☎ *NKr15.* ☉ *Early June and late Aug.–mid-Sept., weekdays 2–4, Sat. noon–2; mid-June–late Aug., Mon.–Sat. 10–5, Sun. 2–4; Oct.–May, Sat. noon–2.*

OFF THE
BEATEN PATH

OLAVSGRUVA – The guided tour of Olaf's Mine, a former copper mine outside town and now a museum, takes visitors into the depths of the earth, complete with sound-and-light effects. Remember to bring warm clothing and good shoes, as the temperature below ground is about 5°C (41°F) year-round. ✉ *Rte. 31,* ☎ *72/41–44–50.* ☎ *NKr45, guided tours early June and late Aug.–Sept., Mon.–Sat. at 1 and 3, Sun. at noon; late June–mid-Aug., daily at 10:30, noon, 1:30, 3, 4:30, and 6 (with entertainment program); Oct.–May, Sat. at 3.*

The **Rørosmuseet** (Røros Museum), in an old smelting plant, documents the history of the mines, with working models in one-tenth scale demonstrating the methods used in mining. ☎ *72/41–05–00.* ☎ *NKr45.*

Dining and Lodging

If you want to explore the green, pastured mountains just south of Røros, more than a dozen farm houses take overnight visitors. Some are hytter, but others, such as the **Vingelsgaard Gjestgiveri** (☎ 62/49–45–43), have entire wings devoted to guest rooms. Call **Vingeln Turistinformasjon** (☎ 62/49–46–65) for more information.

$$–$$$ ✕🖼 **Best Western Bergstadens Hotel.** The lobby here can be very inviting, especially when there's a fire in the stone fireplace. The main draw is the dining room: chef Lars Winther sticks to local traditions and products—fish from mountain streams and berries from the nearby forest. ⊠ *Oslovn. 2, 7460,* ☎ *72/41–11–11,* FAX *72/41–01–55. 73 rooms, 2 suites. 2 restaurants, 2 bars, pool, sauna, nightclub, meeting rooms. AE, DC, MC, V.*

Outdoor Activities and Sports

SKIING

At the northern end of the Gubransdalen region, west of Røros, is **Oppdal** (45 km of alpine pistes, 186 km of cross-country trails; 10 ski lifts), a World Cup venue. Like most other areas, it has lighted trails and snow-making equipment.

Shopping

There are so many craftsmen in downtown Røros that the tourist office will arrange a tour of their workshops for those interested. In the mountains south of Røros, Aashilde Westgaard sells a smattering of antiques and junk from her farmhouse-boutique, **Skraphandlerbua** (⊠ 2542 Vingeln, ☎ 62/49–45–40). If you're planning to explore the area, ask the tourist bureau in Røros (☞ Visitor Information *in* Interior Norway A to Z, *below*) for directions to this odd and wonderful shop.

Interior Norway A to Z

Arriving and Departing

BY CAR

The wide, two-lane Route E6 north from Oslo passes through Hamar and Lillehammer. Route 3 follows Østerdalen (the eastern valley) from Oslo. Route 30 at Tynset leads to Røros and E6 on to Trondheim, 156 km (97 mi) farther north.

BY TRAIN

There are good train connections between Oslo and the major interior towns to the north. The region is served by the Oslo–Trondheim line and two other lines.

Getting Around

BY CAR

Roads in the north become increasingly hilly and twisty as the terrain roughens into the central mountains. The northern end of the region is threaded by E16, E6, and Routes 51 and 3. Don't speed: high-tech markers at the roadside, particularly prevalent in the area of Vinstra and Otta, are actually cameras. Exceed the speed limit and you'll receive a ticket in the mail.

Contacts and Resources

VISITOR INFORMATION

Gjøvik (⊠ Jernbanegt. 2, ☎ 61/17–16–88). **Golå** (⊠ Fjell og Fjord Ferie, DBC–Senteret, ☎ 32/07–45–44). **Hamar** (⊠ Vikingskipet, Olympia Hall, ☎ 62/51–02–17 or 62/51–02–25). **Lillehammer** (⊠ Lilletorget, ☎ 61/ 25–92–99). **Lom** (☎ 61/21–12–86). **Øyer** (☎ 61/27–70–00). **Røros** (⊠ Peder Hiortsgt. 2, ☎ 72/41–00–00). **Vågåmo** (⊠ Brennvegen 1, 2680, ☎ 61/23–78–80).

9 The West Coast: Fjord Country

The Norwegian fjords snake inland from the Russian border in the far north all the way to Norway's southern tip. In spectacular inlets like Sognefjord and Geirangerfjord, vertical walls shoot up out of the water, jagged snowcapped peaks blot out the sky, and water tumbles down off mountains in an endless variety of colors, from thundering turquoise to wispy white.

THIS FJORD-RIDDLED COAST, from south of Bergen to Kristiansund, is stippled with islands and grooved with deep barren valleys, with most of the fertile land edging the water. The farther north you travel, the more rugged and wild the landscape. The motionless Sognefjord is the longest inlet, snaking 190 km (110 mi) inland. It is 4,000 ft deep—a depth that often makes it appear black. Some of its sections are so narrow, with rock walls looming on either side, that they look as if they've been sliced from the mountains.

At the top of Sogn og Fjordane county is a succession of fjords referred to as Nordfjord, with Jostedalsbreen, mainland Europe's largest glacier, to the south. Sunnfjord is the coastal area between Nordfjord and Sognefjord, with Florø, the county seat, on an island close to Norway's westernmost point.

In the county of Møre og Romsdal, you'll see mountains that are treeless moonscapes of gray rock and stone cliffs that hang out over the water far below. Geirangerfjord is the most spectacular fjord, with a road zigzagging all the way down from the mountaintops to the water beside a famous waterfall.

There is more to the central region than fidgety coasts and peaks. In fact, tourists have been visiting central fjord country ever since the English "discovered" the area some 150 years ago in their search for the ultimate salmon. One of these tourists was Germany's Kaiser Wilhelm, who spent every summer except one, from 1890 to 1913, in Molde and helped rebuild Ålesund into one of the most fantastic fits of architectural invention in Scandinavia.

The best way to see the fjord country is to make an almost circular tour—from Oslo to Åndalsnes, out to the coastal towns of Ålesund, Molde, and Kristiansund, then over Trollstigveien to Geiranger, by ferry to Hellesylt, down to Stryn, around Loen and Olden and through the subglacial tunnel to Fjærland, and by ferry to Balestrand, connecting with another ferry down to Flåm, where the railroad connects with Myrdal on the Bergen line (*see* Contacts and Resources *in* Bergen A to Z *in* Chapter 6). Then the trip can either continue on to Bergen or back to Oslo.

While traveling, keep in mind that outside of some roadside snack bars and simple cafeterias, restaurants are few in fjord country. The majority of visitors dine at the hotels, where food is generally abundant and simple. Most feature a cold table at either lunch or dinner.

Åndalsnes

60 *495 km (307 mi) from Bergen, 354 km (219 mi) from Trondheim.*

★ Åndalsnes, an industrial town of 3,000 people, has at least three things going for it: as the last stop on the railroad, it is a gateway to fjord country; Trollstigveien (Trolls' Path); and Trollveggen (Trolls' Wall).

From **Horgheimseidet,** which used to have a gingerbread hotel for elegant tourists—often European royalty—you can view **Trollveggen,** the highest sheer rock wall in Europe (3,300 ft). However, the hotel has been a private home for the past 50 years, and the tourists have been replaced by expert rock climbers from around the world.

Trollstigveien, one of Europe's most fantastic roads, starts in Åndalsnes. This road took 100 men 20 summers (from 1916 to 1936) to build, in a constant fight against rock and water. Trollstigveien and Ørneveien (at the Geiranger end) zigzag over the mountains separating two fjords.

The West Coast

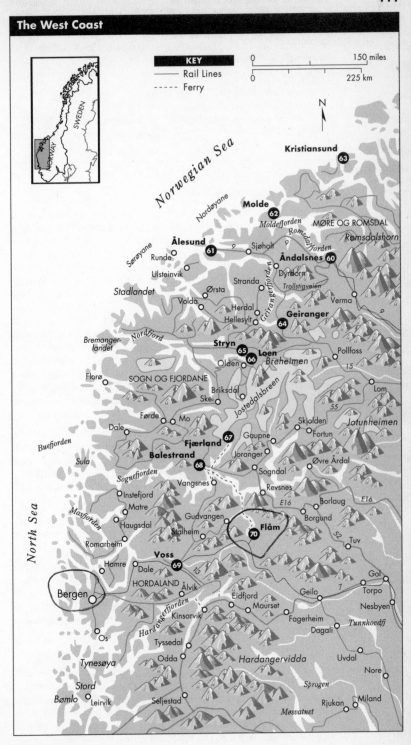

KEY
— Rail Lines
---- Ferry

0   150 miles
0   225 km

N

Norwegian Sea

Kristiansund **63**

Nordøyane

Molde **62**
Moldefjorden   MØRE OG ROMSDAL
       Romsdalsfjorden   *Romsdalshorn*

Sørøyane   **Ålesund** **61**   Sjøholt   9
   Runde   9   **Åndalsnes** **60**
   Ulsteinvik   Stranda   Dyrdorn
Stadlandet   Ørsta   *Trollstigveien*   Verma
     Volda   Herdal
         Hellesylt   **Geiranger** **64**

Bremanger-   *Nordfjord*   **Stryn** **65**   Pollfoss
landet   **Loen** **66**   *Breheimen*
  Florø   Olden   15
   SOGN OG FJORDANE   Lom
      Briksdøl   55
      Skei   *Jostedalsbreen*   *Jotunheimen*
   Førde   Mo   Skjolden
  Dale   Gaupne   Fortun
     Fjærland **67**
   Balestrand **68**   Joranger   Øvre Årdal
Bueffjorden   Vangsnes   Sogndal
Sula   *Sognefjorden*   Revsnes
  Instefjord   E16   Borlaug   E16
   Matre   Gudvangen   Borgund
Masfjorden   Haugsdal   Stalheim   **Flåm** **70**   52   Tuv
  Romarheim
North Sea   **Voss** **69**   Gol
  Hamre   Dale   7   Torpo
Bergen   HORDALAND   Ålvik   Geilo   Nesbyen
      Hardangerfjorden   Eidfjord
  Os   Kinsarvik   Maurset   Fagerheim   *Tunnhovdfj*
         Tyssedal   Dagali
Tynesøya   Odda   *Hardangervidda*   Uvdal
Stord   Nore
Bømlo   Leirvik   Seljestad   *Sprogen*
              Rjukan   Miland
         Møsvatnet

NORWAY   SWEDEN

They're open only during the summer, but there's enough snow for skiing well into July. Trollstigveien has 11 giant hairpin turns, each one blasted from solid rock. Halfway up, the spray from **Stigfoss** (Path Falls) blows across the bridge.

Lodging

$$ 🏨 **Grand Hotel Bellevue.** The cheery rooms have bright carpeting and old prints of the fjord decorating the walls. Most rooms have a view of either the mountains or the fjord. ⊠ *Åndalsgt. 5, 6300,* ☎ *71/22–10–11,* 𝖥𝖠𝖷 *71/22–60–38. 86 rooms. Restaurant, bar, meeting rooms. DC, MC, V.*

Ålesund

⑥ *240 km (150 mi) west of Åndalsnes.*

★ On three islands and between two bright blue fjords is Ålesund, home to 36,000 inhabitants and one of Norway's largest harbors for exporting dried and fresh fish. Nearly 800 buildings in the center of town were destroyed by fire in 1904, said to have been started by a tipped oil lamp. In the rush to shelter the 10,000 homeless victims, Kaiser Wilhelm II, who often vacationed there, led a mercurial rebuilding that married the German Art Nouveau with Viking roots—much of it carried out by an army of young, foreign-educated architects who threw in their own rabid flourishes. Delightfully, little has changed—except that many of the buildings are now painted in pastel colors, a practice thought too eccentric at the time. Winding streets are crammed with warehouses topped with turrets, spires, gables, dragonheads, and curlicues, all in a delirious spirit that's best seen while wandering behind the local dock to Kongensgate, the walking street. To get the most of what you see, try to join one of the tourist office's walking tours; they also put out an excellent descriptive brochure called "On Foot in Ålesund."

To learn more about what they call Jugendstil architecture, visit the exhaustive **Aalesunds Museum,** whose photographs, drawings, and models of the town before and after the fire will make you appreciate the disaster even more. ⊠ *R. Rønnebergsgt. 16,* ☎ *70/12–31–70.* 🎟 *NKr 20.* ☉ *Mid-June–mid-Aug., weekdays 11–4, Sat. 11–3, Sun. noon–3; mid-Aug.–mid-June, Mon.–Sat. 11–3, Sun. noon–3.*

You can drive or take a bus (☎ 70/12–41–70) up nearby Aksla Mountain to a vantage point, **Kniven** (the knife), for a splendid view of the city—which absolutely glitters at night.

If you're traveling by car, you should consider a trip to the islands of **Giske.** A clump of round-topped, temperate islands off the Atlantic coast, they are each newly accessible by tunnel. If you go as far as Godøy in the summertime, stop at the **Alnes Lighthouse** (☎ 70/18–50–90), where owners Eva and Randi Alnes sell local handicrafts and cook delicious homemade fish soup, served with a croissant.

OFF THE
BEATEN PATH

RUNDE – Norway's southernmost major bird rock, Runde, is near Ålesund. It's one of the largest in Europe and a breeding ground for some 130 species, including puffins, gannets, and shags. The island is otherwise known for the "Runde Hoard," 1,300 kilograms (2,860 pounds) of silver and gold coins retrieved from a Dutch ship that sank in 1725. A catamaran leaves from Skateflua quay for the 25-minute trip to Hareid, where it connects with a bus for the 50-km (31-mi) trip to Runde. A path leads from the bus stop to the nature reserve. It is also possible to sail around the rock on the yacht *Charming Ruth,* which leaves from Ulstein-vik at 11 on Wednesday and Sunday. Call the Runde tourist office (☞ Visitor Information *in the West Coast A to Z, below*) for more information.

Dining and Lodging

$$ ✕ **Fjellstua.** This mountaintop restaurant has tremendous views over the surrounding peaks, islands, and fjords. There are several different eating establishments here, but the main restaurant serves a variety of dishes and homemade desserts. ⊠ *Top of Aksla mountain,* ☎ *70/12–65–82. AE, DC, MC, V. Closed mid-Dec.–Feb.*

$$ ✕ **Gullix.** The decor is a bit much, with stone walls, plants hanging from the ceiling, musical instruments, and even the odd old-fashioned record player, but you can't fault the food, which ranges from sautéed monkfish garnished with shrimp, mussels, and crayfish to grilled, marinated filet mignon of lamb. ⊠ *Rådstugt. 5B,* ☎ *70/12–05–48. AE, DC, MC, V.*

$$ ✕ **Sjøbua.** Pick your own lobster from the large tank at one of Norway's most renowned restaurants. The mixed fish and shellfish platter is the most popular dish on the menu. The lobster soup is excellent, too, but leave room for the raspberry ice cream with nougat sauce. ⊠ *Brunholmgt. 1,* ☎ *70/12–71–00. AE, DC, MC, V. Closed Sun.*

$ ✕ **Brosundet Cafe.** This coffee shop in Hotel Atlantica has its own bak-
★ ery, so there are always homemade bread and rolls. You can order anything from bløtkake or the ever-so-popular *nøttekake* (nut cake) to pepper steak. ⊠ *R. Rønnebergsgt. 4,* ☎ *70/12–91–00. Reservations not accepted. AE, DC, MC, V.*

$$–$$$ 🏨 **Rainbow Hotel Atlantica.** Reproduction Van Gogh prints hang on the brightly colored walls of this hotel's cheery guest rooms. A view of the fjord will cost you more, but potted plants and the classic blue-, green-, and yellow-upholstered wood furniture give the rooms a homey feel. ⊠ *R. Rønnebergsgt. 4, 6004,* ☎ *70/12–91–00,* 🅵🅰🆇 *70/12–62–52. 52 rooms. Restaurant, café. AE, DC, MC, V.*

$$ 🏨 **Comfort Home Hotel Bryggen.** This hotel, with stone walls and glassed-in atria, is housed in a converted turn-of-the-century fish warehouse. Strewn with wooden oars, life vests, and fishing tools, the lobby gives a glimpse on the importance of fishing to Ålesund. A light evening buffet is included in the room price, and waffles and coffee are always available. Fishing equipment is available; although Bryggen is on the water, anglers are advised to go farther afield for a better catch. ⊠ *Apotekergt. 1–3, 6021,* ☎ *70/12–64–00,* 🅵🅰🆇 *70/12–11–80. 85 rooms. Sauna, Turkish bath, fishing, meeting rooms. AE, DC, MC, V.*

$$ 🏨 **Quality Scandinavie Hotel.** The impressive building with towers and
★ arches dates from 1905, whereas most rooms are modern and beautifully decorated in shades of blue, peach, and green with reproduction Biedermeier furniture (be sure to ask for a renovated room). Some decorative textiles pay a token tribute to Art Nouveau. ⊠ *Løvenvoldgt. 8, 6002,* ☎ *70/12–31–31,* 🅵🅰🆇 *70/13–23–70. 65 rooms. Restaurant, bar, pizzeria, meeting rooms. AE, DC, MC, V.*

$$ 🏨 **Scandic Hotel.** This large, postmodern building complex stands next to the Exhibition Hall. Its interior design has a maritime theme. The rooms are spacious. ⊠ *Molovn. 6, 6004,* ☎ *70/12–81–00,* 🅵🅰🆇 *70/12–92–10. 117 rooms, 6 suites. Restaurant, bar, indoor pool, sauna. AE, DC, MC, V.*

Molde

㊷ *69 km (43 mi) north of Ålesund on Route 668.*

During World War II the German air force suspected that King Haakon VII was staying in a red house here and bombed every red house in town. These days, Molde is a modern town, after being almost entirely rebuilt. The best time to come is during the town's annual jazz festival in late July. Big names from around the world gather for a huge jam session. Tickets for the fest, where acts like Bob Dylan, Dizzy Gillespie, Miles Davis, and Al Jarreau have performed in the past, can be purchased at all post offices in Norway.

If you like to walk, take the footpath that leads uphill to the charming **Romsdalsmuseet** (Romsdal Open-Air Museum). The path begins on Storgata near the Alexandra Hotel at the King's Birch Tree, named after the place where the king and crown prince were sheltered during the war. On the way to the museum, stop at Reknes Park for a view of the 222 mountain peaks on the other side of the Romdalsfjord. Costumed tour guides will lead you through the open air museum's 40 grass-roofed farm houses and churches dating back to the 14th century. ⊠ *Museumsvn. 14,* ☎ *71/25–25–34.* ⊙ *Early June and late Aug., Mon.–Sat. 10–2, Sun. noon–3; mid-June–mid-Aug., Mon.–Sat. 10–6, Sun. noon–6.*

Dining and Lodging

$$–$$$ ✕⊞ **First Hotel Alexandra Molde.** Named after Britain's Princess
★ Alexandra of Wales, who stayed here in the 1880s, this hotel drew royal visitors from cruise ships as well as Norwegian literary men, such as Ibsen and Bjørnson. Spisestuen, the restaurant of this premier hotel, is worth a special trip. Kåre Monsås prepares such dishes as pepper-marinated veal fillet. The rooms, many of which overlook the water, are nondescript, with dark-brown wood furniture and textiles in shades of blue. ⊠ *Storgt. 1–7, 6400,* ☎ *71/25–11–33,* ℻ *71/21–66–35. 150 rooms, 11 suites. 2 restaurants, bar, sauna, indoor pool, exercise room, meeting rooms. AE, DC, MC, V.*

Kristiansund

➅➂ *68 km (42 mi) north of Molde on Route 64.*

This town was spared the destruction of its historic harbor, Vågen, during World War II. Many buildings in Kristiansund—which celebrated its 250th birthday in 1992—are well preserved, including **Woldbrygga,** a cooper's (barrel maker's) workshop from 1875 to 1965, with its original equipment still operational. ⊠ *Dalevn. 17,* ☎ *71/67–15–78.* ⊟ *NKr25.* ⊙ *Tues.–Fri. 10–2, Sun. noon–3.*

For many years, Kristiansund derived its identity from its unique process of drying cod: on cliffs by the ocean. Called "klippfish," the dried cod then got shipped all over the world for consumption—especially to Portugal, where it became the main ingredient in the Portuguese dish *bacalao.* Housed in an 18th-century warehouse, **Milnbrygge,** the Norwegian Klippfish Museum, pays tribute to the process and the history of the klippfish industry—fishy smells and all. ⊠ *Kristiansund Harbor,* ☎ *71/58–63–80 tourist information.* ⊟ *Nkr 25.* ⊙ *Mid-June–mid-Aug, Mon.–Sat. noon–5, Sun. 1–4.*

Dining and Lodging

$$–$$$ ✕ **Smia Fiskerestaurant.** Dishes like fishballs and whale peppersteak are available here, but the decidedly Mediterranean-tasting dish—bacalao—is strangely part of local culture. Built inside an 18th-century red smithy, the place is decorated with hanging fishnets, Spanish wine bottles, and vintage klippfish tins. ⊠ *Fosnagt. 30B,* ☎ *71/67–11–70. AE, DC, MC, V.*

$$–$$$ ⊞ **Hotel Fosna Atlantica.** Ask for a room with a harbor view in this waterfront hotel. It's not as snazzy as the Rica down the street, but it has more character, with an outdoor café, a mahogany-interiored British-style pub, and a white marble lobby. Rooms vary widely in size. ⊠ *Hauggt. 16, 6501,* ☎ *71/67–40–11,* ℻ *71/67–76–59. 50 rooms. Outdoor café, piano bar, pub, nightclub, meeting rooms. AE, DC, MC, V.*

Geiranger

64 *85 km (52½ mi) southwest of Åndalsnes, 413 km (256 mi) from Bergen.*

★ Geiranger is the ultimate fjord, Norway at its most dramatic, with the finest sightseeing in the wildest nature compressed into a relatively small area. The mountains lining the Geiranger Fjord tower 6,600 ft above sea level. The most scenic route to Geiranger is the two-hour drive along Route 63 over Trollstigveien from Åndalsnes (☞ *above*). Once you are there, the Ørneveien (Eagles' Road) down to Geiranger, completed in 1952 with 11 hairpin turns, leads directly to the fjord.

The 16-km-long (10-mi-long), 960-ft-deep Geirangerfjord's best-known attractions are its waterfalls—the Seven Sisters, the Bridal Veil, and the Suitor—and the abandoned farms at **Skageflå** and **Knivsflå**, which are visible (and accessible) only by boat (☞ Contacts and Resources *in* The West Coast A to Z, *below*). Perhaps the inhabitants left because provisions had to be carried from the boats straight up to Skageflå—a backbreaking 800 ft.

Lodging

$$$ 🏨 **Union Hotel.** This family-owned hotel is more than 100 years old. The old building was torn down, but the present hotel is a tribute to the old style. It is modern and comfortable, with lots of windows facing the view, and light-colored furniture in the rooms, which are relatively large. ✉ 6216, ☎ 70/26–30–00, ℻ 70/26–31–61. *155 rooms, 13 suites. Restaurant, bar, indoor pool, steam room, nightclub. AE, DC, MC, V.*

$ 🏨 **Grande Fjord Hotell.** Idyllically set at the edge of the fjord, this small hotel complex has more charm than the big hotels in the area. The rooms are simple and comfy. ✉ 6216, ☎ 70/26–30–90, ℻ 70/26–31–77. *48 rooms, 18 cabins. Restaurant, bar, boating, fishing. MC, V.*

Stryn

65 *If you continue on to Stryn from Geiranger, take the ferry across the Geiranger Fjord to Hellesylt, a 75-minute ride. It's about 50 km (30 mi) from Hellesylt to Stryn on Rte. 60.*

Stryn, Loen, and Olden, at the eastern end of Nordfjord, were among the first tourist destinations in the region more than 100 years ago. Stryn is famous for its salmon river and summer ski center—**Stryn Sommerskisenter** (✉ 6880 Stryn, ☎ 57/87–19–95).

OFF THE BEATEN PATH | **BRIKSDALSBREEN –** This is the most accessible arm of the Jostedal glacier. Drive along the mountain road or take a bus (from Olden, Loen, or Stryn) to Briksdal. From here, the glacier is a 45-minute walk from the end of the road, or you can ride there with pony and trap, as tourists did 100 years ago. Local guides lead tours (☞ Contacts and Resources *in* The West Coast A to Z, *below*) over the safe parts of the glacier. These perennial ice masses are more treacherous than they look, for there's always the danger of calving (breaking off), and deep crevasses are not always visible.

Lodging

$$$ 🏨 **Kong Oscar's Hall.** Mike and Møyfrid Walston have brought back to life a derelict but magnificent hotel from the heyday of the dragon style, 1896, complete with a tower with dragonheads on the eaves. The Great Hall gives new meaning to the word *great*, and the number of royal guests, both present and past, is impressive. ✉ 6880, ☎ ℻ 57/87–19–53. *5 suites. Restaurant. No credit cards. Closed Sept.–Apr.*

Shopping

Strynefjell Draktverkstad (⊠ 6890 Oppstryn, ☎ 57/87–72–20) specializes in stylish knickers, trousers, and skirts made of heavy wool. It's a 10-minute drive east of Stryn on Route 15.

Loen

66 *10 km (6 mi) southeast of Stryn.*

Loen and Olden are starting points for expeditions to branches of Europe's largest glacier, Jostedalsbreen. Hovering over the entire inner Nordfjord and Sognefjord regions, this glacier covers 800 square km (309 square mi). In geological time, this 5,000-year-old glacier is relatively young. The ice is in constant motion, crawling as much as 2 km (1¼ mi) a day in certain places.

OFF THE BEATEN PATH

KJENNDALSBREEN FJELLSTOVE – It's possible to visit the Kjenndal arm of the glacier on the *M/B Kjendal*, which departs from Sande, near Loen. It sails down the 14-km (9-mi) arm of the lake under mountains covered by protruding glacier arms and past Ramnefjell (Ramne Mountain), scarred by rock slides, to Kjenndalsbreen Fjellstove. A bus runs between the Alexandra lodge (☞ *below*) and the glacier.

Dining and Lodging

$$$ ✕🏨 **Alexandra.** The building that houses Alexandra looks more like
★   a huge white hospital than a hotel. English and German tourists stayed here over 100 years ago. Even though the original dragon-style building exists only in pictures in the lobby, it is still the most luxurious hotel around. The facilities are first-rate, but the food, prepared by chef Wenche Loen, is the best part—the trout is outstanding. ⊠ 6878 Loen ☎ 57/87–50–00, ℻ 57/87–77–70. 193 rooms. 2 restaurants, bar, indoor pool, tennis courts, exercise room, boating, nightclub, convention center. AE, DC, MC, V.

Fjærland

67 *From Olden it's 62 km (37 mi) of easy, though not particularly inspiring, terrain to Skei, at the base of Lake Jølster, where the road goes under the glacier for more than 6 km (4 mi) of the journey to Fjærland.*

Fjærland, until 1986, was without road connections altogether. In 1991 the **Norsk Bremuseum** (Norwegian Glacier Museum) opened just north of Fjærland. It has a huge screen on which a film about glacier trekking plays and a fiberglass glacial maze, complete with special effects courtesy of the *Star Wars* movies' set designer. ☎ 57/69–32–88. 🎟 NKr60. 🕐 June–Aug., daily 9–7; Apr.–May and Sept.–Oct., daily 10–4.

OFF THE BEATEN PATH

ASTRUPTUNET – Halfway across the southern shore of Lake Jølster (about a 10-minute detour from the road to Fjærland) is Astruptunet, the farm of artist Nicolai Astrup (1880–1928). The best of his primitive, mystical paintings sell in the $500,000 range, ranking him among the most popular Norwegian artists. His home and studio are in a cluster of small turf-roofed buildings on a steep hill overlooking the lake. ☎ 57/72–67–82 or 57/72–81–05. 🎟 NKr50. 🕐 July, daily 10–8; late May–June and Aug.–early Sept., Tues.–Sun. 10–5.

Dining and Lodging

$$–$$$ ✕🏨 **Hotel Mundal.** This small, old-fashioned yellow-and-white gingerbread hotel opened in 1891. All rooms are individually and simply decorated. The dining room looks rather dreary, but the food is good.

✉ *5855,* ☎ *57/69–31–01,* FAX *57/69–31–79. 35 rooms. Restaurant, bar, meeting rooms. DC, V. Closed mid-Sept.–mid-May.*

Shopping

Audhild Vikens Vevstove (✉ Skei, ☎ 57/72–81–25) specializes in the handicrafts, particularly woven textiles.

Balestrand

68 *30 km (18½ mi) up the fjord by ferry, 204 km (126 mi) by car to Fjær-land.*

Fjærland is now connected to Sogndal by tunnel (up until 1997 it was only accessible by ferry). Balestrand is on the southern bank of **Sogne-fjord,** one of the longest and deepest fjords in the world, snaking 200 km (136 mi) into the heart of the country. Along its wide banks are some of Norway's best fruit farms, with fertile soil and lush vegetation (the fruit blossoms in May are spectacular). Ferries are the lifeline of the region.

Lodging

$$ ⊡ **Kvikne's Hotel.** This huge, wooden gingerbread house at the edge of
★ the Sognefjord has been a landmark since 1913. It is fjord country's most elaborate old hotel, with rows of open porches and balustrades. The rooms in the old section have personality, but the view is the best part. This spot also has good swimming, hiking, rowing, and fishing possibilities. ✉ *5850, Balholm,* ☎ *57/69–11–01,* FAX *57/69–15–02. 190 rooms. Restaurant, exercise room, fishing, nightclub. AE, DC, MC, V.*

Voss

69 *80 km (50 mi) south of Vangsnes.*

Voss is the birthplace of American football hero Knut Rockne and a good place to stay the night, either in the town itself or 36 km (23 mi) away at Stalheim. The road to Stalheim, an old resort, has 13 hairpin turns in one 1½-km (1-mi) stretch of road that can be almost dizzying—it's 1,800 ft straight down—but well worth the trip for the view. Voss is connected with Oslo and Bergen by train and by roads (some sections are narrow and steep).

Lodging

$$$–$$$$ ⊡ **Stalheim Hotel.** A large, rectangular building, much like other Norwegian resort hotels, the grand Stalheim has been painted dark red and blends into the scenery better than most other hotels. It has an extensive collection of Norwegian antiques and even its own open-air museum, with 30 houses. The view from the large stone terrace is stunning. ✉ *5715 Voss,* ☎ *56/52–01–22,* FAX *56/52–00–56. 127 rooms, 3 suites. 2 restaurants, bar, fishing. AE, DC, MC, V.*

$$ ⊡ **Fleischers Hotel.** The modern addition along the front detracts from the turreted and gabled charm of this old hotel. Inside, the old style has been well maintained, particularly in the restaurant. The rooms in the old section are pleasantly old-fashioned; in the rebuilt section (1993) they are modern and inviting. There is also a children's playroom. The motel section has apartments as well. ✉ *Evangervegen 13, 5700,* ☎ *56/51–11–55,* FAX *56/51–22–89. 90 rooms, 30 apartments. Restaurant, bar, indoor pool, hot tub, sauna, tennis court, nightclub. AE, DC, MC, V.*

Outdoor Activities and Sports

HIKING

Walks and hikes are especially rewarding in this region, with spectacular mountain and water views everywhere. Be prepared for abrupt weather changes in spring and fall. Voss is a starting point for mountain hikes in Slølsheimen, Vikafjell, and the surrounding mountains. Contact the Voss Tourist Board (☞ Contacts and Resources *in* The West Coast A to Z, *below*) for tips.

RAFTING

For rafting in Dagali or Voss, contact **Dagali-Voss Rafting** (✉ Dagali Hotel, ☎ 32/09–38–20) for information on organized trips.

SKIING

Voss (40 km of alpine slopes; 1 cable car, 8 ski lifts; 8 illuminated and 2 marked cross-country trails) is an important alpine skiing center in Norway, although it doesn't have the attractions or traditions of some of its resort neighbors to the east. The area includes several schools and interconnecting lifts that will get you from run to run. Call the Voss Tourist Board (☞ Contacts and Resources *in* The West Coast A to Z, *below*) for details.

Flåm

⑦ *131 km (81 mi) from Voss.*

One of the most scenic train routes in Europe zooms from Myrdal, high into the mountains and down to the quaint town of Flåm. Flåm's waterfront is swamped with day-trippers who stream off of the train at noon, have lunch in a cafeteria, and sweep out of town at about 3. After they leave, a wonderful stillness descends and Flåm becomes a wonderful place to spend the night.

OFF THE BEATEN PATH   **MYRDAL** – It's possible to ride a ferry from Balestrand to Flåm, from which you can make Norway's most exciting railway journey to Myrdal. Only 20 km (12 mi) long, it takes 40 minutes to travel 2,850 ft up a steep mountain gorge and 53 minutes to go down, with one stop for photos each way. Don't worry about the brakes. The train has five separate systems, any one of which is able to stop it. A masterpiece of engineering, the line includes 20 tunnels. From Flåm it is also an easy drive back to Oslo on E16 along the Lærdal River, one of Norway's most famous salmon streams and King Harald's favorite.

Lodging

$$ 🏨 **Fretheim Hotell.** With the fjord in front and mountains in back, the setting is perfect. The hotel is anonymous, white, and functional. The inside has comfy lounges and rooms decorated in a Norwegian folk style. ✉ 5743, ☎ 57/63–22–00, FAX 57/63–23–03. *56 rooms, 28 with shared bath. 2 restaurants, bar, fishing. AE, MC, V.*

The West Coast A to Z

Arriving and Departing

BY BOAT

The **Hurtigruten** (the coastal steamer) stops at Skansekaia in **Ålesund,** northbound at noon, departing at 3, and stops southbound at midnight, departing at 1. A catamaran runs between Ålesund and Molde at least twice daily.

BY CAR

From Oslo, it is 450 km (295 mi) on Route E6 to Dombås and then Route 9 through Åndalsnes to Ålesund. The well-maintained two-lane road runs inland to Åndalsnes and then follows the coastline out to Ålesund.

The 380-km (235-mi) drive from Bergen to Ålesund covers some of the most breathtaking scenery in the world. Roads are narrow two-lane ventures much of the time; passing is difficult, and in summer traffic can be heavy.

BY PLANE

Ålesund's **Vigra Airport** is 15 km (9 mi) from the center of town. **Braathens SAFE** (☎ 81/00–05–55, Ålesund; 70/18–32–45, Vigra) has nonstop flights from Oslo, Bergen, Trondheim, and Bodø.

Between the Airport and Downtown: It's a 25-minute ride from Vigra to town with Flybussen. Tickets cost NKr50. Buses are scheduled according to flights—they leave the airport about 10 minutes after all arrivals and leave town about 60 or 70 minutes before each departure.

BY TRAIN

The **Dovrebanen** and **Raumabanen** between Oslo S Station and Åndalsnes via Dombås run three times daily in each direction for the 6½-hour ride. At Åndalsnes, buses wait outside the station to pick up passengers for points not served by the train. The 124-km (76-mi) trip to Ålesund takes close to two hours.

Getting Around

BY BOAT

In addition to regular ferries to nearby islands, boats connect Ålesund with other points along the coast. Excursions by boat are available through the tourist office.

BY BUS

Bus routes are extensive. The tourist office has information about do-it-yourself tours by bus to the outlying districts. Three local bus companies serve Ålesund; all buses depart from the terminal on Kaiser Wilhelms Gate.

BY CAR

Ferries are a way of life in western Norway, but they are seldom big enough or don't run often enough during the summer, causing built-in delays. Considerable hassle can be eliminated by reserving ahead, as cars with reservations board first. Call the tourist office of the area where you will be traveling for ferry information (☞ Visitor Information, *below*).

Contacts and Resources

EMERGENCIES

Hospital Emergency Rooms/Doctors/Dentists: ☎ 70/12–33–48. **Car Rescue:** ☎ 70/14–18–33.

GUIDED TOURS

Cruises: The M/S **Geirangerfjord** (☎ 70/26–30–07) offers 90-minute guided minicruises on the Geirangerfjord. Tickets are sold at the dock in Geiranger. ☒ NKr67. ☺ June–Aug. *Tours at 10, noon, 2, and 5; late June–mid-Aug., additional tour at 3:30.*

Flying: Firdafly A/S (☎ 57/86–53–88), based in Sandane, has air tours over Jostedalsbreen. Hotel Alexandra in Loen (☞ *above*) arranges group flights.

Glacier: From Easter through September, **Jostedalen Breførlag** (☒ 5828 Gjerde, ☎ 57/68–32–84) offers glacier tours, from an easy 1½-hour family trip on the Nigard branch (equipment is provided) to advanced glacier courses with rock and ice climbing.

Hiking: Aak Fjellsportsenter (☎ 71/22–71–00) in Åndalsnes specializes in walking tours of the area, from rambling in the hills for beginners and hikers to full-fledged rock climbing, along with rafting on the Rauma River. These are the guys who hang out of helicopters to rescue injured climbers, so they know what they're doing.

Orientation: A 1½-hour guided stroll through Ålesund, concentrating mostly on the Art Nouveau buildings, departs from the tourist information center (Rådhuset) Saturday, Tuesday, and Thursday at 1 PM from mid-June to late August. ✉ *NKr45.*

LATE-NIGHT PHARMACIES

Nordstjernen (✉ Kaiser Wilhelms Gate 22, Ålesund, ☎ 70/12–59–45) is open weekdays from 9 AM to 4:30 PM, Wednesday until 6 PM, and Saturday until 2 PM. Sunday hours are from 6 PM to 8 PM.

VISITOR INFORMATION

Ålesund (✉ Rådhuset, ☎ 70/12–12–02). **Åndalsnes** (✉ Corner Nesgt. and Romsdalsvn., ☎ 71/22–16–22). **Balestrand** (✉ Dockside, ☎ 57/69–12–55). **Flåm** (✉ Railroad station, ☎ 57/63–21–06). **Geiranger** (✉ Dockside, ☎ 70/26–30–99). **Hellesylt** (✉ Dockside, ☎ 70/26–50–52). **Lærdal** (☎ 57/66–65–09). **Molde** (✉ Storgt 1, ☎ 71/21–92–62). **Runde** (☎ 70/08–59–96). **Sogndal** (☎ 57/67–30–83). **Stryn** (☎ 57/87–23–32). **Ulvik** (✉ Dockside, ☎ 56/52–63–60). **Voss** (☎ 56/51–00–51). **Fjord Norway** (☎ 55/31–93–00) in Bergen is a clearinghouse for information on all of western Norway.

10 Trondheim to the North Cape

A narrow but immensely long strip of land stretches between Trondheim and Kirkenes in northern Norway. In this vast territory, you'll encounter dramatically different ways of life and a variety of geographical features, from the sawtooth, glacier-carved peaks of the Lofoten Islands to the world's strongest tidal current in Bodø.

THE COAST OF NORTHERN NORWAY fidgets up from Trondheim, scattering thousands of islands and skerries along the way, until it reaches the northernmost point of Europe. Then it continues even farther, straggling above Sweden and Finland to point a finger of land into Russia.

Long and thin, this area covers an astonishing variety of land- and cityscapes, from bustling Trondheim to elegant Tromsø. Some areas, especially when seen from the deck of the mail boats, seem like endless miles of wilderness marked by an occasional dot—a lonely cabin or a herd of reindeer. Views are often exquisite: glaciers, fjords, rocky coasts, and celestial displays of the midnight sun in summer and northern lights (aurora borealis) in winter.

Nordkapp (North Cape) has a character that changes with the seasons. In summer it teems with visitors and tour buses, and in winter, under several feet of snow, it is bleak, subtle, and astonishingly beautiful. It is accessible then only by squealing Sno-Cat snowmobile, a bracing and thoroughly Norwegian adventure.

Keep in mind while traveling, as in the rest of provincial Norway, that most better restaurants are in hotels. If you visit northern Norway between May and August, try the specialty of *måsegg* and *Mack-øl,* more for curiosity value than for taste. *Måsegg* (seagulls' eggs) are always served hard-boiled and halved in their shells. They're larger than chicken eggs, and they look exotic, with greenish-gray speckled shells and bright orange yolks, but they taste like standard supermarket eggs. *Mack-øl* (similar to pils) is brewed in Tromsø at the world's northernmost brewery.

Trondheim

71 *496 km (307½ mi) north of Oslo, 744 km (461 mi) from Bergen.*

Trondheim's original name, Nidaros (still the name of the cathedral), is a composite word referring to the city's location at the mouth of the Nid River. After a savage fire in 1681, the wooden town was rebuilt according to the plan of General Cicignon, a military man from Luxembourg, who also designed Trondheim's fort. The wide streets of the city center are still lined with brightly painted wooden houses and picturesque warehouses.

The Tiffany windows are magnificent at the **Nordenfjeldske Kunstindustrimuseum** (Decorative Arts Museum), which houses one of the finest art collections in Scandinavia. It has superb period rooms from the Renaissance to 1950s Scandinavian modern. ⊠ *Munkegt. 5,* ☎ *73/52–13–11.* ⊡ *NKr30.* ☽ *June–late Aug., weekdays 10–5, Sun. noon–5; late Aug.–May, weekdays 10–3, Thurs. until 7, Sun. noon–4.*

Saint Olav, who formulated a Christian religious code for Norway in 1024 while he was king, was killed in battle against local chieftains at Stiklestad. After he was buried, water sprang from his grave and people began to believe that his nails and hair continued to grow beneath the ground. It is here on the grave of Saint Olav that **Nidaros Domkirke** (Nidaros Cathedral) was built. Following a series of other miracles, the town became a pilgrimage site for the Christians of northern Europe, and Olav was canonized in 1164.

Although construction was begun in 1070, the oldest existing parts of the cathedral date from around 1150. During the Catholic period (circa 1000–1537) it attracted crowds of pilgrims, but after the Re-

Trondheim and the North

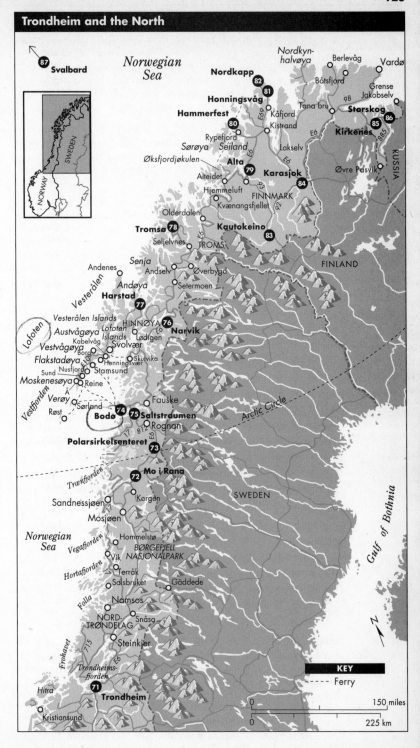

Svalbard **87**

Norwegian Sea

Nordkyn-halvøya

Berlevåg

Vardø

Nordkapp **82**

81

Båtsfjord

Grense Jakobselv

Honningsvåg

Tana bru

98

Hammerfest

Kåfjord

Storskog

85

86

80

Kistrand

Kirkenes

Rypefjord

E6

84

RUSSIA

Sørøya

Seiland

Lakselv

885

Øksfjordjøkulen

Alta **79**

E6

Karasjok

Øvre Pasvik

Alteidet

Hjemmeluft

84

Kvænangsfjellet

93

FINNMARK

Olderdalen

Kautokeino

Tromsø **78**

83

Seljelvnes

TROMS

Senja

Andenes

Andselv

Øverbygd

FINLAND

Vesterålen

Setermoen

Andøya

Harstad

77

Vesterålen Islands

HINNØYA **76**

Austvågøya

Lofoten Islands

Lødingen

Narvik

Kabelvåg

Svolvær

Vestvågøya

Borg

Flakstadøya

Henningsvær

Skutvika

Nusfjord

Stamsund

Sund

Moskenesøya

Reine

Lofoten

Fauske

Å

Verøy

Vestfjorden

Sørland

74

75 **Saltstraumen**

Røst

Bodø

Rognan

Arctic Circle

Polarsirkelsenteret

73

72 **Mo i Rana**

Trænfjorden

SWEDEN

Sandnessjøen

Korgen

Norwegian Sea

Mosjøen

Vegafjorden

Hommelstø

Vik

Hortafjorden

BØRGEFJELL NASJONALPARK

Terråk

Folla

Salsbruket

Gäddede

Gulf of Bothnia

Namsos

NORD-TRØNDELAG

Snåsa

Frohavet

Steinkjer

715

E6

Trondheims-fjorden

Hitra

71

Trondheim

N

Kristiansund

KEY

- - - Ferry

0   150 miles

0   225 km

formation its importance declined and fires destroyed much of it. The crown jewels, which visitors can view, are still kept in the cathedral. Guided tours are offered in English mid-June to mid-August, weekdays at 11, 2, and 4. ⊠ *Kongsgårdsgt. 2,* ☎ *73/52–52–33.* ⊠ *NKr20. Ticket also permits entry to Erkebispegården (☞ below).* ⊙ *Mid-June–mid-Aug., weekdays 9–6:15, Sat. 9–2, Sun. 1–4; May–mid-June and mid-Aug.–mid-Sept., weekdays 9–3, Sat. 9–2, Sun. 1–4; mid-Sept.–mid-Apr., weekdays noon–2:30, Sat. 11–2, Sun. 1–3.*

Scandinavia's oldest secular building (actually two buildings connected by a gatehouse) is the **Erkebispegården** (Archbishop's Palace). Dating from around 1160, it was the residence of the archbishop until the Reformation. After that, it was a Danish governor's palace and later a military headquarters.

Within the Erkebispegården is the **Forsvarsmuseet** (Army Museum), with displays of uniforms, swords, and daggers. The **Hjemmefrontmuseet** (Resistance Museum), also there, documents the occupation of Norway during World War II through objects and photographs. *Archbishop's Palace:* ☎ *73/50–12–12.* ⊠ *NKr20. Ticket also permits entry to cathedral.* ⊙ *June–Aug., weekdays 9–3, Sat. 9–2, Sun. 12:30–3:30. Army and Resistance museums:* ☎ *73/99–59–97.* ⊠ *NKr5.* ⊙ *June–Aug., weekdays 10–3; year-round, weekends 11–3.*

Behind the **Biblioteket** (Library, ⊠ Peter Egges Pl. 1) you can see the **remains of St. Olavskirke** (St. Olav's Church). The crypt of another medieval church can be seen inside Trondhjems og Strindens Sparebank (a savings bank at Søndregate 2) during normal banking hours.

Scandinavia's largest wooden building, **Stiftsgården,** was built in 1778 as a private home, the result of a competition between two sisters who were trying to outdo each other with the size of their houses. Today it is the king's official residence in Trondheim. The interior is sparsely furnished. ⊠ *Munkegt. 23,* ☎ *73/52–13–11.* ⊠ *NKr30.* ⊙ *June–mid-June, Tues.–Sat. 10–3, Sun. noon–5; mid-June–mid-Aug., Tues.–Sat. 10–5, Sun. noon–5; mid-Aug.–May, open 1 day per month.*

Off Munkegate near the water, you can see an immense variety of seafood at **Ravnkloa Fiskehall** (fish market). The **Sjøfartsmuseet** (Maritime Museum), housed in a former prison, displays galleon figureheads, ship models, a harpoon cannon from a whaling boat, and a large collection of seafaring pictures. ⊠ *Fjordgt. 6A,* ☎ *73/52–89–75.* ⊠ *NKr20.* ⊙ *Mon.–Sat. 9–3, Sun. noon–3; closed Sat. in winter.*

Trøndelag Folkemuseum has a collection of rustic buildings from the turn of the century, including a dental office and a lace and ribbon maker's workshop. The museum restaurant is from 1739 and serves traditional Norwegian food. ⊠ *Sverresborg,* ☎ *73/53–14–90.* ⊠ *NKr40.* ⊙ *Late May–Aug., daily 11–6, Sept.–Dec., Sun. noon–4.*

OFF THE
BEATEN PATH

RINGVE MUSIC MUSEUM – For an unusual museum visit, you can take a half-hour ride to Fagerheim and Ringve Gård, the childhood home of the naval hero Admiral Tordenskiold. Guides (music students) demonstrate the instruments on display and tell about their role in the history of music. Concerts are held regularly. ⊠ *Lade Allé 60,* ☎ *73/92–24–11.* ⊠ *NKr50. Guided tours in English late May–June, daily at 11:30 and 2:30; July–mid-Aug., daily at 11, 12:30, 2:30, and 4:30; mid-Aug.– late Aug., daily at 11, 12:30, and 2:30; Sept., daily at noon; Oct.–late May, Sun. at 1:30. Tour lasts about 75 mins.*

Dining and Lodging

Trondheim is known for several dishes, including *surlaks* (pickled salmon), marinated in a sweet-and-sour brine with onions and spices and served with sour cream. A sweet specialty is *tekake* (tea cake), which looks like a thick-crust pizza topped with a lattice pattern of cinnamon and sugar.

$$$ ★ ✕ Bryggen. The furnishings are in bleached wood, with dark-blue and red accessories, and the atmosphere is intimate. The menu features reindeer fillet salad with cranberry vinaigrette and herb cream soup with both freshwater and ocean crayfish for appetizers. ⊠ *Øvre Bakklandet 66,* ☎ *73/52–02–30. Reservations essential. AE, DC, MC, V. Closed Sun. No lunch.*

$$–$$$ ✕ Havfruen. "The Mermaid" has a maritime dining room with an open kitchen at street level. Fish soup is the most popular starter; summer main dishes include poached halibut. ⊠ *Kjøpmannsgt. 7,* ☎ *73/53–26–26. AE, DC, MC, V. Closed Sun. No lunch.*

$$ ✕ Hos Magnus. The price–value ratio is excellent at this old-fashioned restaurant at Bryggen. The menu ranges from old local-specialty surlaks to modern dishes such as salmon cured and marinated with aquavit brandy. Lamb roulade stuffed with cheese and mushroom sauce is on the menu, and there are ample fish and vegetarian choices, too. ⊠ *Kjøpmannsgt. 63,* ☎ *73/52–41–10. AE, DC, MC, V.*

$$ ✕ Lian. In the heights above the city, the views here are spectacular. The oldest part of the restaurant dates from 1700, but the round section, from the 1930s, commands the best view. The food is solid, honest, and hearty, with roast beef, reindeer, smoked pork loin, and the old standby, *kjøttkaker* (Norwegian meat cakes). ⊠ *Lianvn.,* ☎ *72/55–90–77. MC, V.*

$$ ★ ✕ Tavern på Sverresborg. This big, yellow, wooden former ferryman's house at the Trøndelag Folkemuseum has been an inn since 1739. The food is authentic Norwegian, including meat and fish prepared with old methods—pickled, salted, and dried. Choices include a plate with four different kinds of herring, roast lamb ribs, trout, meat cakes, and rømmegrøt. Homemade oatmeal bread and rolls accompany all dishes. ⊠ *Sverresborg Allé,* ☎ *73/52–09–32. MC, V.*

$ ✕ De 3 Stuer. Everything this small bistro chain serves is homemade, and the daily specials may be fish soufflé, fried fish with sour-cream sauce, split-pea soup with sausage, boiled beef, and lamb stew, all served with dessert and coffee. For lunch there's smørbrød, crescent rolls, salads, and cakes. ⊠ *Trondheim Torg,* ☎ *73/52–92–20;* ⊠ *Gågaten Leuthenhaven,* ☎ *73/52–43–42;* ⊠ *Dronningens Gt. 11,* ☎ *73/52–63–20. Reservations not accepted. MC, V. Dronningens Gt. closed Sun.*

$$–$$$$ ▥ Quality Prinsen Hotel. Rooms in this hotel in the center of the city are light—monochromatic to the point of being dull. One of the restaurants here, Pinocchio, serves a good early dinner. ⊠ *Kongensgt. 30, 7002,* ☎ *73/53–06–50,* FAX *73/53–06–44. 81 rooms, 1 suite. 3 restaurants, 3 bars, nightclub. AE, DC, MC, V.*

$$–$$$$ ▥ Radisson SAS Royal Garden. The city's showcase hostelry, right on the river, was built in the same style as the old warehouse buildings that line the waterfront, but in glass and concrete instead of wood. This luxury hotel was renovated before the World Championship in Nordic Skiing in 1997. ⊠ *Kjøpmannsgata 73, 7010,* ☎ *73/52–11–00,* FAX *73/53–17–66. 297 rooms, 8 suites. 3 restaurants, bar, indoor pool, exercise room. AE, DC, MC, V.*

$$$ ▥ Clarion Grand Olav Hotel. Not too many of the impeccably decorated rooms here are similiar—after all, there are 27 different room models. The hotel is part of a complex that contains shops and

Olavshallen Concert Hall (home of the Trondheim Philharmonic). ⊠ *Kjøpmannsgt. 48,* ☎ *73/53–53–10,* FAX *73/53–57–20. 106 rooms. Restaurant, bar, pub, no-smoking rooms, jazz club, meeting rooms. AE, DC, MC, V.*

$$ 🖭 **Ambassadeur.** From the roof terrace of this first-rate modern hotel, you'll see the deep-blue waters of the Trondheimsfjord reflect the dramatic and irregular coastline. The Ambassadeur is about 300 ft from the market square. Most rooms have fireplaces, and some have balconies. ⊠ *Elvegt. 18,* ☎ *73/52–70–50,* FAX *73/52–70–52. 34 rooms. Bar. AE, DC, MC, V.*

$–$$ 🖭 **Comfort Home Hotel Bakeriet.** The hotel opened in March 1991 in
★   a building built as a bakery in 1863. Few of the rooms look alike, but all are large and stylish in their simplicity, with natural wood furniture and beige-and-red-stripe textiles. There's no restaurant, but a hot evening meal is included in the room rate. You can borrow a track suit, and there's free light beer in the lounge by the sauna. ⊠ *Brattørgt. 2, 7011, Trondheim,* ☎ *73/52–52–00,* FAX *73/50–23–30. 99 rooms. In-room VCRs, sauna. AE, DC, MC, V.*

$–$$ 🖭 **Trondheim.** The building is old on the outside, with a curved corner and wrought-iron balconies, but inside it's new. The rooms are big and light, with what is now considered to be classic Scandinavian bentwood furniture. ⊠ *Kongensgt. 15, 7013,* ☎ *73/50–50–50,* FAX *73/ 51–60–58. 131 rooms. Bar, meeting room. AE, DC, MC, V.*

Nightlife

Olavskvartalet is the center of much of the city's nightlife, with a disco, a jazz and blues club, and a bar and beer hall in the cellar. **Monte Cristo** (⊠ Prinsensgt. 38–40, ☎ 73/52–18–80) has a restaurant, bar, and disco under the same roof and is popular with the mid-20s and up age group. Students and younger people in search of cheap drinks, music, and dancing tend to gravitate toward **Strossa** (⊠ Elgeseter Gt. 1, ☎ 73/89–95–10), which is run by students. **Cafe Remis** (⊠ Kjoepmannsgt. 12, ☎ 73/52–05–52) is the center for gay nightlife in Trondheim.

Outdoor Activities and Sports

FISHING

The **Nidelven** (Nid River) in Trondheim is one of Norway's best salmon and trout rivers. You can fish right in the city, but, as usual, you'll need a license. Contact the tourist office.

SKIING

Bymarka and **Estenstadmarka,** the wooded areas on the periphery of Trondheim, are popular among cross-country skiers. At **Skistua** (ski lodge) in Bymarka, and at **Vassfjellet** south of the city, there are downhill runs.

En Route   Nord Trøndelag, as the land above Trondheim is called, is largely agricultural. Taken on its own, it's beautiful, with farms, mountains, rock formations, and clear blue water, but compared with the rest of Norway, it is subtle, with only an undulating landscape—so many tourists just sleep through it on the night train or fly over it on their way to the North. The first town of any size is Steinkjer, a military base, boot camp for 3,000 Norwegian army recruits every year.

Mo i Rana

🔢 *350 km (218 mi) north of Steinkjer.*

Mo i Rana (the poetic name means Mo on the Ranafjord) is a center for iron and steel production using ore from nearby mines.

Setergrotta is one of almost 200 caves 26 km (16 mi) northwest of Mo i Rana. Setergrotta, with 7,920 ft of charted underground paths, many narrow passages, natural chimneys, and an underground river, is for serious spelunkers. The caves are usually open from mid-June to mid-August; however, times vary with conditions. Check with the tourist office (☎ 75/15–06–22, or 75/15–28–87). 🖅 *NKr160 for a 2-hour guided tour.*

Grønligrotta, Scandinavia's best-known show cave, even has electric lights. The 20-minute tour goes deep into the limestone cave to the underground river. ☎ 75/16–23–44. 🖅 *NKr50.* ⊘ *Mid-June–mid-Aug. Tours daily on the hr 10–7.*

OFF THE
BEATEN PATH

SVARTISEN – Glacier fans can hike on the Svartisen—literally, Black Ice— the second-largest glacier in Norway, covering 375 square km (144 square mi). The glacier is 30 km (19 mi) north of Mo i Rana, about 2½ hours by car south of Bodø. OVDS (☎ 75/52–10–20) offers seven-hour boat tours from Bodø to the ice cap on Saturdays in summer. The easiest way to get to the glacier is from Mo, 32 km (20 mi) by car to Svartisvatn lake. A boat crosses the lake every hour to within 2½ km (1½ mi) of the Østerdal arm of the glacier. If you plan to get to the glacier on your own, you should inquire at the Svartisen Tourist Center (☎ 75/75–00–11) about connecting with a guide. Glacier walking is extremely hazardous and should never be done without a professional guide—even though a glacier may appear fixed and static, it is always changing; there's always the danger of calving and hard-to-spot crevasses.

Polarsirkelenteret

🚳 *80 km (50 mi) north of Mo i Rana.*

On a bleak stretch of treeless countryside is the Arctic Circle. The Polarsirkelenteret (Arctic Circle Center), on E6, presents a multiscreen show about Norway. The post office has a special postmark, and you can get your Arctic Circle Certificate stamped. There's also a cafeteria and gift shop. ⊠ *8242 Polarsirkelen,* ☎ *75/16–60–66.* 🖅 *NKr40.* ⊘ *May, daily 10–6; June, daily 10–8; July, daily 8–midnight; Aug., daily 10–6 (Apr., Oct. cafeteria only).*

Bodø

🚴 *174 km (108 mi) north of the Polarsirkelenteret.*

Bodø, a modern city of about 40,000 just above the Arctic Circle, is best known as the end station of the Nordlandsbanen railroad and the gateway to the Lofoten Islands and the North. The midnight sun is visible from June 2 to July 10. Like many other coastal towns, it began as a small fishing community, but today it is a commercial and administrative center. Like much of northern Norway, the Second World War inevitably touched Bodø. In 1940, the town fell victim to German bombs meant to destroy a British air base.

Bodø is the best base for boat excursions to the coastal bird colonies on the Væren Islands. Bodø is also site of the **Nordland County Museum,** which depicts the life of the Sami and the regional history of the area, particularly its rich fishing heritage. ⊠ *Prinsengt. 116,* ☎ *75/52–61–28.* 🖅 *NKr 15.* ⊘ *Weekdays 9–3, weekends noon–3.*

Down the road from Bodø's airport and a good 15 minutes from the town's center, the jumbo **Norsk Luftfartssenter** (Norwegian Aviation Center) tells the story of Norwegian aviation with flight simulators and life-size displays of commercial and military planes dating back to 1912. ☎ *75/50–85–50.* 🖅 *NKr 65.* ⊘ *Early June–mid-Aug., weekdays 10–*

8, Sat. 10–5; mid-Aug.–early June, Mon., Tues., Thurs., Fri. 10–4, Wed. 10–7, Sat. 11–5, Sun. 11–6.

Lodging

$$ ⊞ **Inter Nor Diplomat Hotel.** This hotel near the harbor is a short walk from the shopping district. The modern rooms are somberly decorated. The restaurant has live entertainment, but the food could be more imaginative. ⊠ *Sjøgt. 23, 8000 Bodø,* ☎ *75/52–70–00,* ℻ *75/52–24–60. 109 rooms. 2 restaurants, bar, exercise room, convention center. AE, DC, MC, V.*

$$ ⊞ **Norrøna.** This bed-and-breakfast-style establishment is plain yet comfortable and has a prime downtown location. ⊠ *Storgt. 4B,* ☎ *75/52–55–50,* ℻ *75/52–33–88. 105 rooms. AE, DC, MC, V.*

$$ ⊞ **Radisson SAS Hotel Bodø.** This grandiose hotel pulses with life and has enough services to keep you entertained nearly around the clock. As with all SAS hotels, the rooms have all the amenities, and the service is impeccable. ⊠ *Storgt. 2,* ☎ *75/52–41–00,* ℻ *75/52–74–93. 190 rooms. Restaurant, 2 bars, sauna, health club, nightclub. AE, DC, MC, V.*

Saltstraumen

⑦⑤ *33 km (20 mi) southeast of Bodø on Route 80/17.*

Saltstraumen is a 3-km-long (2-mi-long) and 500-ft-wide section of water between the outer fjord, which joins with the sea, and the inner fjord basin. During high tide, the volume of water rushing through the strait and into the basin is so great that whirlpools form. This is the legendary *malstrøm*—and the strongest one in the world. Sometimes as many as four separate whirlpools can be seen, and the noise made by these "cauldrons" can be both loud and eerie. All that rush of water brings enormous quantities of fish, making the malstrøm a popular fishing spot. The nearby **Saltstraumen Opplevelsesenter** (Adventure Center) houses regional artifacts and a multimedia show that recount the scientific and human tales behind the malstrøm. ☎ *75/56–06–55.* ▦ *NKr50.* ☉ *Mid-May–late May and early-Aug.–mid-Aug., daily 11–8; June–July, daily 11–10; mid-Aug.–late Aug. 11–6*

Dining and Lodging

$$$–$$$$ ✕⊞ **Saltstraumen Hotel.** This hotel is practically on top of the malstrøm. The restaurant serves delicious steamed halibut in butter sauce. ⊠ *1056,* ☎ *75/58–76–85. 28 rooms in hotel, 14 separate bungalows. Restaurant, meeting rooms. AE, DC, MC, V.*

OFF THE **BLODVEIMUSEET** – Ninety minutes southeast of Bodø in Rognan, the
BEATEN PATH Bloodstained Road Museum recreates the sinister atmosphere of an icy North Norway Nazi prison camp where Russian, Serb, and Polish prisoners of war were incarcerated. Photographs and documents displayed in a reconstructed wooden prison cabin show the gradual disintegration of men as they built the roads and railway meant to transport weapons from Mosjøen to Kirkenes. The resulting infrastructure is now known as the Bloodstained Road. **Saltdal Bygdetun,** a collection of historic houses, is a few yards away. Call for a guided tour. ☎ *75/69–06–60.* ☉ *June–Aug., weekdays 9–3, Sat. 12–4, Sun. 1–6.*

Narvik

⑦⑥ *336 km (210 mi) north of Saltstraumen.*

Narvik is more easily reached by rail from Stockholm than from most places in Norway, as it is the end station on the *Ofotbanen,* the Norwegian railroad that connects with the Swedish railroad's northernmost line. Narvik was originally established as the ice-free port for exporting Swedish iron ore mined around Kiruna. From mid-June to mid-August, you can take a cable car 2,132 ft above town for a view of the city and Ofotenfjord.

On May 9, 1940, the German army invaded Norway through Narvik, and German occupying forces stayed for more than five years. After the war, Narvik, which had been leveled by the bombing, was rebuilt. The **Krigsminnemuseet** (War Memorial Museum) documents wartime events with artifacts, models, and pictures. ⊠ *Torget,* ☎ *76/94–44–26.* ▣ *NKr25.* ☉ *March–mid June and mid-Aug.–late Sept., daily 11–2; mid-June–mid-Aug., daily 10–10.*

Lodging

$$–$$$ ▥ **Inter Nor Grand Royal.** It looks like an office building from the outside, but inside it is a top-class hotel, with big, rather formal rooms. ⊠ *Kongensgt. 64, 8500 Narvik,* ☎ *76/94–15–00,* ℻ *76/94–55–31. 108 rooms. 2 restaurants, 2 bars, sauna, exercise room, nightclub, convention center. AE, DC, MC, V.*

Lofoten and the Islands of the North

Extending out into the ocean north of Bodø are the Lofoten Islands, a 190-km (118-mi) chain of jagged peaks and mountaintops rising from the bottom of the sea like open jaws. In summer the idyll of farms, fjords, and fishing villages draws caravans of tourists, whereas in winter the coast facing the Arctic Ocean is one of Europe's stormiest. The midnight sun is visible here from May 26 to July 17. If you are lucky enough to be visiting on a clear midnight, drive over to the western side, where the spear-shaped mountains give way to flat, sandy beaches that look oddly fluorescent in the hush of night. The sight is spectacular.

Until about 50 years ago fishing was the only source of income for the area (today tourism helps bolster the still thriving fisheries). Cod and haddock were either dried or salted and sold in other parts of Europe. As many as 6,000 boats with 30,000 fishermen would mobilize between January and March for the Lofotfisket, the world's largest cod-fishing event. During the season they fished in open boats and took shelter during stormy nights in *rorbuer,* simple cabins built right on the water. Today many rorbuer have been converted into lodgings, but Lofotfisket is still an annual tradition. In the summer, crisscrossing wooden racks are densely hung with drying cod while the midnight sun plays on the wooden boats in the harbor.

The best way to visit Lofoten is by car. **Svolvær,** the main town and administrative center for the villages on the islands, is connected with the other islands by express boat and ferry, and by coastal steamer and air to Bodø. It has a thriving summer art colony.

A drive on E10, from Svolvær to the outer tip of Lofoten (130 km [80 mi])—the town with the enigmatic name of **Å**—is an opportunity to see how the islanders really live.

The **Norwegian Fishing Village Museum** (☎ 76/09–14–88) at Å is a spread-out living fishing village with houses, a 19th-century cod-liver-oil factory, and a bread bakery. ▣ *NKr35.* ☉ *June–Aug., daily 10–6; Sept.–May, weekdays 10–4.*

Just south of Svolvær, the hamlet of **Kabelvåg** provides the perfect introduction to the string of islands, their history, and their inhabitants. A cluster of museums less than a mile from the quiet village center sits on the site of an old fishing settlement. Restored fishing cabins displayed at the **Lofotmuseet** (Lofoten Island Museum, ☎ 76/07–82–23) depict the rigorous life of a fishing community on the grassy edge of a fjord inlet. Next door, the **Galleri Espolin** (☎ 76/07–64–05) exhibits the dark, haunting paintings and lithographs of fishermen in stormy weather. Kaare Espolin Johnsen, who died in 1994, was a nationally renowned artist. The **Lofot-Akvariet** (Aquarium, ☎ 76/07–86–65) proves you can't understand a fishing culture without knowing what's in the water. Exhibits include a salmon farm, a seal pond, and a slide show of sea creatures. ⊠ Storvågan. ☉ Mid-June–mid-Aug., daily 10–9; mid–late Aug., daily 10–6; Sept.–Apr., weekdays and Sun. 11–3; May–early June, daily 11–3.

Southwest of Kabelvåg is **Henningsvær.** This enchanting village is home to **Karl Erik Harr Gallery** (☎ 76/07–15–73), which exhibits Lofoten-inspired paintings by acclaimed Norwegian artists, including the gallery's namesake. Upstairs is more on fishing and a reconstructed cod-liver-oil factory.

Viking enthusiasts might want to veer northwest to **Borg,** where archeologists unearthed a long, low chieftain's house—the largest Viking building ever discovered. Now rebuilt exactly as it was, the **Viking Museum Lofotr** houses the 1,000-year-old artifacts discovered there. Tour guides in Viking garb sit around crackling fires and demonstrate the crafts, customs, and cookery of their ancestors. ⊠ Borg i Lofoten. ☎ 76/08–49–00. 🖭 NKr70. ☉ Late May–mid-June, daily 10–5; mid-June–early Aug., daily 10–7; early Aug.–Sept., daily 10–5.

Other scenic stops include tucked-away **Nusfjord,** a 19th-century fishing village on an official European Conservation list; **Sund,** with its smithy; and festive **Reine.**

NEED A BREAK?   The rustic **Gammelbua,** in Reine, serves excellent salmon mousse and chilled Norwegian beer. Locals and tourists flock here to eat, drink, and gossip.

Off the tip of Moskenesøy, the last island with a bridge, is **Moskenesstraumen,** a malstrøm not quite as dramatic as Saltstraumen (☞ above) but inspiration to both Jules Verne, who wrote about it in Journey Beneath the Sea, and Edgar Allan Poe, who described it in his short story "A Descent into the Maelstrom."

North of the Lofotens are the **Vesterålen Islands,** with more fishing villages and rorbuer, and diverse vegetation. There are fewer tourists in Vesterålen, but more whale sightings. Puffins populate area cliffs, as in the Lofotens. The Coastal Steamer (☞ Arriving and Departing by Boat in Trondheim A to Z, below) slithers in and around fjords along the coastline of these more subtle islands, such as the steep-cliffed **Trollfjord.** The first arctic cod of the year is caught in Vesterålen.

⑦ East of Vesterålen on Hinnøya, Norway's largest island, is **Harstad,** where the year-round population of 22,000 swells to 42,000 during the annual June cultural festival (the lineup includes concerts, theater, and dance) and its July deep-sea fishing festival.

Dining and Lodging

A word on the fishermen's cabins: although hotels have popped up in some of the bigger fishing villages, rorbu lodging is essential to the Lofoten experience. Rorbuer vary in size and comfort, some date back to the last century and others are new imitations. If you do stay in a rorbu, it is worth your while to bring a few days' worth of food to stick in the refrigerator. Some villages have few cafés, and you may find that the closest thing to a grocery store is a gas station. Unless you have your own linens, remember you'll have to pay extra—usually about NKr100.

$$$ ✕ **Røkenes Gård.** The farm was originally homesteaded in AD 400, and the large white wooden building with an intricately carved portal opened in 1750 as a commercial trading house and inn. The ninth generation of descendants restored it, and it is now a cozy restaurant serving regional specialties, such as marinated reindeer and cloudberry parfait. ⊠ *9400 Harstad,* ☎ *77/01–74–65. Reservations essential. AE, DC, MC, V.*

$$ ✕ **Fiskekrogen.** This quayside restaurant in the fishing village of Henningsvær will prepare your own catch. Chef-owner Otto Asheim's specialties include smoked gravlaks (smoking the dill-marinated salmon gives it extra depth of flavor) and sautéed ocean catfish garnished with mussels and shrimp. ⊠ *8330 Henningsvær,* ☎ *76/07–46–52. Reservations essential. AE, DC, MC, V.*

$$–$$$ ▥ **Grand Nordic.** This hotel is housed in a redbrick Bauhaus-style building; the public rooms are decorated with Norwegian leather furniture from the 1970s. Bedrooms, no bigger than necessary, have dark-wood furnishings. The restaurant and conference rooms are lighter and more modern. ⊠ *Strandgt. 9, 9400 Harstad,* ☎ *77/06–21–70,* 𝖥𝖠𝖷 *77/ 06–77–30. 82 rooms, 3 suites. Restaurant, bar, nightclub, convention center. AE, DC, MC, V.*

$$–$$$ ▥ **Nyvågar Rorbu og Aktivitetssenter.** This lodging and recreation complex is a 15-minute drive from the Svolvær airport and a five-minute walk from the Storvågan museum complex. Activities are well organized, with fishing-boat tours, eagle safaris, and deep-sea rafting, as well as planned evening entertainment. The cabins, which are not especially authentic (they're new), are spotless. ⊠ *8310 Kabelvåg, Storvågan,* ☎ *76/07–89–00,* 𝖥𝖠𝖷 *76/07–89–50. 30 rooms. Restaurant, meeting rooms. AE, DC, MC, V.*

$$–$$$ ▥ **Rainbow Vestfjord Hotel.** This simple hotel has spacious rooms and a lovely view of the harbor beyond. It used to be a cod-liver-oil factory. ⊠ *8301 Svolvær,* ☎ *76/07–08–70,* 𝖥𝖠𝖷 *76/07–08–54. 63 rooms, 3 suites. Restaurant, bar, conference room. AE, DC, MC, V.*

$$–$$$ ▥ **Rica Hotel Svolvær.** One of the rooms in this spruced-up fisherman's inn comes with a hole through which to fish one's dinner. Don't be fooled by the Rica's rorbu look. It's just an elegant hotel on the inside. ⊠ *Lamholmen, 8301 Svolvær,* ☎ *76/07–22–22,* 𝖥𝖠𝖷 *76/07–20–01. 147 rooms. Restaurant, bar, convention center. AE, DC, MC, V.*

$ ▥ **Henningsvær Rorbuer.** This small group of turn-of-the-century rorbuer, all facing the sea, is just outside the center of Lofoten's most important fishing village. Breakfasts can be ordered from the cafeteria-reception, where there's a fireplace and a TV. Reservations are essential for July. ⊠ *8330 Henningsvær,* ☎ *76/07–46–00,* 𝖥𝖠𝖷 *76/07–49–10. 16 1- or 2-bedroom rorbuer. Cafeteria, grill, sauna, laundry service. V.*

$ ▥ **Nusfjord Rorbuer.** Families stay at these secluded cabins for weeks at a time. There's plenty to do—hiking, fishing, boating—in the surrounding area, which is crawling with natural life: giant moss-covered boulders seem frozen in motion, and small herds of sheep wander freely along the one-lane highway. For a glimpse at the midnight sun, drive to the other side of the island at Flakstad. Rowboats are included in the price of a rorbu, and you can rent out fishing gear and motor boats. The completely preserved village of Nusfjord with its string of colorful rorbuer is quaint at every turn, starting with the old-fashioned general store. ⊠ *8380 Ramberg,* ☎ *76/09–30–20,* 𝖥𝖠𝖷 *76/09–33–78. 15 1- or 2-bedroom rorbuer. Restaurant, bar, coin laundry. DC, MC, V.*

$ ▥ **Reine Rorbuer.** In the heart of Reine, which was named the country's prettiest village by Norwegian travel agents, these authentic fishing cabins are down the hill from Gammelbua (☞ *above*), a local eatery and social spot. The cabins all have typical Norwegian names, like Gro and

Liv. The furniture and kitchenware look and feel as old and Norwegian as the cabins. Make reservations early as the cabins tend to get booked early in summer. ⊠ *8390 Reine,* ☎ *76/09–22–22,* FAX *76/09–22–25. 26 1-, 2-, or 3-bedroom rorbuer, most with shower. AE, MC, V.*

$ ⌷ **Wulff-Nilsens Rorbuer.** A five-minute drive from Reine, this tidy cluster of 19th-century rorbuer is an excellent starting point for fishing excursions and mountain walks. Seagulls nest only yards from the cabins, and workers unload fish shipments on the dock below. The rorbuer are rustic but comfortably equipped; they have stoves and refrigerators. Breakfast and light meals are served in the restaurant by request. ⊠ *Hamnøy, 8390 Reine,* ☎ *76/09–23–20,* FAX *76/09–21–54. 14 1-, 2-, or 3-bedroom rorbuer, all with shower. Restaurant, kitchenettes. AE, MC, V.*

Outdoor Activities and Sports

BIRD-WATCHING

There's a constant shrieking hum that emanates from some of North Norway's arctic island cliffs, which virtually pulsate from the thousands of birds perching their sides. From Moskenes, just north of Å (or from Bodø), you can take a ferry to the bird sanctuaries of **Værøy** and **Røst.** Many different types of seabirds inhabit the cliffs, in particular the eider ducks, favorites of the local population, which build small shelters for their nests. Eventually the down collected from these nests ends up in *dyner* (down comforters).

WHALE-WATCHING

The stretch of sea that lies north of Lofoten and Vesterålen is perhaps the best place to sight whales, porpoises, and white-beaked dolphins. Whale safari boat tours leave from the tip of Andøy, a salamander-shaped island northwest of Hinnøya. Contact Andøy Nature Center (☎ 76/14–26–11) for more information. Brush up on your knowledge of the seafaring mammal at the island's **Whale Center** (Destination Lofoten, ☎ 76/07–30–00) before the trip. Farther south from the Vesterålen coastal town of Stø, **Whale Watch A/S** (☎ 76/13–44–99) also scours the sea for sperm, minke, and killer whales. Reservations are necessary for both excursions.

Shopping

Lofoten is a mecca for artists and craftspeople, who come for the spectacular scenery and the ever-changing subtle light; a list of galleries and crafts centers, with all locations marked on a map, is available from tourist offices.

Probably the best-known craftsperson in the region is Tor Vegard Mørkved, better known as **Smeden i Sund** (the blacksmith at Sund, ☎ 76/09–36–29). Watch him make wrought-iron cormorants in many sizes, as well as candlesticks and other gift items. Another fun stop is Åse and Åsvar Tangrand's **Glasshytta and Ceramics Workshop** (☎ 76/09–44–42), near Nusfjord. **Sakrisøy Antiques & Second Hand Store** (☎ 76/09–21–43), which is just outside of Reine (above Dagmar's Museum of Dolls and Toys), sells sundry Lofoten keepsakes.

Tromsø

❼❽ *318 km (197 mi) northeast of Harstad.*

The most important city north of the Arctic Circle, Tromsø looks the way a polar town should—with ice-capped mountain ridges and jagged architecture. The midnight sun shines from May 21 to July 21, and the city's total area—2,558 square km (987 square mi)—is the most expansive in Norway. Still, Tromsø is just about the same size as the country of Luxembourg, but home to only 55,000 people. The city's picturesque center itself sits on a small, hilly island connected to the mountainous mainland by a long-legged, slender bridge with a subtle peak that mimics the craggy surroundings. The 13,000 students at the world's northernmost university are one reason the nightlife here is more lively than in many other northern cities.

Certainly, the **Ishavskatedralen** (Arctic Cathedral) is the city's best-known structure. A looming peak of 11 descending triangles of concrete and glass, it is meant to evoke the shape of a Sami tent and the iciness of a glacier. Inside, an immense jewel-colored stained-glass window by Norwegian artist Viktor Sparre depicts the Second Coming. ☎ *77/63–76–11.* ☑ *NKr10.* ☉ *June–Aug., Mon.–Sat. 10–8, Sun. 1:30–6. Times may vary according to church services.*

The **Tromsø Museum,** part of Tromsø University, offers an extensive survey of local history, lifestyles, and nature, with dioramas on Sami culture, arctic hunting practices, and wildlife. Children can listen to animal sounds over earphones, match animals to tales about them, and play with a nearly life-size dinosaur. An open-air museum is on the same grounds. ☒ *Universitetet, Lars Thøringsvei 10,* ☎ *77/64–50–00.* ☑ *NKr20.* ☉ *June–Aug., daily 9–9; Sept.–May, Mon., Tues., Thurs., and Fri. 8:30–3:30, Wed. 7 PM–10 PM, Sat. noon–3, Sun. 11–4.*

The **Polarmuseet** (Polar Museum), in an 1830s customs warehouse, documents the history of the polar region, with skis and equipment from Roald Amundsen's expedition to the South Pole and a reconstructed Svalbard hunting station from 1910. ☒ *Søndre Tollbugt. 11b,* ☎ *77/68–43–73.* ☑ *NKr30.* ☉ *Mid-May–mid-June, daily 11–6; mid-June–Aug., daily 11–8; Sept.–mid-May, daily 11–3.*

To get a real sense of Tromsø's northerly immensity and peace, take the **Fjellheisen** (cable car) from behind the cathedral up to the mountains, just a few minutes out of the city center. You'll get a great view of the city from **Storsteinen** (Big Rock), 1,386 ft above sea level. In the late afternoon and on weekends, summer and winter, this is where locals go to ski, picnic, walk their lucky dogs, and admire the view. ☎ *77/63–87–37.* ☑ *NKr 50.* ☉ *Late Apr.–mid-May, daily 10–5; late May–Sept., daily 10–1 AM if it's sunny. At other times, call for hours.*

OFF THE BEATEN PATH
NORDLYSPLANETARIET – At the Northern Lights Planetarium, 112 projectors guarantee a 360° view of programs, which include a tour through the northern lights, the midnight sun, and geological history, as well as a film and multimedia show about the city. It's just outside town in Breivika. ☎ *77/67–60–00.* ☑ *NKr50.* ☉ *June–Aug., shows in English weekdays at 12:30 and 4:30, Sat. 4:30; Sept.–May call for show times.*

Dining and Lodging

$$–$$$ ✕ **Brankos.** Branko and Anne Brit Bartolj serve authentic Slovenian dishes here. Try the *pleskavica* (grilled beef with zesty spices and garlic), accompanied by their own imported wines from the former Yugoslavia. The bistro on the ground floor serves an affordable lunch. ☒ *Storgt. 57,* ☎ *77/68–26–73. Reservations essential. AE, DC, MC, V.*

$$–$$$ ✕ **Compagniet.** An old wooden trading house from 1837 is now a stylish restaurant serving modern Norwegian food. Chef Anders Blomkvist prepares cream of lobster soup with a dash of brandy and escargot in garlic sauce for starters; main dishes include grilled crayfish and reindeer fillet in a sauce seasoned with blueberries. ☒ *Sjøgt. 12,* ☎ *77/65–57–21. Reservations essential. AE, DC, MC, V. No lunch in winter.*

$$–$$$ 🏨 **Comfort Home Hotel With.** This hotel on the waterfront's dock area has spacious rooms decorated in shades of gray with occasional colorful accents. The sauna-relaxation room on the top floor has the best view in town. As part of the Home Hotel chain, Hotel With offers al-

cohol-free beer, a hot meal, and waffles and coffee at all times and at no charge. ⊠ *Sjøgt. 35–37, 9000,* ☎ *77/68–70–00,* FAX *77/68–96–16. 76 rooms. Sauna, Turkish bath, meeting rooms. AE, DC, MC, V.*

$$–$$$ 🏨 **Radisson SAS Hotel.** You'll get splendid views over the Tromsø shoreline at this modern hotel, but standard rooms are tiny, and even the costlier "Business Club" rooms aren't big enough for real desks and tables, so modular ones have been attached to the walls. ⊠ *Sjøgt. 7, 9001,* ☎ *77/60–00–00,* FAX *77/66–42–60. 195 rooms with bath, 2 suites. Restaurant, bar, pizzeria, sauna, nightclub. AE, DC, MC, V.*

$$–$$$ 🏨 **Rica Ishavshotel.** Tromsø's snazziest hotel sits atop a deck that stretches over the sound toward the Arctic Cathedral, its icicle-like spire mirroring the cathedral's own triangular ridges. Inside, shiny wood furnishings with brass trimmings evoke the maritime life that is inescapable in this North Sea region. A colorful tapestry depicting life in the Arctic city brightens the bustling dining room, where the adjacent bar's piano chimes away. The soft-carpeted rooms are decorated in bold golds, reds, and navy blues, and the bathrooms are shiny and white. Guests represent a mixture of business executives, tourists, and scientific conference attendees. ⊠ *Fr. Langes gt. 2, Box 196, 9001,* ☎ *77/66–64–00,* FAX *77/66–64–44. 180 rooms. 2 restaurants, 2 bars, meeting rooms. AE, DC, MC, V.*

$$ 🏨 **Saga.** The central location on a pretty town square and a helpful staff make the Saga a good place to stay. Its restaurant has affordable, hearty meals, and the rooms—though somewhat basic—are quiet. ⊠ *Richard Withs Pl. 2,* ☎ *77/68–11–80,* FAX *77/68–23–80. 66 rooms. Restaurant, cafeteria. AE, DC, MC, V.*

$–$$ 🏨 **Polar Hotell.** This no-frills hotel gives good value for the money in winter, when none of the bigger hotels have special rates. Rooms are small, and the orange-brown color scheme is a bit dated, but it's a pleasant, unassuming place. ⊠ *Grønnegt. 45, 9000,* ☎ *77/68–64–80,* FAX *77/68–91–36. 68 rooms. Restaurant in a separate building across from the hotel, bar, meeting rooms. AE, DC, MC, V.*

Nightlife

Tromsø brags that it has 10 nightclubs, not bad for a city of 50,000 at the top of the world. **Compagniet** (☞ Dining, *above*) has the classiest nightclub; **Charly's** (⊠ Sjøgt. 7) at the SAS Royal Hotel is also popular. **Victoria/Klubb Circus/Amtmannen** (⊠ Amtmann Gt., ☎ 77/68–49–06), a good bar and restaurant complex, has live bands and attracts a younger crowd. **Dampen** (⊠ Kai Gt. 1) is more alternative than any other venue in Tromsø in terms of live music and clientele. The train motif at **Tromsø Jernbanestation** (⊠ Strandgt. 33-35, ☎ 77/61–23–48) suggests that some locals are still crossing their fingers to get a railway. The smoky bar attracts a young crowd who sit in booths akin to train compartments.

Outdoor Activities and Sports

HIKING

In Tromsø there's good hiking in the mountains above the city, reachable by funicular. Other regional possibilities begin anywhere outside the town's limits (usually only a few minutes away).

SKIING

In Tromsø, the mountains, only eight minutes away by funicular, are a great place to ski. Elsewhere, you'll have to ask specifics from the tourist board. Listen to the weather reports and heed warnings. Blizzards come in quickly over the water; the wind alone can knock a sizable person clear off his or her feet.

En Route The drive from Tromsø to Alta is mostly on a coastal road. At one point you'll drive along the **Kvænangsfjellet ridge,** where Kautokeino Sami spend the summer in turf huts—you might see a few of their reindeer along the way. Thirteen kilometers (8 miles) west of Alteidet you'll pass by Øksfjordjøkelen, the only glacier in Norway that calves into the sea.

Alta

⑦⑨ *409 km (253 mi) north of Tromsø, 217 km (134 mi) from the North Cape.*

Alta is a major transportation center into Finnmark, the far north of Norway. Most people come just to spend the night before making the final ascent to the North Cape.

OFF THE BEATEN PATH **ALTA MUSEUM –** It's worth a trek to Hjemmeluft, southwest of the city, to see four groupings of 2,500- to 6,000-year-old prehistoric rock carvings, the largest in northern Europe. The pictographs, featuring ships, reindeer, and even a man with a bow and arrow, were discovered in 1973 and are included on the UNESCO World Heritage List. The rock carvings form part of the Alta Museum. The museum has displays delineating the history of the area from the Stone Age until today, including its destruction in World War II. ☎ 78/43–53–77. 🎟 *Summer NKr40; winter NKr35.* ☉ *May and Sept. daily 9–6; early-June–mid-June and mid-Aug.–late Aug., daily 8–8; mid-June–mid-Aug., daily 8 am–11 pm; Oct.–Apr., weekdays 9–3, weekends 11–4.*

Lodging

$$$ 🏨 **North Cape Hotel Alta.** This glass-and-white hotel does everything it can to make you forget that you are in a place where it is dark much of the time. Everything is light, from the reflectors on the ceiling of public rooms to the white furniture in the bedrooms. ⊠ *Lokkevn. 1, 9500,* ☎ *78/48–27–00,* 🆁🆇 *78/43–58–25. 154 rooms. 2 restaurants, 2 bars, lobby lounge, sauna, nightclub, meeting rooms. AE, DC, MC, V.*

Outdoor Activities and Sports

DOGSLEDDING

Canyon Huskies (☎ 78/43–33–06), in Alta, arranges all kinds of personalized tours, whether you want to stay in a tent or hotel, and whether you want to drive your team or stay in the sled. Like most Norwegian sled dogs, these are very friendly.

Shopping

Manndalen Husflidslag (☎ 77/71–62–73) at Løkvoll in Manndalen, on E6 about 15 km (9 mi) west of Alta, is a center for Coastal Sami weaving on vertical looms. Local weavers sell their rugs and wall hangings along with other regional crafts.

Hammerfest

⑧⓪ *145 km (90 mi) north of Alta.*

The world's northernmost town is Hammerfest, an important fishing center. At these latitudes the "most northerlies" become numerous, but certainly the lifestyles here are a testament to determination, especially in winter, when night lasts for months. In 1891 Hammerfest decided to brighten the situation and purchased a generator from Thomas Edison. It was the first city in Europe to have electric street lamps.

Hammerfest is home to the **Royal and Ancient Polar Bear Society.** Since the exhibits all depict some aspect of Arctic hunts, don't visit the society if you don't like taxidermic displays. ⊠ *Town Hall Basement.*

Free. ⊙ *June–Aug., weekdays 8–8, weekends 10–3. Sept.–May, noon–3:30, or by appointment.*

Dining and Lodging

$$–$$$ ✕▦ **Rica Hotel Hammerfest.** The rooms are functional and small, but the furniture is comfortable. There is also an informal pizza pub and a spacious bar. ⊠ *Sørøygt. 15,* ☎ *78/41–13–33,* FAX *78/41–13–11. 94 rooms. Restaurant, bar, pizzeria, sauna, convention center. AE, DC, MC, V.*

$$$ ▦ **Quality Hammerfest Hotel.** Right on the pleasant Rådhusplassen, this guest house has handsome, harbor-view rooms for tolerable prices in a town where hotels are expensive. The hotel is very accessible for travelers with disabilities. ⊠ *Strandgt. 2–4,* ☎ *78/41–16–22,* FAX *78/41–21–27. 53 rooms. Restaurant, cafeteria, pub, sauna. AE, DC, MC, V.*

Honningsvåg

❽❶ *130 km (80.6 mi) from Hammerfest.*

The last village before the Cape, Honningsvåg was completely destroyed at the end of World War II, when the Germans retreated and burned everything they left behind. Only a single wood church, which still survives, was not left in embers. The **Nordkappmuseet** (North Cape Museum), on the third floor of Nordkapphuset (North Cape House), documents the history of the fishing industry in the region as well as the history of tourism at the North Cape. ⊠ *9750 Honningsvåg,* ☎ *78/47–28–33.* *NKr20.* ⊙ *Mid-June–mid-Aug., Mon.–Sat. 9–8, Sun. 1–8; mid-Aug.–mid-June, weekdays 11–4.*

Lodging

$ ▦ **Hotel Havly.** This simple hotel is cozy and centrally located, with small, spic-and-span rooms and an ample breakfast buffet. Because this is a seamen's hostel, no alcohol is served. ⊠ *9751 Honningsvåg,* ☎ *78/47–29–66,* FAX *78/47–30–10. 35 rooms. Cafeteria, meeting rooms. AE, MC, V.*

Outdoor Activities and Sports

BIRD-WATCHING

There are tons of birds in Gjesvær on the east coast of the Honningsvåg. Contact **Ola Thomassen** (☎ 78/47–57–73) for organized outings.

Nordkapp

❽❷ *34 km (21 mi) from Honningsvåg.*

On your journey to the Nordkapp (North Cape), you'll see an incredible treeless tundra, with crumbling mountains and sparse dwarf plants. Although this area is notoriously crowded in the summer, with endless lines of tour buses, it's completely different from fall through spring, when the snow is yards deep and the sea is frosty gray. Because the roads are closed in winter, the only access is from the tiny fishing village of Skarsvåg via Sno-Cat, a thump-and-bump ride that's as unforgettable as the beautifully bleak view. For winter information, contact North Cape Travel (☎ 78/47–25–99). Knivsjellodden, slightly west and less dramatic than the North Cape, is actually a hair farther north.

The contrast between this near-barren territory and the **North Cape Hall** is striking. Blasted into the interior of the plateau, the building is housed in a cave and includes a restaurant with incredible views. A tunnel leads past a small chapel to a grotto with a panoramic view of the Arctic Ocean and to the cliff wall itself, passing exhibits that trace the history of the Cape, from Richard Chancellor, an Englishman who drifted around it and named it in 1533, to Oscar II, king of Norway and Sweden, who climbed to the top of the plateau in 1873, and King Chulalongkorn of Siam (now Thailand), who visited the Cape in 1907. Out on the plateau itself, a hollow sculptured globe is illuminated by the midnight sun, which shines from May 11 to August 31. ✉ *9764 Nordkapp,* ☎ *78/47–25–99. Entrance to the hall:* ✆ *NKr175.* ☉ *Mid-Apr.–mid-May and late Sept.–early Oct., daily, 2–5; mid-May–mid-June, daily, noon–1 AM; mid-June–mid-Aug., daily, 10–2 AM; mid-Aug.–early Sept., daily, 10–midnight; early Sept.–mid-Sept., daily, noon–5.*

Outdoor Activities and Sports

RAFTING

Deep-sea rafting is a relatively new sport in the area, but one that is as exhilarating as it is beautiful. Among the several tours is a three-hour trip to the North Cape. Call **Nordkapp Safari** (☎ 78/47–27–94).

Trondheim to the North Cape A to Z

Arriving and Departing

BY BOAT

Hurtigruten (the coastal express boat, which calls at 35 ports from Bergen to Kirkenes) stops at Trondheim, southbound at St. Olav's Pier, Quay 16, northbound at Pier 1, Quay 7. Other stops between Trondheim and the North Cape include Bodø, Stamsund (Lofotens), Svolvær, Sortland (Vesterålen), Harstad, Tromsø, Hammerfest, and Honningsvåg. Call ☎ 73/52–55–40 for information on Hurtigruten and local ferries.

BY BUS

Buses run only from Oslo to Otta, where they connect with the train to Trondheim. Buses connect Bergen, Molde, Ålesund, and Røros with Trondheim.

Nor-Way Bussekspress (☎ 22/17–52–90) can help you to put together a bus journey to the North. The Express 2000 travels three times a week between Oslo, Kautokeino, Alta, and Hammerfest. The journey, via Sweden, takes 24, 26, and 29 hours, respectively.

BY CAR

Trondheim is about 500 km (310 mi) from Oslo: seven to eight hours of driving. Speed limits are 80 kph (50 mph) much of the way. There are two alternatives, E6 through Gudbrandsdalen or Route 3 through Østerdalen. Roads are decent for the most part but can become thick with campers during midsummer, sometimes making the going slow. It's 727 km (450 mi) from Trondheim to Bodø on Route E6, which goes all the way to Kirkenes. There's an NKr20 toll on E6 just south of Trondheim for travelers in both directions. Cars entering the downtown area must pay an NKr10 toll (6 AM–10 PM). Anyone who makes it to the **North Cape** *sans* tour bus will be congratulated with an NKr150 toll.

BY PLANE

Trondheim's **Værnes Airport** is 35 km (22 mi) northeast of the city. **SAS** (☎ 74/84–34–00), **Braathens SAFE** (☎ 73/89–57–00), and **Widerøe** (☎ 73/89–67–00) are the main domestic carriers. **SAS** also has one flight between Trondheim and Copenhagen daily, except Sunday, and daily flights to Stockholm.

With the exception of Harstad, all cities in northern Norway are served by airports less than 5 km (3 mi) from the center of town. Tromsø is a crossroads for air traffic between northern and southern Norway and is served by Braathens SAFE, SAS, and Widerøe. SAS flies to eight destinations in northern Norway, including Bodø, Tromsø, Alta, and Kirkenes. Braathens SAFE flies to five destinations, including Bodø and

Tromsø. Widerøe specializes in northern Norway and flies to 19 destinations in the region, including Honningsvåg, the airport closest to the North Cape.

The *Dovrebanen* has five departures daily, four on Saturday, in both directions on the Oslo–Trondheim route. Trains leave from Oslo S Station for the seven- to eight-hour journey. Trondheim is the gateway to the North, and two trains run daily in both directions on the 11-hour Trondheim–Bodø route. For information about trains out of Trondheim, call ☎ 73/53–00–10. The *Nordlandsbanen* has two departures daily in each direction on the Bodø–Trondheim route, an 11-hour journey. The *Ofotbanen* has one departure daily in each direction on the Stockholm–Narvik route, a 21-hour journey. In summer, a tourist train travels at 4:30 daily from Narvik to the Swedish border and back.

Getting Around

Boat is the ideal transportation in Nordland. The *Hurtigruten* stops twice daily (north and southbound) at 20 ports in northern Norway. It is possible to buy tickets between any harbors right on the boats. **OVDS** (Narvik, ☎ 76/92–37–00) ferries and express boats serve many towns in the region. **TFDS, Troms Fylkes Dampskibsselskap** (Tromsø, ☎ 77/64–81–00) operates various boat services in the region around Tromsø.

Most local buses in **Trondheim** stop at the Munkegata/Dronningens Gate intersection. Some routes end at the bus terminal (✉ Skakkes Gt. 40, ☎ 73/82–22–22). Tickets cost NKr12 and allow free transfer between buses (☎ 73/54–71–00) and streetcars (Gråkallbanen, ☎ 72/55–23–55).

North of **Bodø** and **Narvik** (a five-hour bus ride from Bodø), beyond the reach of the railroad, buses go virtually everywhere, but they don't go often. Get a comprehensive bus schedule from a tourist office or travel agent before making plans. Local bus companies include **Harstad Oppland Rutebil** (☎ 77/06–81–70), **Saltens Bilruter** (Bodø, ☎ 75/50–90–00), **Ofotens Bilruter** (Narvik, ☎ 76/92–35–00), **Tromsbuss** (Tromsø, ☎ 77/67–02–33), **Midttuns Busser** (Tromsø, ☎ 77/67–27–87), and **Finnmark Fylkesrederi og Ruteselskap** (FFR, Alta, ☎ 78/43–52–11; Hammerfest, ☎ 78/41–10–00).

The roads aren't a problem in northern Norway—most are quite good, although there are always narrow and winding stretches, especially along fjords. Distances are formidable. Route 17—the *Kystriksvegen* (Coastal Highway) from Namsos to Bodø—is an excellent alternative to E6. Getting to Tromsø and the North Cape involves additional driving on narrower roads off E6. In the northern winter, near-blizzard conditions and icy roads sometimes make it necessary to drive in a convoy. You'll know it when you see it: towns are cut off from traffic at access roads, and vehicles wait until their numbers are large enough to make the crossing safely.

You can also fly the extensive distances and then rent a car for sightseeing within the area, but book a rental car as far in advance as possible. There's no better way to see the Lofoten and Vesterålen islands than by car. Nordkapp (take the plane to Honningsvåg) is another excursion best made by car.

The best way to see the Lofoten Islands is by car since bus service is often limited and there is just so much to see. The main tourist office in Svolvær can point you to local rental agencies, whose rates tend to be quite high. Short distances between neighboring villages are doable by bicycle if you plan to stay in one village for several days.

BY PLANE

Northern Norway has excellent air connections through SAS, Braathens SAFE, and Widerøe (☞ Arriving and Departing by Plane, *above*).

BY TAXI

Taxi stands are located in strategic places in downtown **Trondheim.** All taxis are connected to the central dispatching office (☎ 73/50–50–73). Taxi numbers in other towns include the following: **Harstad** (☎ 77/06–20–50), **Narvik** (☎ 76/94–65–00), and **Tromsø** (☎ 77/60–30–00).

Contacts and Resources

GUIDED TOURS

Tromsø: The tourist information office (⊠ Storgt. 61/63, 9001, ☎ 77/61–00–00) sells tickets for **City Sightseeing** (Dampskipskaia) and **M/F Karlsøy**, an original Arctic vessel that runs a fishing tour in the waters around Tromsø Island.

Trondheim: The Trondheim Tourist Association offers a number of tours. Tickets are sold at the tourist information office or at the start of the tour.

LATE-NIGHT PHARMACIES

Trondheim: St. Olav Vaktapotek (⊠ Kjøpmannsgt. 65, ☎ 73/52–66–66) is open Monday through Saturday 8:30 AM–midnight and Sunday 10 AM–midnight.

Tromsø: Svaneapoteket (⊠ Fr. Langes Gt. 9, ☎ 77/68–64–24) is open daily 8:30–4:30 and 6–9.

VISITOR INFORMATION

Alta (⊠ Top Of Norway, 9500, ☎ 78/43–54–44). **Bodø** (⊠ Sjøgt. 21, 8006, ☎ 75/52–60–00). **Hammerfest** (⊠ 9600, ☎ 78/41–21–85). **Harstad** (⊠ Torvet 8, 9400, ☎ 77/06–32–35). **Lofoten** (⊠ 8301 Svolvær, ☎ 76/07–30–00). **Mo i Rana** (⊠ Polarsirkelen Reiselivslag, 8600 Mo, ☎ 75/15–04–21). **Narvik** (⊠ Kongensgt. 66, 8500, ☎ 76/94–60–33). **Nordkapp** (⊠ Nordkapphuset, Honningsvåg, ☎ 78/47–28–94). **Rognan** (Salten Tourist Board, ☎ 75/64–33–03). **Tromsø** (⊠ Storgt. 61/63, 9001, ☎ 77/61–00–00). **Trondheim** (⊠ Munkegt. 19, 7000, ☎ 73/92–93–94). **Vesterålen Reiselivslag** (⊠ 8400 Sortland, ☎ 76/12–15–55).

11 Samiland to Svalbard and the Finnish-Russian Connection

On the roof of Europe, atop the vast, windswept Finnmarksvidda, roam the Continent's only nomadic indigenous people, the reindeer-herding Sami. Most still live in traditional tents and dress in colorful costumes, although the most visible evidence of their lifestyle consists of roadside souvenir stands and tourist exhibits. The desolate expanses and treeless tundra of this area is an inspiring trekking destination—you're almost guaranteed an encounter with reindeer.

EVERYONE HAS HEARD OF LAPLAND, but few know its real name, Samiland. The Sami recognize no national boundaries, as their territory stretches from the Kola Peninsula in the Soviet Union through Finland, Sweden, and Norway. These indigenous reindeer herders are a distinct ethnic group, with a language related to Finnish. Although still considered nomadic, they no longer live in tents or huts, except for short periods during the summer, when their animals graze along the coast. They have had to conform to today's lifestyles, but their traditions survive through their language, music (called *joik*), art, and handicrafts. Norwegian Samiland is synonymous with the communities of Kautokeino and colorful Karasjok, capital of the Sami, in Finnmark.

Numbers in the margin correspond to points of interest on the Trondheim map in chapter 10.

Kautokeino

83 *129 km (80 mi) southeast of Alta.*

Kautokeino is the site of the Sami theater and the Nordic Sami Institute, dedicated to the study of Sami culture. It is a center for Sami handicrafts and education, complete with a school of reindeer herding.

Guovdageainnu (Kautokeino in the Sami language) **Gilisillju,** the local museum, documents the way of life of both the nomadic and the resident Sami of that area before World War II, with photographs and artifacts, including costumes, dwellings, and art. ⊠ *9520 Kautokeino,* ☎ *78/48–58–00.* ⊠ *NKr10.* ☉ *Mid-June–mid-Aug., weekdays 9–7, weekends noon–7; mid-Aug.–mid-June, weekdays 9–3.*

The Arts

During Easter, Kautokeino holds its annual **Easter Festival,** including theater, joik (a haunting, ancient form of solo, a cappella song, often in praise of nature), concerts, weddings, and exhibits of traditional crafts. Contact **Top Of Norway** (⊠ 9500 Alta, ☎ 78/43–54–44).

Shopping

Locals say **Juhl's Silver Gallery** (☎ 78/48–61–89) was Finnmark's first silversmith. Also sold are handicrafts and art from around the world.

Karasjok

84 *178 km (110 mi) from Kautokeino.*

Karasjok, on the other side of the Finnmark Plateau, is the seat of the 39-member Sami Parliament and capital of Samiland. It has a typical inland climate, with the accompanying temperature extremes. The best time to come is at Easter, when the communities are celebrating the weddings and baptisms of the year and taking part in reindeer races and other colorful festivities. In summer, when many of the Sami go to the coast with their reindeer, the area is not nearly as interesting.

The **Samid Vuorka-Davvirat** (Sami Collections) is a comprehensive museum (indoor and open-air) of Sami culture, with emphasis on the arts, reindeer herding, and the status of women in the Sami community. ⊠ *Museumsgt. 17,* ☎ *78/46–63–05.* ⊠ *NKr25.* ☉ *Mid-June–late Aug., Mon.–Sat. 9–6, Sun. 10–6; late Aug.–Oct., weekdays 9–3, weekends 10–3; Nov.–Mar., weekdays 9–3, weekends noon–3; Apr.–mid-June, weekdays 9–3, weekends 10–3.*

From late fall to early spring you can go **reindeer sledding.** A Sami guide will take you out on a wooden sled tied to a couple of unwieldy reindeer, and you'll clop through the barren, snow-covered scenery of Finnmark. Wide and relatively flat, the colorless winter landscape is veined by inky alder branches and little else. You'll reach a *lavvu,* a traditional Sami tent, and be invited in to share a meal of boiled reindeer, bread, jam, and strong coffee next to an open alder fire. It's an extraordinary experience. Contact Karasjok Opplevelser (☎ 78/46–69–00).

Dining and Lodging

$$$–$$$$ ✕🏨 **North Cape Hotel.** This establishment feels more like a ski chalet
★ than a hotel, with bright rooms, done in warm blues and reds, that are cozy rather than industrial. The lobby is more staid. The hotel's wonderful Sami restaurant, Storgammen, serves traditional fare, including reindeer cooked over open fires. ⊠ *Box 38, 9731 Karasjok,* ☎ *78/46–74–00,* 𝖥𝖠𝖷 *78/46–68–02. 56 rooms. 2 restaurants, bar, saunas, meeting rooms. AE, DC, MC, V.*

Outdoor Activities and Sports

DOGSLEDDING

Sven Engholm, who has won the longest sledge race in Europe, leads tours with his pack dogs. In winter, you can lead your own dog sled, accompany one on skis, or just go along for the ride. In summer, you can hike with the huskies. Contact **Husky Adventure** (☎ 78/46–71–66) for information.

HIKING AND FISHING

In between the Alta and Karasjok areas, the **Finnmarksvidda** has marked trails with overnight possibilities in lodges. Contact the Norske Turistforening (⊠ Buks 1963 Vika, 0125 Oslo, ☎ 22/83–25–50) and the Finnmark Travel Association (☎ 78/43–54–44). Finnmark boasts some of Norway's best fishing rivers. For more information, call **Top Of Norway** (☎ 78/43–54–44.)

Shopping

The specialties of the region are Sami crafts, particularly handmade knives. In **Samelandssenteret** (☎ 78/46–71–55) is a large collection of shops featuring northern specialties, including **Knivsmed Strømeng** (☎ 78/46–71–05).

Kirkenes

 At its very top, Norway hooks over Finland and touches Russia for 122 km (75 mi). The towns in east Finnmark have a more heterogeneous population than those in the rest of the country. A century ago, during hard times in Finland, many industrious Finns settled in this region, and their descendants keep the language alive there.

A good way to visit this part of Norway is to fly to Kirkenes and then explore the region by car. Only Malta was bombed more than Kirkenes during World War II—virtually everything you see in town has been built within the past 45 years.

In winter this entire region, blanketed by snow and cold, is off the beaten track. As the Norwegians say, there is no bad weather, only bad clothes—so bundle up and explore.

During the more than 300 bombings of Kirkenes, its residents sought cover in subterranean tunnels under the town's center. One of them, **Andersgrotta,** is open to the public. ☎ 78/99–25–01. 🎟 NKr40. ☉ *Opening hours vary.*

From mid-June to mid-August, the **FFR** (⊠ Hammerfest, ☎ 78/41–10–00) operates visa-free day cruises to Murmansk, Russia, on a high-speed catamaran. Booking is required two weeks in advance.

OFF THE BEATEN PATH

ST. GEORGS KAPELL – Forty-five kilometers (28 miles) west of Kirkenes is the only Russian Orthodox chapel in Norway, where the Orthodox Skolt-Sami had their summer encampment. It's a tiny building, and services are held outside, weather permitting.

Lodging

$$–$$$$ 🏨 **Rica Arctic Hotel.** Do not confuse this hotel with the Rica Hotel Kirkenes, an older establishment, which ends up costing the same during the summer. Rooms here are spacious and pretty, with white-painted furniture and light print textiles. ✉ *Kongensgt. 1–3, 9900,* ☎ *78/99–29–29,* 🖷 *78/99–11–59. 80 rooms. Restaurant, bar, indoor pool, beauty salon, sauna, exercise room, nightclub, convention center. AE, DC, MC, V.*

Storskog

🚳 *About 60 km (37 mi) from Kirkenes.*

Just east of Kirkenes is Storskog, for many years the only official land crossing of the border between Norway and Russia. The tiny village of **Grense Jakobselv** on the Russian border is where King Oscar II built a chapel right at the border in 1869 as a protest against constant Russian encroachment in the area.

OFF THE BEATEN PATH

ØVRE PASVIK – The southernmost part of Finnmark, about 118 km (73 mi) south of Kirkens, is Øvre Pasvik national park, a narrow tongue of land tucked between Finland and Russia. This subarctic evergreen forest is the western end of Siberia's taiga and supports many varieties of flora found only here. The area is surprisingly lush, and in good years all the cloudberries make the swamps shine orange.

Svalbard

🚳 *640 km (400 mi) north of the North Cape.*

The islands of Svalbard, the largest of which is Spitsbergen, have officially been part of Norway only since 1920. They might have remained wilderness, with only the occasional visitor, if coal had not been discovered late in the 19th century. Today both a Norwegian and a Russian coal company have operations there, and there are two Russian coal miners' communities. The islands offer ample opportunities for ski, dogsled, boat, and snowmobile exploring.

Because Svalbard is so far north, it has four months of continual daylight, from April 21 to August 21. Summers can be lush, with hundreds of varieties of wildflowers. The season is so compressed that buds, full-blown flowers, and seed appear simultaneously on the same plant.

The capital, **Longyearbyen,** is 90 minutes by air from Tromsø. Named for an American, John Monroe Longyear, who established a mining operation there in 1906, the "settlement" is home to only about 1,200 Norwegians. Only three species of land mammal besides humans (polar bears, reindeer, and Arctic foxes) and one species of bird (ptarmigan) have adapted to Svalbard winters, but during the summer months, more than 30 species of bird nest on the steep cliffs of the islands, and white whales, seals, and walruses also come for the season. Do heed warnings about polar bears: they can be a real hazard.

Traditionally, only the richest tourists and the most serious scientists traveled to Svalbard. Now the islands have become more accessible. If Hammerfest felt like the edge of Europe, Svalbard feels like the edge of the world. Striations of snow have singed their way across the wild, jagged mountains, splintered down by millennia of arctic conditions. In early summer, antlerless reindeer lounge on the soot-colored tundra. Rumors of hungry polar bears looking to gobble up lonesome travelers tend to precede a trip to the icy island. But adventurous trekkers should not miss the chance to experience this strange, icy wilderness, with its arctic animals and frozen rock formations. Just go with caution, and only travel outside Longyearbyen with an experienced tour guide.

Lodging

$$$–$$$$ ⊡ **Svalbard Polar Hotel.** Svalbard's only full-service hotel consists of rooms originally built to house the U.S. team sponsor during the Winter Olympics in Lillehammer. An enormous panoramic window in the hotel's dining and bar area provides a view of Mount Hjorthavnfjellet across the waters of the Icefjord. In summer, you can watch the sun cross from one side of the mountain at dusk to the other at dawn—many locals do this from the hotel's bar. ⊠ *Box 544, 9170,* ☎ *79/02–35–00,* FAX *79/02–35–00. 67 rooms, 4 suites. Restaurant, 2 bars, sauna. AE, DC, MC, V.*

The Arts

To get a sense of the frosty place during other times of the year, see the **Kaare Tveter Collection** slide presentation. One of Norway's most admired artists, Tveter donated 40 illustrations of Svalbard's pink mountains, black fjords, and charcoal gray skies to the new Galleri Svalbard. There are more than 60 Arctic region maps, which are centuries old, that fill an adjacent exhibition room. ⊠ *Galleri Svalbard.* ☎ *79/02–23–40.* ⊙ *Tues.–Thurs, 5–7, Sat. 4–6, Sun. 4–9.*

Samiland to Svalbard A to Z

Arriving and Departing

BY BOAT

Hurtigruten now cruises from Tromsø to Svalbard, dipping down to the North Cape afterwards. Contact Bergen Line (☞ Boat Trips *in* the Gold Guide).

(☞ Trondheim to the North Cape A to Z *in* Chapter 10).

Getting Around

(☞ Trondheim to the North Cape A to Z *in* Chapter 10).

Contacts and Resources

GUIDED TOURS

Contact **Sami Travel A/S** (⊠ Kautokeino, ☎ 78/48–56–00) for adventure trips to Sami settlements. Because of extreme weather conditions and the dangers of polar bears, the best way to see Svalbard is through an organized tour. Longyearbyen's tour operators lead even very small groups on exploring trips lasting anywhere from a day to several weeks. **Svalbard Polar Travel** (⊠ 9170 Longyearbyen, ☎ 79/02–19–71) arranges combination air-sea visits, from five-day minicruises to 12-day trekking expeditions on the rim of the North Pole. **Spitsbergen Travel** (⊠ 9170 Longyearbyen, ☎ 79/02–24–00) offers specialized "exploring" walks and hikes that focus on the plant and animal life of the region. If you're short on time, the daylong boat trip to Barentsburg provides a snapshot of the surrounding area's icy beauty.

VISITOR INFORMATION

Karasjok (⊠ 9730 Karasjok, ☎ 78/46–73–60). **Lofoten** (⊠ 8300 Svolvær, ☎ 76/07–30–00). **Svalbard** (⊠ 9170 Longyearbyen, ☎ 79/02–23–03).

12 Portraits of Norway

NORWAY AT A GLANCE: A CHRONOLOGY

c 1200 BC The earliest human settlers reach Norway.

2,000 BC Tribes from Southern Europe migrate toward Denmark. The majority of early settlers in Scandinavia were of Germanic origin.

c AD 770 The Viking Age begins. For the next 250 years, Scandinavians set sail on frequent expeditions stretching from the Baltic to the Irish seas and even to the Mediterranean as far as Sicily, employing superior ships and weapons and efficient military organization.

c 870 The first permanent settlers arrive in Iceland from western Norway.

c 900 Norwegians unite under Harald I Haarfager.

995 King Olaf I Tryggvasson introduces Christianity into Norway.

1000 Leif Eriksson visits America. Olaf I sends a mission to Christianize Iceland.

1016–1028 King Olaf II Haraldsson (St. Olaf) tries to complete conversion of Norway to Christianity. Killed at Stiklestad in battle with Danish king, he becomes patron saint of Norway.

1028–1035 Canute (Knud) the Great is king of England, Denmark (1018), and Norway (1028).

1045–1066 King Harald III (Hardraade) fights long war with Danes, then participates in and is killed during Norman invasion of England.

1217 Haakon IV becomes king of Norway, beginning its "Golden Age." His many reforms modernize the Norwegian administration; under him, the Norwegian empire reaches its greatest extent when Greenland and Iceland form unions with Norway in 1261. The Sagas are written during this time.

1319 Sweden and Norway form a union that lasts until 1335.

1349 The Black Death strikes Norway and kills two-thirds of the population.

1370 The Treaty of Stralsund gives the north German trading centers of the Hanseatic League free passage through Danish waters. German power increases throughout Scandinavia.

1397 The Kalmar Union is formed as a result of the dynastic ties between Sweden, Denmark, and Norway, the geographical position of the Scandinavian states, and the growing influence of Germans in the Baltic. Erik of Pomerania is crowned king of the Kalmar Union.

1520 Christian II, ruler of the Kalmar Union, executes 82 people who oppose the Scandinavian union, an event known as the "Stockholm blood bath." Sweden secedes from the Union three years later. Norway remains tied to Denmark and becomes a Danish province in 1536.

1536 The Reformation enters Scandinavia in the form of Lutheranism through the Hanseatic port of Bergen.

1559–1648 Norwegian trade flourishes.

1660 Peace of Copenhagen establishes modern boundaries of Denmark, Sweden, and Norway.

1814 Sweden, after Napoleon's defeat at the Battle of Leipzig, attacks Denmark and forces the Danish surrender of Norway. On 17 May, Norwegians adopt constitution at Eidsvoll. On 4 November, Norway is forced to accept Act of Union with Sweden.

1811 University of Oslo is established.

1884 A parliamentary system is established in Norway.

1903 Bjørnstjerne Bjørnson awarded Nobel Prize for literature.

1905 Norway's union with Sweden is dissolved.

1914 At the outbreak of World War I, Norway declares neutrality but is effectively blockaded.

1918 Norwegian women gain the right to vote.

1920 Norway joins the League of Nations. Novelist Knut Hansun receives Nobel Prize.

1928 Sigrid Undset receives Nobel Prize for literature.

1929–1937 Norway is ruled by a labor government.

1939 Norway declares neutrality in World War II.

1940 Germany occupies Norway.

1945 Norway joins the United Nations.

1946–1954 Norwegian statesman Trygve Lie presides as first Secretary-General of UN.

1949 Norway becomes a member of NATO.

1952 The Nordic Council, which promotes cooperation among the Nordic parliaments, is founded.

1968 Norway discovers oil in the North Sea.

1971 North Sea oil extraction begins, transforming the Norwegian economy.

1972 Norway declines membership in the EC.

1981 Gro Harlem Brundtland, a member of the Labor party, becomes Norway's first female prime minister.

1991 King Olav V dies. King Harald V ascends the throne. His wife, Queen Sonja, becomes first queen since the death of Maud in 1938.

1993 Norway's Minister of Foreign Affairs Thorvald Stoltenberg is appointed peace negotiator to Bosnia and Herzegovina.

1994 Norway hosts the XVII Olympic Winter Games at Lillehammer.

1995 In a national referendum, Norwegians again decline membership in the EC.

IN NORWAY AT CHRISTMAS

EVERY CULTURE REINVENTS the wheel. But every culture reinvents it slightly differently. In Norway, a traditional dining table may rest not on four legs, as tables usually do elsewhere, but on a cubic frame, like an imaginary cage that imprisons your feet while you eat.

I am a Chinese who has fallen in love with Norway. I was invited by my good friends Ole and Else to spend Christmas and New Year's with them in Oslo. It turned out to be the most marvelous Christmas of my fifty-two years.

It was one long feast, moving from household to household. On Christmas Eve we held hands and sang carols and danced ring-around-the-Christmas-tree. We skied at night on an illuminated track, whose lights switched off at ten, plunging us into obscurity on the downward slope. We played squash on the Norsk Hydro court and afterward relaxed in the sauna. We ushered in the New Year with fireworks on Oslo's frozen streets.

I am probably one of the few Chinese in two thousand years to have had such an intimate glimpse of Norwegian life. Of course, it is presumptuous of me to write about a people after an eight-day visit. Yet I have the feeling that Norwegians don't very much mind presumption (as long as it is straightforward and honest). Indeed, this exceptional tolerance of friendly rudeness bespeaks their generosity and is, to me, one of their most endearing qualities.

To begin with, to a Chinese who has seen something of the world, Norway is a most exotic country. Even ordinary, everyday things are done exotically here. For example, I saw my Norwegian friends: drink aquavit at breakfast; eat breakfast in the afternoon; turn on an electric switch to heat the sidewalk in front of their house; get a thrill out of driving their car like a bobsled; leave the house lights on day and night, when they went out and when they slept; wash their dishes with soap without rinsing them.

Norwegians also love to give gifts and make philosophical speeches at festive dinners. They decorate their Christmas trees not with angels but with strings of Norwegian flags. They don't find it necessary to have curtains around their showers, because it's simpler to build a drain on the bathroom floor. Cold dishes are de rigueur in the winter. There is a national horror of hot, spicy foods, and a national pact to ignore vegetables.

The Norwegians and the Chinese share certain cultural traits. The most striking is their common fondness for rituals. Confucius insisted on the importance of rituals as a collective code of behavior that gives order to life. The Master said, "To suppress the self and submit to ritual is to engage in Humanity." This precept might just as well apply to the Norwegians as to the Chinese.

At Christmas, all the traditional rituals are performed, some older than Christianity in Norway. A great deal of effort goes into making sure that they are done right. After each one—the baking of the gingerbread houses, the decorating of the tree—the excitement palpably mounts.

Christmas begins on the eve, with the hostess welcoming the guests to the dinner table. She assigns to each a specific seat according to a careful arrangement. The seating plan is the one touch of originality that marks the occasion. It is, in some ways, the hostess's signature for the evening. (You find seating charts of past banquets faithfully recorded in a family book.) It's quite touching to see a young hostess assign a seat to her own mother, who has undoubtedly done the same many times herself. It signals the passing of the torch from one generation of women to another.

Once the guests are seated and the candles lit, the feast begins. It begins with the dessert: rice pudding (reminiscent of the rice gruel that Chinese eat for breakfast and when ill, albeit without milk and butter). Toasts are offered, followed by a chorus of *skaals*.

Then comes raw fish of every kind—salmon, eel, herring, enough to send a sashimi-loving Japanese into ecstasy. From the sea, the food parade marches onto land. A whole side of roast pork, skin done to a golden crisp, is served with meatballs and sausage, and buried under potatoes. Throughout there is much toasting with aquavit.

Finally, after two hours the meal is done. You get up from the table and stagger into the living room. There, in a role reminiscent of her mother's, the little daughter of the house hands out the gifts—there is a mound of them under the tree—to each recipient with charming solemnity.

Great care is taken by each household to do everything the same way, so that, as with the retelling of a familiar tale, all expectations are happily satisfied. Once in a while, one may introduce an oddity, such as a Chinese guest from afar, to liven up the routine. But in general surprises tend to raise eyebrows.

If, for the Chinese, rituals recall the teachings of Confucius, for the Norwegians they go back to the pagans. In spite of the electric sidewalks, the past is very much alive in the modern Norwegian psyche. The feasting, the speech-making, the gift-giving, and especially the generous hospitality and the importance of friendship are all part of the Viking tradition. Yuletide was a pagan celebration of the winter solstice. The birth of Christ was a later liturgical imposition. In some families these days, it is celebrated almost as an afterthought.

The other thing that the Norwegians share with the Chinese is their strong attachment to the family. Like the Chinese, the Norwegians belong to extended families, practically clans. But what defines a family in Norway is not at all clear. The relations are so complex and intertwined that, rather than family trees, the Norwegians seem to have family bushes. To begin with, there is one's spouse and one's brothers and sisters and their spouses. And then there is one's former spouse and his or her present spouse. And then there is the former spouse of the present spouse of one's former spouse, who in some cases also happens to be one's present spouse. The children of the former spouse of one's spouse are somewhat like nephews and nieces. Beyond that, there are the living-together arrangements and the progeny thereof, which take on quasi-family status.

It's not unusual for people who are divorced to remain good friends. Their old pictures sometimes hang in each other's bedrooms, Christmastime finds them reunited with their old partners and all of their children, old and new. At first, this kind of marital pluralism is slightly unsettling. What, no bad blood? No bitterness or jealousy?

I ASKED A YOUNG NORWEGIAN if it upset him to be shuttling between his father's and mother's separate households. He looked at me with astonishment. "But that's normal," he said. "Every kid in my class is in the same situation."

His guileless reaction gave me food for thought. "And indeed what's wrong with that?" I asked myself. Why try to stay with an unhappy relationship when one feels the need to change? And once changed, why not try to reconcile the past with the present?

The Chinese family is a vertical structure. Like the society itself, it is hierarchical, ruled from the top down. Confucius said, "Let the prince be prince, the minister be minister, the father be father, the son be son." Patriarchy and gerontocracy are the order of things: old men will rule, and the young will obey. Repression is inevitable under such a hierarchy. The collective always takes precedence over the individual; order always takes precedence over freedom. This denial of the self is responsible for much of the envy, backbiting, and hypocrisy common in Chinese communities.

The Norwegian family, on the other hand— or perhaps I should say the *new* Norwegian family—is horizontal. Like a strawberry plant, it spreads in all directions. Wherever it touches soil, it sprouts a new shoot. An obvious sign of this strawberry-patch kinship is the diminished importance of the family name. These days people are known mostly by first names. Children, too, often address their parents by their first names. As more and more households are headed by women, the old nuclear family is giving way to a fluid tribalism.

One way to understand the difference between the vertical and the horizontal cultures is to compare their concepts of space. To the Chinese, any space must have a center. The Chinese name for China, Zhongguo, means precisely Center Country. Every Chinese knows that the center of China is Beijing. Why? Because the vast expanse of China is not divided into time zones, and from the Pacific to Tibet every watch is set to Beijing time. Every Chinese also knows that the center of Beijing is the Forbidden City, the symbol of governmental power, and that inside the Forbidden City sits an old man whose word is law.

NO ONE WOULD DREAM of ordering Norway's space this way. Unlike elsewhere in Europe, you seldom see a square in a Norwegian town. People don't seem to feel the need to meet and sit in the sun and feed the pigeons. In some rural communities, the church stands not in the center of town but on a hill somewhere on the outskirts. The houses, in all forms and dispositions, are widely dispersed, disdaining to line up along a straight road. One gets the impression that zoning laws are not very strict in Norway.

The big question is, if the Norwegians are such confirmed individualists, how come they are so conformist? It's voluntary, true, they choose it, but it's conformity all the same. This is the question posed—but never answered—by Ibsen's plays.

For me, the key to understanding the Norwegians is to recognize that they are a nation of irreconciled opposites. They have taken on the contradiction of their seasons: the long happy summer days alternating with the gloomy nights of winter. They have inherited two pasts with totally different characters. For more than two hundred years, from the ninth to the eleventh centuries, they were the scourge of Europe. They raided Britain and discovered America; they ruled Kiev and besieged Paris; they served at the court of Byzantium, and—who knows?—maybe some of them even made it to China. Lusty, adventurous, destructive, and curious about the world, they were sea nomads, the maritime counterpart of the horsemen of Genghis Khan, who conquered Russia and China. Then, as suddenly as they burst upon the world in their splendid ships, they retreated, went back to their home in the north. They were converted to Christianity and not heard from again.

Why the seafaring Vikings turned into God-fearing Christians is one of those mysteries that history doesn't explain very well. What made them turn their gaze inward? Why did they change from thinking big to thinking small? What, finally made them give up violence for peaceful ways? There is no satisfactory answer.

In any case, as the final image of Ingmar Bergman's *Fanny and Alexander* so powerfully shows, there are two ghosts walking beside the Scandinavian soul: the ghost of the hard-drinking father and the ghost of the psalm-singing stepfather. They walk beside the boy, each with a hand on his shoulder, never exchanging a word.

So the Norwegian labors under a double identity. In one ear, the Viking ghost tells him to leave Norway, this cold, homogeneous, incurious community, and discover the world. Go! The center is elsewhere! There are wonderful places to see and fabulous riches to be had!

In his other ear, the Christian ghost tells him Stay! Go back to your roots! Embrace the tradition and preserve the social order.

This ambivalence is at the heart of Norway itself. You see it reflected on canvas in the National Gallery in Oslo. Among the painters of the late nineteenth century, one finds two divergent sensibilities: the naturalists, who took as their subject the Norwegian folk, and the cosmopolitans, who, having spent time in Paris or Rome, insisted that art was not sociology or geography but, simply and purely, a composition of color and light.

For eight centuries, Christian ethics held sway in Norway as in the rest of Europe. But since 1945 something important has changed. There is a gap between the values of the prewar and the postwar generations. Between the threat of nuclear destruction and the temptation of America, the influence of the church waned. More and more, people have stopped practicing their faith. As they do so, they are reverting to their ancestral Viking instincts.

One clue to this reemergence of pagan consciousness is the marital pluralism that I observed. Another clue, probably closely related, is women's push for equality, a push that has been more forceful and more widely accepted in Scandinavia than anywhere else. A third indication of this new pagan way, I believe—and here I'm sticking my neck out—is the nation's collective decision, in the seventies, to turn Norway overnight into an oil economy.

There have been a lot of arguments about the reasoning behind this decision, but none of them address the Viking-versus-Christian dilemma. If Norway had listened to its Christian voice, it would have been content to remain a frugal, hard-working nation, tending the farm or the machine. Instead, after the oil crisis of 1973, Norway chose the Viking solution and went for broke. It decided to plunder the sea.

Agrarian people, like the Chinese, are naturally patient: it takes time to make things grow. The Vikings, on the other hand, never had patience. If they could survive by fishing and gathering berries, they would not care to cultivate. Whatever they could get by raiding, they would not care to make. It is still so today. Norwegians are willing to put all their ingenuity and technical skill into building gigantic derricks and drilling kilometers beneath the sea. They will do so in order to avoid making clothes and toys to compete with Hong Kong. This is the message I got from that magnificent Christmas feast: If it tastes good raw, *don't bother to cook it*. Take it raw. Don't transform. And nothing is rawer than oil.

In 1066, King Harald Hardraade left the shores of Norway to grab the big prize: the throne of England. At Stamford Bridge, he was offered by his enemy seven feet of English ground, "and more—if you are taller." Harald fought and lost. By nightfall, mortally wounded, he said, "I will accept that piece of kingdom that was offered me this morning."

I said to my friend Ole—who, as an oil engineer at Norsk Hydro, has staked his whole future on a challenge against the North Sea—"One day your oil will be depleted, and then where will you be?" He grinned and said, echoing King Harald's insouciance, "And then I will have nothing."

— By Chunglu Tsen

Born in Shanghai, Chunglu Tsen grew up in Paris and received his education in England and the United States. Since 1974 he has worked as a translator for the United Nations in Geneva. This article appeared originally in the December 1990 issue of *Wigwag*.

NORWEGIAN VOCABULARY

	English	Norwegian	Pronunciation
Basics			
	Yes/no	Ja/nei	yah/nay
	Please	Vær så snill	**vehr** soh snihl
	Thank you much.	Tusen takk	**tews**-sehn tahkvery
	You're welcome.	Vær så god	**vehr** soh goo
	Excuse me.	Unnskyld	**ewn**-shewl
	Hello	God dag	goo **dahg**
	Goodbye	Ha det	**ha** day
	Today	i dag	ee **dahg**
	Tomorrow	i morgen	ee **moh**-ern
	Yesterday	i går	ee **gohr**
	Morning	morgen	**moh**-ern
	Afternoon	ettermiddag	**eh-terr**-mid-dahg
	Night	natt	naht
Numbers			
	1	en	ehn
	2	to	too
	3	tre	treh
	4	fire	**feer**-eh
	5	fem	fehm
	6	seks	sehks
	7	syv, sju	shew
	8	åtte	**oh**-teh
	9	ni	nee
	10	ti	tee
Days of the Week			
	Monday	mandag	mahn-dahg
	Tuesday	tirsdag	**teesh**-dahg
	Wednesday	onsdag	**oonss**-dahg
	Thursday	torsdag	**tohsh**-dahg
	Friday	fredag	**fray**-dahg
	Saturday	lørdag	**loor**-dahg
	Sunday	søndag	**suhn**-dahg
Useful Phrases			
	Do you speak English?	Snakker De engelsk?	snahk-kerr dee ehng-ehlsk
	I don't speak Norwegian.	Jeg snakker ikke norsk.	yay **snahk**-kerr **ik**-keh nohrshk
	I don't understand.	Jeg forstår ikke.	yay fosh-**tawr** **ik**-keh
	I don't know.	Jeg vet ikke.	yay veht **ik**-keh
	I am American/British.	Jeg er amerikansk/engelsk.	yay ehr ah-mehr-ee-kahnsk/ehng-ehlsk
	I am sick.	Jeg er dårlig.	yay ehr **dohr**-lee

Please call a doctor.	Vær så snill og ring etter en lege.	vehr soh snihl oh ring **eht**-ehr ehn **lay**-geh
Do you have vacant room?	Har du et rom som er ledig?	yay vil **yehr**-neh hah eht room
How much does it cost?	Hva koster det?	vah **koss**-terr deh
It's too expensive.	Det er for dyrt.	deh ehr for **deert**
Beautiful	vakker	**vah**-kehr
Help!	Hjelp!	yehlp
Stop!	Stopp!	stop
How do I get to . . .	Hvor er	voor ehr
the train station?	jernbanestasjonen	yehrn-bahn-eh sta-**shoon**-ern
the post office?	posthuset	**pohsst**-hewss
the tourist office?	turistkontoret	tew-**reest**-koon-toor-er
the hospital?	sykehuset	**see**-keh-hoo-seh
Does this bus go to . . . ?	Går denne bussen til . . . ?	gohr **den**-nah boos teel
Where is the W.C.?	Hvor er toalettene?	voor ehr too-ah-**leht**-te-ne
On the left	Til venstre	teel **vehn**-streh
On the right	Til høyre	teel **hooy**-reh
Straight ahead	Rett fram	reht **frahm**

Dining Out

menu	meny	meh-new
fork	gaffel	gahff-erl
knife	kniv	kneev
spoon	skje	shay
napkin	serviett	ssehr-vyeht
bread	brød	brur
butter	smør	smurr
milk	melk	mehlk
pepper	pepper	pehp-per
salt	salt	sahlt
sugar	sukker	sook-kerr
water/bottled water	vann	vahn
The check, please.	Jeg vil gjerne betale.	yay vil **yehr**-neh beh-**tah**-leh

INDEX

Index

Index

Index

WHEREVER YOU TRAVEL, *H*ELP IS NEVER FAR AWAY.

From planning your trip to providing travel assistance along the way, American Express® Travel Service Offices are always there to help you do more.

Norway

American Express Foreign Exchange
Karl Johansgatan 33
509 Sentrum
Oslo
47/22/98 37 20

American Express TFS/Bureau De Change
Fridtjof Nansens Pl 6
509 Sentrum
Oslo
47/22/98 37 30

do more AMERICAN EXPRESS
Travel

http://www.americanexpress.com/travel
American Express Travel Service Offices are located throughout Norway.